MANAGEMENT STRATEGY AND BUSINESS DEVELOPMENT

MANAGEMENT STRATEGY AND BUSINESS DEVELOPMENT

An Historical and Comparative Study

edited by
LESLIE HANNAH

First published 1976 by
THE MACMILLAN PRESS LTD
London and Basingstoke
Associated companies in New York
Dublin Melbourne Johannesburg and Madras

SBN 333 19816 6

Printed in Great Britain by
THE BOWERING PRESS LTD
Plymouth

Contents

PART THREE : SECTORAL STUDIES

PART FOUR : CONCLUSION

Preface

The present volume has its origins in a conference of business and economic historians, archivists, management scientists, economists and sociologists held in London on 10 June 1975. The central threads which drew the participants together were an interest in the evolution of modern business and a common admiration for the work of Professor Alfred D. Chandler, who was at the time visiting All Souls College, Oxford. There was also a strong belief that generalisations by business historians had, with notable exceptions such as Chandler's own work, so far been disappointing, but that there was considerable potential in problem-centred business history research in contributing to an understanding of the modern corporate economy. In the event, the quality of both papers and discussion was high and it was clear that the publication of the proceedings in edited form would be a valuable stimulus to further research in this important field.

It remains for me, as editor, to thank those who made both the conference and this volume possible. Alfred Chandler provided the inspiration, and my co-chairmen, Bernard Alford, Donald Coleman and Peter Payne ensured that we proceeded smoothly through a large conference programme with the maximum of fruitful discussion. The prompt submission of papers by the participants greatly assisted me in my editorial capacity. Although the discussion at the conference is not reprinted here, my own and the authors' thanks must also go to all participants, many of whose suggestions have been taken into account both by the authors of the papers and by William Kennedy and Peter Payne, whose concluding contribution to the collection is based on their reflections on the very full and stimulating discussions which took place. The Social Science Research Council provided a grant towards conference travel and organisation. The Electricity Council kindly loaned their excellent conference facilities, and their staff saw us through a remarkably full one-day conference programme speedily and efficiently. Mrs Sue Aylott and Mrs Jackie Maynard capably organised the administration of the conference and the typing of the final versions of papers. To all of them : grateful thanks, on my own behalf and on behalf of the conference participants.

Leslie Hannah

Wivenhoe Park
October 1975

Notes on Contributors

BERNARD ALFORD is Reader in economic history at the University of Bristol. His publications include *Depression and Recovery? British Economic Growth 1918–1939* (1972) and *W. D. & H. O. Wills and the Development of the U.K. Tobacco Industry 1786–1965* (1973). He is currently completing a book on Britain and the International Economy since 1880.

T. C. BARKER was a member of the economic history staff at the LSE from 1953 to 1964 and has since been Professor of Economic and Social History at the University of Kent at Canterbury. His publications include histories of Pilkington Brothers, of London Transport and of the London livery companies and (with J. R. Harris) *A Merseyside Town in the Industrial Revolution* (1954) and (with C. I. Savage), *An Economic History of Transport in Britain* (1975). He has been secretary of the Economic History Society since 1960. His revised and enlarged edition of the Pilkington history will be published in 1976 as *The Glassmakers*.

ALFRED D. CHANDLER Jr is the author of numerous books and articles on the development of modern business in the USA, and his book *Strategy and Structure: Chapters in the History of the Industrial Enterprise* (MIT Press, 1962) has been the inspiration for much recent work in the US and abroad on business history and management organisation. He is currently Professor of Business History at the Harvard Graduate School of Business Administration.

DEREK F. CHANNON was a Ford Foundation European doctoral fellow at the Harvard Business School, where his thesis was awarded the Richard D. Irwin prize for the best doctoral dissertation. It has now been published as *The Strategy and Structure of British Enterprise* (Macmillan, 1973). He has returned to teaching at the Manchester Business School and is currently directing an SSRC project on the strategy and structure of the UK Service sector.

S. D. CHAPMAN is Pasold Reader in the Department of Economic and Social History at Nottingham University. He is the author of several books on modern industrial history, including *The Early Factory Masters* (1967), *Cotton in the Industrial Revolution* (1972), and *Jesse Boot of Boots the Chemists* (1974); and edited *The History of Working Class Housing: A Symposium* (1971). He has also contributed articles to a number of scholarly journals and is co-editor of *Textile History*. Dr Chapman's current research is concerned with capital formation in the Industrial Revolution, and he is also adding to his knowledge of the recent development of Boots.

R. W. FERRIER is currently Group Historian at BP. After leaving Oxford he lectured abroad in France and Persia. Subsequently at Cambridge as a research student with Professor Charles Wilson he completed a doctoral thesis in the History Faculty. He is the author of a number of articles on international trade in the seventeenth and eighteenth centuries.

LESLIE HANNAH has held appointments in economics and history at Nuffield and St John's Colleges, Oxford and the University of Essex, and is currently university lecturer and fellow of Emmanuel College, Cambridge. He is the author of *The Rise of the Corporate Economy* (1976), and (with J. A. Kay) *Concentration in Modern Industry – Theory, Measurement and the U.K. Experience* (forthcoming). He is now working on a study of the British electricity supply industry.

W. P. KENNEDY graduated from Rice University in 1966 and obtained his PhD from Northwestern University. He is currently a lecturer in economics at the University of Essex and is working on overseas investment and growth in the British economy. Some early results of this work were published as 'Foreign Investment, Trade and Growth in the United Kingdom, 1870–1913' in *Explorations in Economic History*, XI (1974).

PETER L. PAYNE was the first holder of the Colquhoun lectureship in business history at the University of Glasgow and is now professor and head of the department of economic history at the University of Aberdeen. His publications include *Rubber and Railways in the Nineteenth Century* (1961), and *British Entrepreneurship in the Nineteenth Century* (Macmillan, 1974) and he has edited *Studies in Scottish Business History* (1967). He is currently working on a study of the Scottish steelmakers.

W. J. READER was research assistant (1947–9) to Professor C. H. Wilson in preparing *The History of Unilever*, and then worked for Unilever from 1950 to 1965. Since then he has been a free-lance historian. He is a Fellow of the Royal Historical Society and during the summer of 1973 taught at the University of Delaware. His published works include *Professional Men: The Rise of the Professional Classes in 19th Century England* (1966), *Architect of Air Power: The Life of the First Viscount Weir of Eastwood* (1968), and *Imperial Chemical Industries: A History* (2 vols, 1970–75).

ANDREW WILSON graduated in economics and economic history from the University of Bristol and completed his MA in Social Studies at the University of Saskatchewan, Regina, in 1973 with a thesis on the British Papermaking Industry. He is currently lecturer in economic and social history in the department of economics, Loughborough University, and is working on the British electricity supply industry in the interwar period.

Introduction: Business Development and Economic Structure in Britain since 1880

LESLIE HANNAH

In the last twenty years, the subject of business history has developed rapidly in the United Kingdom, largely because of the initiatives of major companies in commissioning business histories by professional historians. The histories of Unilever, ICI, W. D. and H. O. Wills, Boots, and Courtaulds[1] have set a high standard and now offer to the economic historian a wealth of case study material with which to enrich his analysis of Britain's recent economic development. Yet there seems to be general agreement that the harvest from these rich possibilities has so far been a limited one. There has been too great a temptation to generalise from the single case, or – it is difficult to see it as the lesser failing – not to generalise at all. The intellectual 'spin-off' from business history to economic history and economics has not been as great as might reasonably have been hoped. Yet two works which have attempted to generalise from business history case study material have been widely welcomed by economic historians and social scientists in general. I refer, of course, to Professor Edith Penrose's *Theory of the Growth of the Firm*[2] and Professor Alfred D. Chandler's *Strategy and Structure. Chapters in the History of Industrial Enterprise.*[3] The intellectual traffic has thus not all been one-way, from the older disciplines to business history: the historical case study method exemplified in the work of Chandler has made an important contribution to the development of new ideas in the theory of the firm,[4] and this prompts legitimate expectations of further generalisations.

A relatively neglected aspect of the current work in British business history is the relationship between management organisation and strategic decisions at the level of the firm, on the one hand, and, on the other, the effect of these decisions on the growth of the firm and, ultimately, on the growth of the economy as a whole. There are excellent reasons why the study of business history has not developed in these directions. Firstly an individual company history – like political biography – has a fascination in its own right, irrespective of any broader spin-offs to other social sciences. Secondly – and more fundamentally – there are intellectual problems in developing generalisations from case studies which are perhaps more serious in business history than in other social sciences. Business historians, have, of course, made their dutiful obeisance to the role of Schumpeter's creative entrepreneur, and the self-evident truth that businessmen in one form or another, are the agents, and possibly the engines, of economic growth has not been ignored. To go beyond that, however, and assess the contribution of entrepreneurship to the growth of firms and the growth of the economy more precisely, raises difficult problems. How is entrepreneurship to be defined and measured? How representative are the firms being studied? Is there not a bias in the sample inherent in the fact that only successful firms survive to commission their own histories? Is the success we observe the result not of a series of decisions taken *ex ante* with good information and clear-sighted entrepreneurship but merely the outcome of a stochastic process in which good luck rather than good management has been important to the firm we observe as the survivor? Is our diagnosis of good judgement an attempt to endow with significance an entrepreneurial function which we do not fully understand; our concept of entrepreneurship a mere rag-bag of residuals which clothes our ignorance of the real determinants of business performance? My own instinct – and I use the word instinct, rather than conviction, advisedly – is to believe that the answer to this last question is no; that entrepreneurship – the realisation of new production functions, the strategic allocation of scarce investment resources among alternative possibilities, the winning of new markets – is a skill which is a major and systematic determinant of business growth and of the growth of the economy.[5] If this instinct is right, then business history has an important part to play in the explanation of economic growth, and we are justified in devoting attention – as did the conference to which the papers published in this volume were presented – to examining the extent to which international contrasts in business organisation and strategic economic decisions can illuminate international contrasts in economic performance.

It is natural to compare British and American business for a number of reasons. Both are large industrialised economies which have been industrial leaders of the world at different periods in the last hundred years; both have similar economic institutions – business corporations, capital markets, systems of law, and democratic political traditions sanctioning a mixed economy. They have both been treading similar industrial paths towards technology-intensive industry. Yet there are also significant differences. Large corporations came to America somewhat earlier than to Britain; the American economy has grown more rapidly than Britain's since 1870, though it too has recently performed more sluggishly compared with other western industrial nations. It is, then, appropriate to consider whether some of the contrasts in performance may be connected with substantial differences in the strategy and structure of British and American corporate enterprises.

Professor Chandler has identified three major types of improvement in efficiency which can be traced to new strategies adopted by American entrepreneurs from the mid-nineteenth century onwards.[6] The first is the integration of industrial operations under the control of one enterprise, extending from raw materials extraction through the various manufacturing operations to wholesaling and in some cases as far as retailing. The logic of such integration is not immutable; it may often pay a firm to remain unintegrated, buying its raw materials on the market and selling its products through agents. The key to successful entrepreneurial innovation is that the integration of the operation within the firm must reduce costs below those achieved by the 'invisible' – but not costless! – hand of the market. There may be a number of reasons why entrepreneurs can reduce costs through integration within the firm. In some industries the quality, or speed of movement, of raw materials may be increased if it is controlled by one management. Alternatively, expenses in manufacturing may be reduced, as for example, when ironmaking and steelmaking are integrated so there is no loss of heat between the two processes. Another possibility is that when a firm integrates forward to distribution and servicing – as for example, in the case of the Singer sewing machine enterprise – it may build consumer confidence and hence create markets which would not otherwise have been available. Chandler sees these strategies – usually formulated by strong management units organised on a functional basis (that is with centralised control and separate departments for purchasing, production, research, marketing etc.) – as being a major aspect of the growth of firms and entrepreneurial innovation in the United States between 1880 and 1920, though in Britain they appear to have been less common.[7] Although the railways in Britain, as in America, were the pioneers of large scale, functionally-differentiated professional management, there appears to have been little spin-off from this sector to other industrial fields, and new management methods tended to come from engineers and accountants rather than from men with railway experience.[8] However British firms like Boots and Pilkingtons do appear to have integrated at an early stage,[9] and it has to be remembered also that British firms which did not integrate could rely on a well-established and efficient network of merchants, wholesaling houses and interlocking markets which may have been superior to those available in the American economy.[10] Moreover, since Britain was less well-endowed with raw materials than the United States, her entrepreneurs' experiments in integration took an international rather than national form. If we considered the British steel companies with their interests in Spanish ore mines, and enterprises such as Shell, which rivalled Standard Oil as an integrated petroleum producer on a world scale but under Anglo-Dutch management and control, it would be more difficult to sustain the view that the opportunities for economies of integration were not being seized by British entrepreneurs.

A second important area of innovation by American enterprises was in large scale organisation and its associated mass production technology. In continuous process and metalworking industries, in particular, improved management techniques in the US increased the speed and volume of through-put and thus often laid the foundations for a mass production technology which was frequently both capital- and management-intensive. In industries like automobiles, electrical engineering, and the modern sector of chemical production, firms in the United States – and later, but more hesitantly, in Britain – expanded and were able to achieve substantial economies of large scale production. Some, like Ford in the US and Morris in the UK, grew internally, relying on their ability to build new, large-throughput, low cost production lines and cutting prices to win larger markets. In other industries where demand for the product of an individual firm was more differentiated and relatively inelastic, entrepreneurs found that they could achieve economies best by merging with competitors. The major task was to seek an organisation structure which was capable of overcoming the managerial diseconomies of growth which, especially in the turn of the century merger waves, had created difficulties in both countries, though perhaps more especially so in Britain.[11] Economies of large scale marketing, finance and research were equally, if not more important than economies in industrial plant size, and the technical expertise embodied in firms like Westinghouse and Du Pont in the US, and Associated Electrical Industries and Imperial Chemical Industries in Britain, were an important source of the flow of new products and processes to the market.[12]

The strategy of diversification into such new and rapidly growing markets was the third major source of business growth isolated by Professor Chandler in his analysis of American business development. As the process of innovation in products and markets became institutionalised in large firms the multidivisional management structure[13] was widely adopted. The relationship was at first seen as one in which strategy determined structure : firms adopting a strategy of diversification were among the first to adopt the new structure.[14] It is now clear, however, that the relationship is best seen as a mutually reinforcing, dynamic one – strategy does indeed induce a change in management structure, but the creation of the multidivisional management structure may also in its turn facilitate the adoption of a strategy of diversification.[15] By the same token the failure to adopt an appropriate organisation structure – for example the failure to create a strong head office with a good eye for new technical and market opportunities – can inhibit a large firm from seizing such opportunities, and hence lead to its stagnation. Multidivisional organisation appears then to have been an important, efficiency-improving innovation for US manufacturing firms and, as Dr Channon's initial report on his research on the British service industries suggests, the adoption of such a structure has also been important in industries such as banking and retailing, particularly in the postwar era when regional decentralisation in a form of multidivisional structure enabled some firms in such service sectors to overcome the problems of managerial diseconomies of scale.[16]

If the business historian is interested in the success or failure of individual firms, the strategy and structures which they adopted will clearly be a key variable to examine – but what of the macroeconomic significance of these changes? Apart from the obvious fact that, prior to the contemporary era of national statistical services, such information as we have about the economy is often available only at the level of individual firms, there is a good reason to believe that a study of the growth strategies of major firms will tell us a great deal about the general performance of the economy in the twentieth century. As Chart 1 shows, the largest 100 firms in the United States already accounted for over 20 per cent of its manufacturing output in the first decade of the century and in the 1920s, by which time large firms were also gaining ground in Britain, this share was equalled by the largest 100 British firms. Today in Britain almost one-half of manufacturing output is accounted for by the largest 100 firms, and the corresponding figure for America – by now a much larger economy – is one-third. The composition of the 100 largest firms has been constantly changing, but over the course of the century the mobility among the largest has become less pronounced and, if this trend continues, existing giants will have a more secure future than their predecessors. Moreover, the acquisition of vigorous young firms by large established ones means that innovation is often brought under the control of dominant firms even where it does not originate with them. The power which large firms exert over their suppliers – especially in industries such as automobile and aircraft manufacture, where a high proportion of parts are bought from outside – also implies that their influence on the set of strategic decisions, through the medium of which changes in the structure of national output occur, is greater than the statistics of their market share alone suggest.

In the light of these facts it is clear that the view sometimes ad-

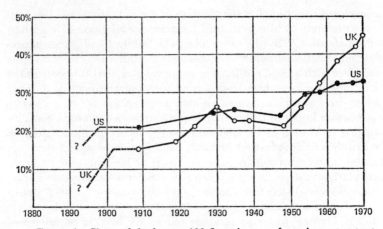

CHART 1   Share of the largest 100 firms in manufacturing net output

Sources: UK—L. Hannah, *The Rise of the Corporate Economy* (1976).
US—S. J. Prais and C. Reid, 'Large and Small Manufacturing Establishments in Europe and America' (forthcoming proceedings of Nijenrode Conference on Industrial Economics, ed. H. W. de Jong).

vanced that, because a process of natural selection operates in the economy whereby good firms drive out bad, the study of purposive behaviour in individual firms is of little value,[17] can legitimately be questioned. There are clearly some cases in which such a view has superficial plausibility. If we accept W. J. Reader's suggestions that many of the strategic decisions of entrepreneurs can only be explained in terms of their personal drives[18] – or even if we, more extremely, assume that there is at any one time a large array of small firms taking an equally large array of decisions on a quite random, whimsical basis – then those entrepreneurs whose fads pass the production test of technical feasibility and the market test of consumer acceptability will survive, whilst all others will go bankrupt and lose their importance. In such cases we may trouble ourselves little about the management practices and motivations of the myriads of individual small entrepreneurs involved, yet still gain some understanding of the process by which the observed result has been achieved. If, however, as in W. J. Reader's case studies, the entrepreneurs involved are large corporate ones such as Unilever and ICI, the chances are that they will survive, even if some of their decisions do prove to be great mistakes, and the resources which they commit to their mistakes may be a large proportion of the total investment resources of the economy. (For example, one investment project of ICI, that at Billingham, which Reader describes as a failure, involved an investment of £20m in 1927–1930;

in 1930 the whole of fixed capital formation in domestic manufacturing industry was only £68m.)[19] To point out the dominant role of such corporate investment decisions is not, of course, to say that it is of no importance to consider the role of newcomers, the displacement of leading firms, and the performance of smaller firms in the economy; nor is it to say that large firms are not subject to market forces – as ICI found to their cost at Billingham. But it does suggest that the larger firms have to some extent supplemented – some would say supplanted – market forces as the centres of resource allocation in the modern economy, and that their major strategic decisions are likely to be of decisive importance to the future of such an economy. The skill with which they formulate and choose between investment strategies, and their efficiency in executing them, ought, then, to be a major preoccupation of social scientists concerned with explaining economic performance and of management scientists seeking to improve it.

We may take as an example the possible influence of corporate investment decisions on the diversification of output and structural change in the economy. Historically, economic growth has occurred not merely through the more efficient production of a given set of products but also, importantly, through the transfer of resources to the production of new products in which opportunities to achieve high productivity of both capital and labour were frequently more easily realised. In the present century the production of automobiles, electrical and electronic equipment, fine chemicals, plastics, and artificial fibres has, for example, been an important source of growth in America and in Europe, and the speed with which a given economy has been able to develop high-technology production capability in these areas and transfer investment resources to them has been an important determinant of its overall rate of growth.[20] Now such a transfer of resources can occur, in principle, without the intervention of existing large firms at all. There are many cases of important innovations being made by entrepreneurs with little capital and experience, or by small firms in a different industry. A large firm like Courtaulds, for example, which pioneered rayon (artificial silk) manufacture in Britain and America before the First World War, relied for its initial cash flow and business skills on its experience as a small firm specialising in the production of that important but distinctly Victorian product, mourning crêpe.[21] In addition to such ploughback of profits within existing enterprises, loans between local capitalists, made on the basis of close personal and social ties, were an important source of capital for new ventures and could overcome some of the rigidities implicit in an industrial system in which firms were specialised by product but in which there was also a need for structural change. The growth of the highly successful electricity supply undertakings on the north-east coast of Britain, for example, was possible because of the investments made in them by the families which owned the prosperous local ship-building concerns.[22]

In industries where the capital requirements are large, and where profit ploughback or local borrowing are an inefficient way of build-ing up a capital stock of the appropriate size within the firm, the capital market may provide a useful additional source of funds. Capital issues on the stock market can channel savings from the investing public to those industrialists with such urgent and large capital requirements, and in Britain, the institutional arrangements available for capital issues were more advanced than those in the United States, indeed, more advanced than those in any other country.[23] However, high costs may inhibit firms from applying to the formal capital markets, and, as W. P. Kennedy argues,[24] there is reason to believe that, despite its undoubted maturity, the London stock market did not adequately fulfil the function of diversifying investment strategy toward the new industries with rapid growth potential. The bias against such risky, but potentially lucrative investments, which Kennedy diagnoses, may have been a reflection of the lack of skills in the City for evaluating the performance of industrial enterprises. Other institutions like in-dustrial banks,[25] or large industrial corporations, may in fact be more appropriate financial intermediaries in that they possess closer know-ledge of both markets and production technology, on which the evalua-tion of future investment strategy is ideally based. Such at least was the view of the US Chase Bank, for when in the 1920s the bank de-cided that British industry represented a potentially profitable field for investment, it established a joint subsidiary with a major British corporation, Imperial Chemical Industries. This subsidiary, the Finance Corporation of Great Britain and America, drew heavily on the exper-tise of ICI's head office in determining its investment strategy and ICI was also extensively engaged on assessing new profit opportunities in a wide range of metal processing, engineering and chemical in-dustries on its own account.[26]

Chandler has also stressed that the search for the fast growing and profitable markets of the future is an important strategic function of the general office of large corporations, and many of the innovations in the fast growing industries have come from the major corporations – ICI, for example, pioneered polythene, and Du Pont pioneered nylon. In each of these cases it was, of course, logical for a chemical firm to be involved in research and development in these fields,[27] but, as we have seen, there are other non-technical reasons why existing large firms may be the vehicles of important diversifications in the output of an economy. In an economy in which firms are typically specialised by industry, in which the majority of new capital investment is financed by the ploughback of profits, and in which the formal capital markets have little experience or information on which to base an assessment of new and untried capital projects, structural change can be given an important boost if existing large corporations take it upon themselves to finance innovations. The structure of an economy *may* change rapidly without the intermediation of large diversifying firms, but it will almost certainly grow more rapidly if the services of such firms are available to smooth the transition. The most important exception will be where management skills are industry-specific. If, say, the skills of steelmen can be applied only to their own industry then any attempt by them to enter a new industry could reduce the overall efficiency of the economy.

How then do the US and the UK rate for their performance in changing the structure of their economy towards the rapidly growing, high productivity industries?

If we look at the manufacturing sector it seems clear that Britain was a laggard in diversifying into the new industries before the First World War and it is generally accepted that the main growth of the automobile, chemical and electrical industries was delayed until the interwar years in Britain.[28] The alibis for this have been well rehearsed,[29] but they cannot yet be considered conclusive. An important chicken-and-egg problem arises for example in the view that since the British market was growing more slowly than that in the US the market for new products was simply smaller.[30] No doubt in part the US market was growing rapidly because of factors beyond the control of British entrepreneurs, factors such as the high rate of immigration and her wealth of natural resources, but equally it is possible that, if entrepreneurial choices in Britain had been more skilfully directed, the British economy would have grown faster than in the event it did, and larger markets would thus have been attainable.[31] W. P. Kennedy has presented[32] some compelling evidence that the choices made by UK wealthholders – and in the period before the divorce of ownership and control this is in many cases synonymous with the choices made by entrepreneurs – were biased by institutional forces against needed structural change and that this failing was a major cause of the slow growth of the new industries. There is also evidence that some British firms which attempted to diversify their production portfolio from old industries to new ones did so less skilfully and less successfully than some of their American counterparts.[33] Even more damningly, a high proportion of the output of the new industries in Britain was produced by American firms operating in Britain, rather than by native British capitalists and entrepreneurs. Before the First World War for example, two of the four largest electrical machinery producers in the United Kingdom, British Westinghouse and British Thomson-Houston, were American-owned, whilst a third, Siemens, was German-owned. The remaining one, GEC, was under nominal British ownership, being controlled and managed by an immigrant from Germany![34] Germany also appears to have led Britain in the newer sectors of the chemical industry; and Brunner Mond, one of the leading technical innovators in the UK chemical industry, was founded by Ludwig Mond, a German Jewish immigrant, and J. T. Brunner, son of a Swiss immigrant.[35] Such borrowing of expertise from abroad was, of course, an important source of the international diffusion of skills and technology and it was also used by America and Germany. Nevertheless the degree of foreign influence is in the British case so great, and it is located in such important growth sectors of the economy, that unfavourable inferences about British entrepreneurship are difficult to avoid. Moreover, once American and German firms had established large organisations in their home markets, with specialised marketing services, higher overall volume, and lower unit costs, it became increasingly difficult for new British competitors to establish themselves. Hence in many cases this pattern of foreign domination of key sectors persisted in the interwar years – it was Gerard Swope of US General Electric, for example, who organised the Associated Electrical Industries merger in 1926–8, and two American automobile firms were among the market leaders in the rapidly growing UK car industry – Ford through their British subsidiary and General Motors through their acquisition in 1925 of Vauxhall.[36] In these industries the market opportunities can hardly be said to have been lacking since American interlopers were able to seize them, and the suspicion of a failure of British entrepreneurship must be strong. The early lead which the Americans gained appears to have been consolidated with time and today one-fifth of British manufacturing industry is under American control; furthermore US firms in the UK persistently show a higher rate of profit than native UK firms.[37]

Outside manufacturing industry the case is weaker, partly because there are remarkably few studies of other sectors by business historians,[38] though, as Dr Channon suggests, the service sector has been a rapidly expanding one and its management structure and strategy can be analysed in Chandlerian terms.[39] The public utility sector also deserves more attention, for whilst public utilities do not normally compete directly with their foreign counterparts, they have an important influence on the underlying costs which the manufacturing and service sectors face. Before nationalisation in 1948, the control of services such as electricity supply lay in the hands of municipalities and private companies, and it might be thought that contrasts in ownership would have had important influences on the goal structure of managers. In the electricity supply industry however, the ideology of the senior managers and engineers – Galbraith's 'technostructure' – appears to have been the crucial determinant of the strategies of undertakings, though Andrew Wilson reports that municipally-owned undertakings were more likely than privately owned ones to charge lower prices and adopt a vigorous strategy of expansion.[40] Whilst this undoubtedly promoted the expansion of this important productivity-improving industry, it would, of course, be necessary to establish that the lower prices charged by municipalities were not below long-run marginal costs before we could confidently generalise about their implications for growth and welfare.[41] For the public sector more generally, there is evidence that in the 1960s its record on pricing, profitability and productivity compares favourably with that of private manufacturing industry,[42] though Dr Channon views the recent impact of Treasury control as potentially harmful to strategic decision-making and managerial efficiency.[43]

If there was entrepreneurial failure in Britain – and the circumstantial evidence for it, at least in the manufacturing sector, is certainly sufficient to justify initiating the prosecution's case – why, then, did it occur? Is it really plausible that the country whose entrepreneurs seemed so active and enterprising in the first hundred years of the industrial revolution, should suddenly have become sleepy and stagnant in the new phase of industrialisation based on automobiles, electricity and chemicals? One important point to remember is that the British in the crucial period of the closing years of the nineteenth century and much of the first half of the twentieth century saw themselves not as maximising the development of their own small island but rather as developing a large part of the world and particularly the British Empire. Among the many millions of emigrants from Britain to the United States and the White Commonwealth in the late nineteenth and early twentieth centuries must have been some of the more enterprising of her citizens, and even those who retained their British allegiance and did not become citizens of the foreign lands in which they worked would represent an important loss to the stock of British entrepreneurs.

It is arguable that the overseas enterprise of Britons created substantial benefits for the home economy, as in the case of the discovery of oil in Persia and the subsequent development of the whole Middle Eastern oil industry whose early management by Britons is described by Dr Ferrier.[44] This secured not only plentiful and cheap supplies of petroleum for the home economy but also the rents of pioneering entrepreneurship in an underdeveloped country with no technical or management skills, and contemporaries were well aware of the advantages of these investments.[45] However, such direct investment was the exception rather than the rule, and, as Dr Kennedy argues,[46] the case for portfolio investment overseas being beneficial to the home economy is less clear cut.

Another favourite explanation for entrepreneurial failure which has been advanced is the unsuitability of the family firm – and especially the old-established family firm – to the task of transition which the British economy has faced in the present century. Yet, as the conference papers and discussion demonstrated, there are many difficulties with this hypothesis. Professor Barker, for example, has shown[47] from his case study of Pilkingtons that a wide definition of the family and a willingness to recruit outside talent through marriage created a pool of management potential which enabled the firm to survive and prosper whilst remaining under family control.[48] On the other hand there is no shortage of examples of family firms which failed to make the adjustments required in changing economic circumstances,[49] and it seems unlikely that there were very many family firms – in the classic sense of those remaining under family ownership – which, like Pilkingtons, were large enough to be included – and to remain – among the dominant firms in the economy.[50] It may be, however, that the 'problem' of the family firm should be more widely defined to include the cases, which were very common in Britain, in which founding families had given up majority voting control but retained a minority financial interest sufficient to preserve their management positions. Even when the shares were sold, the original family owners could retain some influence on the important management decisions of a company – as is shown in the extraordinary deference shown to the founder's son (and future chairman) at Boots, even *after* it was sold to the American-owned Liggett International drugstore group.[51] The problems which were caused when firms grew by the merger of a number of family firms are now well known,[52] and many of the dominant British companies are best seen as federations of family firms under a holding company umbrella, rather than as centralised units in which strategic decision-making is firmly under the control of a head office. Not all such arrangements were unsuccessful,[53] but it is difficult to resist the conclusion that in many companies the family vested interest inhibited change which would have been desirable.[54]

There were, of course, potential pressures which could change this situation. Crises in the development of the firm caused by technical change, or the collapse of traditional markets, or the failure of the family to produce sufficient male issue to take on the major management functions might produce a reassessment of organisation and strategy.[55] One insistent and powerful incentive to change – the pressure of competition – was, however, somewhat muted in Britain compared with the United States, particularly in the period between the 1930s and the 1950s, when restrictive practices and cartel arrangements (which were illegal in the United States) proliferated in Britain as firms attempted to protect themselves against the depression by reducing the penalties of failure. The role of restrictive agreements in inhibiting managerial innovation and reorganisation is now widely recognised.[56] In addition, agreements between firms may have had some effect not only on competition within industries but on competition between industries, and hence on the rate at which diversification contributed to the growth of new sectors in the economy. Courtaulds, for example, had an agreement with ICI that they would not diversify into the chemical industry, in return for which ICI undertook not to diversify into rayon fibres, a field in which they had considerable background knowledge and development potential.[57] The widespread adoption of new strategies and structures by British firms in the 1960s – following the tightening up of competition legislation in the Restrictive Trade Practices Act of 1956 and other changes in the economic environment[58] – provides further confirmation of the earlier role of competitive restrictions in inhibiting change, though the problems of the British economy have by no means been eliminated by these new departures.[59]

This introduction – like the conference whose proceedings it introduces – has raised a number of questions, but cannot claim to have answered them. Nonetheless, it has, I hope, made a convincing case for the view that by asking these questions we may gain a fuller understanding not only of the process of the growth of industrial firms but also of the development of whole economies through time. What then is needed to realise this goal? There is still room for further work on the traditional 'case study' basis of individual companies : the histories of the majority of the largest companies in Britain still remain to be written.[60] Encouragingly, as a result of the work of Chandler and others, there is a growing awareness among the potential writers of such histories of the importance of seeking answers to the sort of problems raised here, and the contributions of Alford, Kennedy and Payne should reinforce this awareness.[61] Nonetheless to look for an answer to these questions primarily in case studies – even case studies rooted in well-conceived problem-centred research – is inappropriate. A proliferation of examples will not by itself resolve the issues. Indeed almost all of the points that have been made here and backed by examples could equally be refuted by counter-examples. It is not difficult in this period to find firms in Britain which exhibited the favourable traits which Chandler has identified in the innovating American corporations; equally there are many examples – in this and earlier periods – of US corporations which failed to seize opportunities to innovate in strategy and structure, and of British corporations entering the American market in competition with them and beating them at their own game.[62] On the basis of aggregate performance, also, there is scope for constructive scepticism about the recurrent criticisms of British entrepreneurial failure. In the interwar period, and in the 1930s especially, Britain's industrial performance – by then stimulated by competition from innovating corporations in the United States and, to a lesser extent, in Germany – did in fact compare creditably with that of these major industrial rivals. Moreover, there is increasing evidence that this may have been at least in part the result of substantial initiatives in the direction of rationalising industrial structure, diversifying output into the new industries, and investing in managerial innovation and in research and development.[63] The picture is thus not black and white, there is neither blanket entrepreneurial failure nor total success. Hence the issues are hardly likely to be advanced further by the mere multiplication of contending examples and counter-examples.

The key to future constructive research must surely be in two major directions : the more careful definition of yardsticks and the examination of wider and more representative samples of firms. Agreed yardsticks for measuring performance are important if we are to get away from the more naïve assessments which tend to be made of the historical performance of businessmen. These generally conclude, somewhat predictably, that on the one hand business decisions were not wholly illogical, whilst on the other hand it is with hindsight possible to envisage an alternative course of action which would have been superior. This will, of course, be true, and indeed uncontentious, in 99 out of 100 cases : businessmen achieve higher marks than monkeys, but they are not supermen. The real problem is to define an intermediate scale on which to measure performance without descending to self-evident banality. International comparisons of entrepreneurial performance may, we have suggested, provide one of the best yardsticks, at least for countries which have access to a common fund of technology and are at broadly similar stages of economic development. It is important, however, in drawing such comparisons to make allowance for differing resource endowments, market opportunities, and any other factors which are beyond the control of the entrepreneurs in the economy in question. Yardsticks have been suggested by the 'new' economic historians[64] which have the merit of abstracting from such differences. Essentially they involve an examination of whether entrepreneurs in various countries were maximising profits, given the constraints placed on their behaviour by such factors. Many studies in this vein have cast doubt on the thesis of British entrepreneurial failure and hence provided a salutary warning against casual criticism of entrepreneurs, but it is noteworthy that the majority of the studies have been concerned with the choice of techniques *within* individual industries, rather than with the broader strategic question of diversification of output. The management skills required for these two functions probably differ considerably and the broader question still awaits study. Whilst the 'new' economic historians have made an important contribution in improving the rigour of work on entrepreneurship, then, much work remains to be done on devising yardsticks for a wider range of entrepreneurial skills than those examined so far.[65] Once yardsticks are established, it is equally important to study a sample of firms which is statistically appropriate and relevant to the issue being investigated. Already there are signs of interesting longitudinal studies of the determinants of the performance of UK firms in the postwar years, and, encouragingly, these are linked to a similar study in Germany, which may yield interesting comparative performance yardsticks.[66] Similar representative international comparisons may well provide insights – and more rigorous testing of hypotheses – for the business historian and economic historian also. The prize – a deeper understanding of the microeconomic foundations of economic growth – is one which is well worth competing for. The questions raised by the contributions which follow will give some useful pointers for potential entrants to the competition.

NOTES

1   C. Wilson, *The History of Unilever*, 2 vols (London, 1954); W. J. Reader, *Imperial Chemical Industries: A History*, 2 vols (London, 1970, 1975); B. W. E. Alford, W. D. and H. O. Wills and the development of the U.K. Tobacco Industry 1786–1965 (London, 1973); S. D. Chapman, *Jesse Boot of Boots the Chemists* (London, 1974); D. C. Coleman, *Courtaulds: An Economic and Social History*, 2 vols (Oxford, 1969).
2   (Oxford, 1959).
3   (Cambridge, Mass., 1962). See also R. S. Edwards and H. Townsend, *Business Enterprise* (London, 1958); Bruce R. Scott, 'Stages in Corporate Development', unpublished paper, (Harvard Business School, 1971).
4   e.g. O. E. Williamson, 'Managerial Discretion, Organisational Form and the Multi-Division Hypothesis' in R. Marris and A. Wood (eds), *The Corporate Economy* (London, 1971).
5   For a fuller consideration of the nature of the stochastic process which may determine the growth of firms, see L. Hannah and J. A. Kay, *Concentration in Modern Industry: Theory, Measurement and the U.K. Experience* (London, 1976).
6   A. D. Chandler, *Strategy and Structure*; also his 'Management Decentralisation: An Historical Analysis', *Business History Review*, xxx (1956); 'The Role of Business in the U.S.: A Historical Survey', *Daedalus*, xcviii (1969): 'The Beginnings of Big Business in American Industry', *Business History Review*, xxxiii (1959); 'Development Diversification and Decentralisation' in R. Freeman (ed.), *Postwar Economic Trends in the United States* (New York, 1960); 'The Large Corporation and the Making of the Modern American Economy' in S. E. Ambrose (ed.), *Institutions in Modern America* (Baltimore, 1967); 'The Structure of American Industry in the Twentieth Century: A Historical Overview', *Business History Review*, xliii (1969); 'Structure and Investment Decisions in the United States' in H. Daems and H. van der Wee (eds), *The Rise of Managerial Capitalism*

(Louvain, 1974); with F. Redlich, 'Recent Developments in American Business Administration and their Conceptualisation', *Weltwirtschaftliches Archiv*, (1961); with L. Galambos 'The Development of Large Scale Economic Organisations in Modern America', *Journal of Economic History*, xxx (1970); with S. Salsbury, 'Le Role de la Firme dans L'Economie Americaine', *Economie Appliqué* (1964).

7   Chandler, 'The Development of Modern Management Structure in the US and UK', pp. 23–51 below.

8   G. R. Hawke, *Railways and Economic Growth in England and Wales 1840–1870* (Oxford, 1970), pp. 384–8; L. Hannah, 'Managerial Innovation and the Rise of the Large Scale Company in Interwar Britain', *Economic History Review*, xxvii (1974); B. Supple, 'Aspects of Private Investment Strategy in Britain' in Daems and van der Wee (eds), *Rise of Managerial Capitalism*, pp. 87–8.

9   S. D. Chapman, 'Strategy and Structure at Boots the Chemists', pp. 95–107 below; T. C. Barker 'A Family Firm becomes a Public Company: Changes at Pilkington Brothers Limited in the Inter-war Years', pp. 85–94 below. See also R. Ferrier, 'The Early Management Organisation of British Petroleum and Sir John Cadman', pp. 130–47 below.

10 Cf. pp. 32–40 below.

11 P. L. Payne, 'The Emergence of the Large-Scale Company in Great Britain, 1870–1914', *Economic History Review*, xx (1967).

12 On the growth of large firms in Britain by 1930 see my *The Rise of the Corporate Economy* (1976), passim.

13 See Chandler, 'The Development of Modern Management Structure in the US and UK' pp. 23–32 below.

14 Chandler, *Strategy and Structure*, p. 324.

15 e.g. B. W. E. Alford, 'Strategy and Structure in the UK Tobacco Industry', pp. 79–82 below.

16 D. F. Channon, 'Corporate Evolution in the Service Industries', pp. 213–34 below.

17 A. A. Alchian, 'Uncertainty, Evolution and Economic Theory', *Journal of Political Economy*, lviii (1950).

18 W. J. Reader, 'Personality, Strategy and Structure: Some Consequences of Strong Minds', pp. 108–29 below.

19 C. H. Feinstein, *National Income, Expenditure and Output of the United Kingdom* (Cambridge, 1972) p. T92.

20 A classic statement of the importance of structural change in economic growth may be found in I. Svennilson, *Growth and Stagnation in the European Economy* (Geneva, 1954).

21 Coleman, *Courtaulds*, ii, passim.

22 L. Hannah, unpublished paper. Similarly in Germany, the most successful electricity undertaking, the Rhenish-Westphalian company, was financed by the Stinnes-Thyssen coal interests, see R. Tilly, 'The Growth of Large Scale Enterprise in Germany since the middle of the Nineteenth Century' in Daems and van der Wee, *Rise of Managerial Capitalism*, p. 157. The incentives for such diversification are normally enhanced for mature industries as they encounter market saturation and declining marginal productivity of capital in their traditional fields. However, the staple industries – cotton, coal and shipbuilding – did, of course, remain prosperous in Britain up to the interwar period, and this may in some cases have encouraged 'satisficing' rather than risk-diversifying and profit maximising behaviour.

23 L. Davis, 'The Capital Markets and Industrial Concentration in the U.S. and U.K., a Comparative Study', *Economic History Review*, xix (1966).

24 Kennedy, 'Institutional Response to Economic Growth', pp. 151–83 below.

25 A. D. Chandler and H. Daems, 'The Rise of Managerial Capitalism and its impact on investment strategy in the Western World and Japan' in Daems and

van der Wee, *Rise of Managerial Capitalism*, p. 32; Kennedy, op. cit. pp. 155–8 below. However, diversification strategies can also be missed by financial groupings: the Japanese *zaibatsu*, for example, were slow to realise the potential of investments in electric utilities, see K. Nakagawa, 'The Structures and Motives of investment by private enterprises in Japan before the Second World War', in idem, p. 206.

26 Information from ICI archives. I am grateful to W. J. Reader for drawing my attention to this case. The FCGBA faded out in the slump of the 1930s.

27 Though the element of luck should not be underrated and ICI was slow to respond to the challenge of the developing plastics industry, see Reader, *ICI*, II, 318–410.

28 H. W. Richardson, 'Overcommitment in Britain before 1930', *Oxford Economic Papers*, XVII (1965).

29 For a favourable view of British entrepreneurship see D. N. McCloskey and L. G. Sandberg, 'From Damnation to Redemption: Judgements on the Late Victorian Entrepreneur', *Explorations in Economic History*, IX (1971); T. C. Barker, 'History: Economic and Social', in C. B. Cox and A. E. Dyson (eds), *The Twentieth Century Mind* (London, 1972); C. Wilson, 'Economy and Society in Late Victorian England', *Economic History Review*, XVIII (1965). The more pessimistic view is represented by D. Landes, *The Unbound Prometheus* (Cambridge, 1969) ch. 5; A. L. Levine, *Industrial Retardation in Britain, 1880–1914* (London, 1967); D. H. Aldcroft, 'The Entrepreneur and the British Economy 1870–1914', *Economic History Review*, XVII (1964).

30 Chandler, 'The Development of Modern Management Structure in the US and UK', p. 47 below. Of course there is also the problem, though Chandler considers it the less important one, that tastes were more differentiated in Britain, so that as well as facing a small market the British entrepreneur faced a 'class' rather than 'mass' market.

31 Similar points are made in B. Supple, 'Aspects of Private Investment Strategy in Britain', in Daems and van der Wee, *Rise of Managerial Capitalism*, p. 79.

32 W. P. Kennedy, 'Institutional Response to Economic Growth: Capital Markets in Britain to 1914', pp. 151–83 below; see also his 'Foreign Investment, Trade and Growth in the United Kingdom', *Explorations in Economic History*, XI (1974).

33 L. Hannah, 'Strategy and Structure in the Manufacturing Sector', pp. 184–202 below.

34 I. C. R. Byatt, 'Electrical Products', in D. H. Aldcroft (ed.), *The Development of British Industry and Foreign Competition 1875–1914* (London, 1968).

35 Reader, *ICI*, I, 37–56; H. W. Richardson, 'Chemicals', in Aldcroft, op. cit. On innovative investment strategies in Germany more generally see R. Tilly, 'The growth of large scale enterprise in Germany since the middle of the nineteenth century', in Daems and van der Wee, *Rise of Managerial Capitalism*.

36 On American investment generally see J. H. Dunning, *American Investment in British Manufacturing Industry* (London, 1958).

37 See p. 69, note 62, below.

38 Honourable exceptions include P. Mathias, *Retailing Revolution* (London, 1967); B. Supple, *The Royal Exchange Assurance 1720–1970* (Cambridge, 1970).

39 D. Channon, 'Corporate Evolution in the Service Industries', pp. 213–34 below.

40 A. Wilson, 'The Strategy of Sales Expansion in the British Electricity Supply Industry between the Wars', pp. 203–12 below.

41 Cf. I. M. D. Little, *The Price of Fuel* (Oxford, 1953).

42 R. Pryke, *Public Enterprise in Practice* (London, 1971).

43 pp. 230–1 below.

44 R. Ferrier, 'The Early Management Organisation of British Petroleum and Sir John Cadman', pp. 130–47 below.

45   [Macmillan] Committee on Finance and Industry, *Report* (Cmd 3897, 1931), para 384.

46   pp. 158–77 below. Recently direct investment has been subjected to greater criticism, see W. B. Reddaway, *Effects of U.K. Direct Investment Overseas* (Cambridge, 1968).

47   Barker, 'A Family Firm becomes a Public Company', pp. 85–94 below. See also his *The Glassmakers* (1976).

48   In France, also, it appears that many family firms were able to survive, perhaps without detriment to the economy, by creating a skilled and *polytechnique*-educated cadre of potential managers within the family, see M. Levy-Leboyer, 'Le patronat français a-t-il été malthusien?', *Le Mouvement Social* (1974).

49   e.g. W. G. Rimmer, *Marshalls of Leeds, Flax-Spinners 1788–1886* (Cambridge, 1960).

50   A. J. Merrett and M. E. Lehr, *The Private Company Today* (London, 1971) 67–70. However, outside manufacturing industry, owner- or family-dominated enterprises still played a major role in the postwar era, see S. Aris, *The Jews in Business* (London, 1970), passim.

51   Chapman, 'Strategy and Structure at Boots the Chemists', pp. 97–100 below. For a similar phenomenon in another European context, see Tilly, 'Growth of Large Scale Enterprise in Germany', in Daems and van der Wee, *Rise of Managerial Capitalism*, p. 157.

52   Payne, 'Emergence of the Large-Scale Company in Great Britain', *Economic History Review*, xx (1967) 527–36. L. Hannah, 'Mergers in British Manufacturing Industry 1880–1918', *Oxford Economic Papers*, xxvi (1974) pp . 13–14.

53   Alford, pp. 73–5 below.

54   Hannah, 'Strategy and Structure in the Manufacturing Sector', pp. 195–200 below. Of course it would be too simplistic to suggest that the personality of a family heir or dominant manager in the United States did not also sometimes inhibit change; see e.g. Chandler, *Strategy and Structure*, pp. 365–6.

55   e.g. Barker, 'A Family Firm becomes a Public Company', p. 89 below.

56   Chandler, 'The Development of Modern Management Structure in the US and UK', pp. 48–9 below; Hannah, 'Strategy and Structure in the Manufacturing Sector', p. 200 below. In Germany, however, cartels were tolerated, and even encouraged, by government until recently, without obviously sapping the dynamism of her industry.

57   D. C. Coleman, *Courtaulds, An Economic and Social History* (Oxford, 1969) ii, 264–5.

58   D. F. Channon, *The Strategy and Structure of British Enterprise* (London, 1973) pp. 25–32.

59   R. E. Caves (ed.), *Britain's Economic Prospects* (Brookings Institution, Washington and London, 1968), passim.

60   One unlooked for advantage of the recent waves of merger activity and the advance of nationalisation, is that it will be possible to study whole industries – or at least the history of the dominant firms within them – from the archives which have thus come under central control. Recent studies of the electrical engineering industry by R. Jones and O. Marriott, *Anatomy of a Merger: A History of GEC, AEI and English Electric* (London, 1970), and of the steel industry by J. Vaizey, *A History of British Steel* (London, 1974), provide some interesting insights into the possibilities of such research based on the archives of a number of firms in the same industry, though they cannot claim to equal the high standards set by some of the better business histories.

61   B. W. E. Alford, 'The Chandler Thesis—some General Observations', pp. 52–70 below; W. P. Kennedy and P. L. Payne, 'Directions for Future Research', pp. 237–58 below.

62 It comes as a surprise to many Americans to learn that Lever Brothers is owned not by an American company but by the Anglo-Dutch Unilever enterprise!

63 B. Supple, 'Aspects of Private Investment Strategy in Britain', in Daems and van der Wee, *Rise of Managerial Capitalism*; H. W. Richardson, *Economic Recovery in Britain 1932–1939* (London, 1967); and his 'New Industries in Britain between the Wars', *Economic History Review*, xiii (1961); Hannah, *The Rise of the Corporate Economy*, ch. 3, 7, 8 and 9; M. Sanderson, 'Research and the Firm in British Industry, 1919–1939', *Science Studies*, ii (1972).

64 e.g. P. H. Lindert and K. Trace, 'Yardsticks for Victorian Entrepreneurs', in D. N. McCloskey (ed.), *Essays on a Mature Economy: Britain after 1840* (London, 1971); McCloskey and Sandberg, 'From Damnation to Redemption'.

65 Serious problems arise for the 'new' economic history if the 'counter-factual', strategies which are posited involve substantial, rather than marginal, changes, as, for example, in structural change. The general equilibrium solutions to such systems may be very different from those so far obtained by the 'new' economic historians.

66 This research is being undertaken at Nuffield College, and at the Free University of Berlin; see e.g. S. Nyman and A. Silberston, 'An Approach to the Study of the Growth of Firms', paper delivered to the Second Conference on the Economics of Industrial Structure, Nijenrode, Netherlands, April 1975.

Part One

THE DEVELOPMENT OF MODERN MANAGEMENT

1 The Development of Modern Management Structure in the US and UK*

ALFRED D. CHANDLER JR

In recent years business practices in the United States and the United Kingdom have been converging. In both countries the largest and most powerful industrial enterprises now use much the same basic type of organisational structure. In 1970, according to one careful study, 72 of the 100 largest industrial enterprises in Britain were administered through some variation of the multidivisional form.[1] The percentage had become higher in the United States.

This multidivisional structure is depicted on Chart 1. It consists of a number of operating divisions administered by a general office. The divisions are responsible for the production and marketing of a major line for a major product market or geographic territory and for the coordination of flow of materials and funds through processes of production and distribution from the suppliers of raw materials to the ultimate consumer. The general or corporate office includes general executives and a large advisory and financial staff. Besides coordinating, monitoring, and evaluating divisional performance, the general office plans for the continuing health and growth of the enterprise and allocates the funds, equipment and personnel required to carry out such plans. In both the US and UK the large industrial enterprises that adopted the multidivisional structure were those that had moved into new geographical areas and into new product markets.

In both countries, too, the large industrial enterprises, whether they had adopted the multidivisional structure or not, were clustered in relatively few sets of industries. These were industries where the technology of production involved capital intensive, high volume large-batch or continuous processes and where the output of such processes of production was mass marketed in national and international mar-

* The author gratefully acknowledges the support of the Division of Research at the Harvard Graduate School of Business for this study.

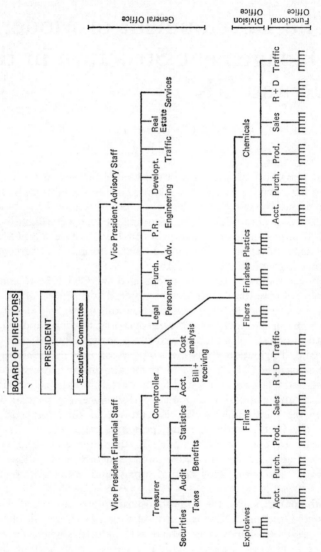

CHART 1   The multidivisional structure

kets. By mid-century in Britain and earlier in the United States, the large industrial enterprise had come to dominate those chemical, pharmaceutical, rubber, glass, newsprint and food industries using flow processes. It had triumphed in metal-working industries using mass production techniques involving the fabricating and assembling of interchangeable parts to manufacture agricultural, office, electrical and electronic machinery, automobiles, and similar products.[2] By 1970 firms using flow and interchangeable parts processes had diversified into new product markets and geographical areas and had adopted the multidivisional structure.

On the other hand, in both countries the large enterprises in textiles and metal-making were slow to adopt the multidivisional form. They continued to serve much the same markets in much the same areas. In both countries too there were labour-intensive industries in which the large enterprise rarely appeared at all. These included the apparel, lumber, furniture, leather and publishing and printing industries, those processing foods on a seasonal basis, those making simple tools, hardware and other easily fabricated products, and those producing complex, unstandardised machines and instruments.

In a general way, then, the same type of organisation has come to be used in the US and the UK to administer large enterprises in the same types of industries. But that is about as far as the similarities go. A closer view of the operation of large industrial firms in the two countries brings out many contrasts in the forms and procedures used to manage big business. It also reveals that relationships between managers and owners differed in the two nations. These dissimilarities, in fact, help to explain fundamental differences in the rise of modern industrial enterprise in the US and the UK. In this paper I would like to use such contrasts as a way to make a most tentative comparative analysis of the historical development of this most important modern economic institution in these two advanced economies.

The analysis can be begun by looking at the differences in the ways in which British and Americans were using the multidivisional form in the early 1970s. Here I rely almost wholly on Derek Channon's valuable *Strategy and Structure of British Enterprise*. Channon points out that multidivisional structures used by British enterprises were less carefully defined and articulated than those of American firms. The duties and functions of the general office and the divisions were less clearly spelled out. Individual authority and responsibility were not as sharply pinpointed. British firms employed more committees and boards in managing day-to-day operations than did American ones. The distinction between policy and operations was often blurred. In many cases the general office included the heads of the operating divisions, who were responsible for current operations as well as for long-term policies and plans. The group executive (a general officer with supervision over several divisions and a standard position in American management) was in 1970 a position still little used in British business. The general service and financial staffs, though extensive, were usually smaller and less comprehensive than those in the United States. Thus, although there were some differences in divisional organisation and activities, the basic contrast in the operation of the multidivisional form in the two nations has come in the make-up and functions of the general office.[3]

For this reason over-all control and planning has been less extensive and less sophisticated in British than in American multidivisional enterprises. By 1970 few British firms had gone beyond financial performance as the criterion used in monitoring and evaluating the performance of the divisions. Nearly all used rate of return on capital employed, normally using a cash flow discount method. For some, turnover and share of market were also used to evaluate divisional performance. Forecasting was still not widely employed for short-term adjustment of flows or for long-term capital allocation. Although nearly all used budgets for both control and planning, some had only introduced such procedures in the 1960s. Relatively few firms had formal planning offices and even fewer had offices that concentrated on management development. In both control and planning, the top executives relied more on personal contact in office visits and committee meetings than did their American counterparts. Channon did find, however, that the diversified firms in the most technologically advanced industries – large chemical, pharmaceutical, electrical and electronics firms – had control and planning procedures as sophisticated and clearly defined as those of any of the multidivisional American firms.

The differences in how the multidivisional form is used suggest two basic differences between the American and British enterprises themselves.

First, the British firms are smaller in size, and, secondly, they have adopted the multidivisional structure more recently. Because these firms are not as big as those in the United States, a smaller number of top executives can have closer personal contact with each other and with their operating managers. Because the techniques are still new, they have not yet been fully tested and adjusted to the specific needs of the enterprises adopting them.

Channon's information emphasises how recently British enterprise adopted the new form. In 1950 it was still almost unknown in Britain. Of the 92 firms Channon studied, only 12 were using a variation of the multidivisional form, and of these, 8 were units of foreign, largely American, enterprises.[4] Both the size of the British firms and the newness of their organisational structure reflects the very different historical development of large industrial enterprise in the UK and the US.

One of Channon's most striking findings was the different ways in which the multidivisional form came into being in the two countries.[5] In the United States it replaced the centralised, functionally departmentalised structure. In Britain it evolved largely out of the loose-knit, decentralised holding company. In fact, between 1950 and 1960, the holding company form had become the most widely used by large British industrial enterprises. Of the 92 companies in Channon's earlier 1950 sample, 52 employed some variation of the centralised, functionally departmentalised structure (that is, a structure in which each major function – manufacturing, sales, purchasing, finance, or research – was managed through its own department). By 1960, however, only 21 were using the centralised form and 40 the holding company structure. Of these 40, 35 had diversified product lines. By 1970 only 8 companies in Channon's sample had a functionally departmentalised structure, 15 used the holding company type, and 72 some variation of the multidivisional form. Many firms had only just made the transformation to the multidivisional structure.

In Britain, then, the most common organisational challenge facing the reorganisers of large-scale enterprise was to transform the holding company into a multidivisional type of structure. This involved the building of a large general office, with extensive general service and financial staffs and the development of new sets and types of operating controls and planning techniques. These firms had to meet much the same type of problems and challenges faced by the organisational innovators at General Motors in 1921 – the response to which I have analysed in detail in *Strategy and Structure*.[6]

In the United States the multidivisional structure usually appeared when an enterprise employing a centralised, functionally departmentalised form began to encounter a wide range of management problems resulting from diversification into new product lines or into new geographical areas. Such large, integrated, centralised companies had in nearly all cases devised their central office controls and planning systems and had developed large central staffs before carrying out such expansion. Their challenge was to create the new operating divisions and then to define their procedures, and to set their boundaries. Their organisational problems were similar to those that faced the reorganisers at du Pont in 1920 and 1921. These were spelled out in another chapter of *Strategy and Structure*. Many of the contrasts between the multidivisional structure in the US and the UK can, then, be accounted for by the fact that in Britain it has appeared only recently and evolved out of the holding company form; whereas in the United States, it came earlier, being first adopted in the 1920s and 1930s, and grew out of the functionally departmentalised structure.

II

The reason the multidivisional type of organisation developed in these different ways in the two countries can best be understood by going back into history and contrasting the nature of large-scale industrial enterprise in the two nations half a century ago. For in business, as in every other activity, the past has a powerful impact on the present.

In making this contrast it may be helpful to define large-scale enterprise in terms of ownership and control, as well as of strategy and structure. Until the late nineteenth century, owners nearly aways managed their enterprises. Those few that hired managers rarely employed as many as four or five, and they retained a close personal relationship with their managers, often making them partners in the firm. Such an enterprise may be termed a *personal* one. As firms grew large and began to carry out more than one function, the number of salaried managers increased, reaching 20 or 30 or even 50. Such employees or, to use the British term, servants of the company rarely held large holdings of its stock. These shares remained in the hands of the entrepreneurs who built the company, or in those of their families. These share-holders continued to have a major say in the selection of managers, in the making of over-all policy, and in long-term planning and allocation of resources. Such manager-manned but owner-controlled enterprises can be termed *entrepreneurial* ones. As firms grew larger and as their activities were extended and diversified, stock ownership tended to become widely scattered. Full-time, salaried career managers who owned little or no stock took over positions in top as well as middle and lower management. They made long-term as well as short-term decisions. Owners became rentiers, more concerned with the dividends than the operation of their company. The owners had neither the time, information, experience nor commitment required to manage. Such manager-dominated enterprises can properly be termed *managerial*.

By World War I the large managerial firm was becoming commonplace in the United States. Personal enterprises had entirely disappeared in American big business, and entrepreneurial enterprises were giving way to managerial ones. This was not yet the case in Great Britain. In 1919 the managerial enterprise was still a rarity; many large firms had become entrepreneurial, and a few were still personal ones owned and managed by a small group of partners. Often these entrepreneurial and family enterprises had joined with others in the same industry, either in an informal cartel or a more formal holding company to control price, output and competition in general.

I recently completed a study of the American experience by making a survey of the strategy and structure of all industrial enterprises capitalized in 1917 at $20 million or more. This review of 278 companies, of which 236 were classed as manufacturing companies, brought out two basic points.[7]

One was that the large enterprise had become integrated, that is, besides manufacturing, it did its own marketing, purchasing and even controlled its own supplies of raw and semifinished materials. Over 85 per cent of the 236 manufacturing companies in this sample used some type of centralised, functionally departmentalised structure. The rest employed the holding company as an operating as well as legal form. The administration of all these large manufacturing companies required the service of a corps of lower level managers to run their many plants, offices, mines and other units and a sizeable number of middle managers to supervise the functional departments (or subsidiaries) and staff offices.

The second point was that these enterprises were clustered in a relatively few industries. Of the 236 manufacturing firms (the rest were mostly mining and crude oil producing companies), 171 were concentrated in 6 of the 20 two-digit industrial groups as defined by the US Census Standard Industrial Classification (SIC). The six groups were food, chemicals, petroleum, primary metals, machinery and transportation equipment. Nearly all of these 171 and most of the others were operating in industries that used capital-intensive, high-volume methods of production to make standardised goods for mass markets.

These large, centralised industrial enterprises that integrated mass production with mass distribution had first appeared in the 1880s. They had grown large in two quite different ways.

One was through internal expansion. Manufacturing or processing companies built national and often international marketing and distributing organisations and as extensive purchasing ones. The enterprises to follow this path to size during the decade of the 1880s included producers of perishable products who began to sell in the new national market created by the railroads; producers who developed a new technology that led to a sudden and massive increase in the output of a single manufacturing establishment; and firms which began to make in volume new standardised machinery whose marketing required specialised services, such as, demonstration, installation, after-sales repair and service, and consumer credit. The best-known examples of the first type to appear in the 1880s were the meat packers (Swift, Armour and three smaller national packers) and the national brewers (Pabst, Miller, Schlitz and Anheuser-Busch). The second type occurred among producers of low-priced packaged goods which could be differentiated through advertising. During the decade of the 1880s, pioneering interprises appeared in the making of cigarettes (American Tobacco), matches (Diamond Match), breakfast cereals (Quaker Oats), flour (Washburn and Pillsbury), canned goods (Campbell, Heinz, Borden and Libby), soap (Procter & Gamble) and photographic film (Eastman Kodak). In that same decade of the 1880s, a third set of manufacturers, the makers of new types of standardised machines, particularly sewing, office and agricultural machinery, perfected their national and international sales networks. These enterprises included Singer Sewing, McCormick, Harvester, Deere and Company, J. I. Case Threshing Machine, Fairbanks Scales, Remington Typewriter, National Cash Register and in the 1890s, A. B. Dick (mimeograph), Burroughs Adding Machine and the forerunners of IBM. In these same years, companies making standardised heavy machinery built comparable worldwide marketing organisations to demonstrate and install equipment and to provide service, repair and consumer credit. This was true for Westinghouse Air Brake, Westinghouse Electric, the predecessors of General Electric, Babcock and Wilcox, Otis Elevator, Worthington Pump, E. W. Bliss and Merganthaler Linotype.

These three types of firms had many similarities. A good number built manufacturing plants overseas becoming the nation's first multinationals.[8] When they did buy another company, they incorporated its activities into their own centralised functionally departmentalised structure. Nearly all financed their expansion out of retained earnings. And because they were financed from within, these builders and their families continued to control the stock in these firms. They remained entrepreneurial enterprises for a generation and often even longer.

The other route to size was through the merger of a large number of small, single function manufacturing firms. The process was one of legal combination, followed by administrative centralisation and then vertical integration forward into marketing and backwards into purchasing and the controlling of raw or semifinished materials. This path to size was first taken in the 1880s by combinations in processing industries which used the new trust form of legal organisation. These included Standard Oil, American Cotton Oil, National Linseed Oil, American Sugar Refining, the Wiskey Trust, and National Lead.

By the 1890s, the success of the early integrated enterprises and the passage of the Sherman Anti-Trust Act, led to an increasing number of mergers. Then in 1898 a buoyant capital market and Supreme Court rulings defining the Sherman Act brought the first great merger movement in American history. For the Court declared cartels illegal but the holding company legal. Mergers came in every industry . The most profitable ones, however, were those whose managers consolidated and rationalised their production facilities, placed them under a central administrative office and then built their own national and international marketing and purchasing organisation. By 1910 the most successful enterprises to follow this strategy of integration were Corn Products Refining, National Biscuit, Standard Milling, and American Chicle in foods; Du Pont, General Chemical, National Analine, Virginia-Carolina Chemical, American Agricultural Chemical, and United Drug in chemicals and pharmaceuticals; and General Electric, International Harvester, Allis-Chalmers, and American Radiator in machinery.

In the first years of the twentieth century the number of large integrated centralised functionally departmentalised enterprises increased rapidly. They came fast in oil. By 1909, two years before the Supreme Court broke up Standard Oil, the Texas Company, Tidewater and Union were listed among the nation's largest 100 firms.[9] By 1917, Texas, Gulf, Pure Oil and Magnolia and four of the former Standard Companies were in the top 50 and seven more integrated oil companies were in the top 100. In rubber, Goodrich, Goodyear, Firestone – all integrated, functionally departmentalised firms – had by 1917 joined U.S. Rubber in the top 100. By then those new automobile companies that had built the extended marketing organisations essential to providing specialised services had become among the largest in the land. These included Ford, Chevrolet, Studebaker, Willys-Overland, Maxwell, Dodge and the subsidiaries of General Motors (Buick, Olds and Cadillac).

By 1917 then, large industrial enterprises in the United States had become integrated and centralised. They clustered in the technologically advanced, mass production, mass distribution industries. Even in the metal making industries – iron, steel, copper and other nonferrous metals – many of the firms had integrated production with distribution. Few metal makers, however, had integrated forward into the fabrication of metal products and few fabricators had moved backwards into metal making. Nearly all those enterprises which had integrated were administered through a centralised, functionally departmentalised structure. Only the giant US Steel Corporation, Standard Oil (New Jersey) and a handful of smaller metals and oil firms continued to use the holding company form. All these enterprises employed a large force of managers. Most of those that had grown internally by financing their growth from retained profits were still entrepreneurial enterprises. The founders or their families continued to control and to make top management decisions. On the other hand, nearly all of those firms created by merger had become managerial with career managers administering the firm at all levels.

Besides dominating mass production industries, the large managerial firm had appeared earlier in American transportation and communication. By 1890 the American railroad, telegraph and embryonic telephone networks were controlled by a small number of very large managerial enterprises. By the beginning of the twentieth century mass marketers had created large entrepreneurial enterprises that wholesaled and retailed goods in massive volume. The requirements of these large enterprises had by 1917 brought into existence a still small but most influential managerial class.

By World War I that class was becoming increasingly professional. In the 1880s in railroads, and in the first decade of the twentieth century in industry, specialists in different functional activities had set up their own quasi-professional associations. At semiannual meetings of these associations, accountants, auditors, several types of engineers, and traffic, purchasing, marketing and general managers met to read papers and discuss mutual problems in their different specialties. These associations had their own journals which were supplemented by other specialised periodicals. In addition, American education had responded quickly to the needs for trained managers. First came the specialised schools and institutes to provide training in civil, mechanical, mining, electrical and later chemical engineering. Then came the first business schools at Cornell, Pennsylvania, Harvard and elsewhere offering courses in finance, production, marketing and general management. At the same time professional consultants and consulting firms appeared to advise on factory and corporate management and on such functional activities as marketing, finance, labour relations and even public relations. By the 1920s then, specialised consultants, courses, journals and associations were as established a part of the American business scene as the managerial enterprise and the managerial class were of the national economy.

III

At the end of the First World War, the business scene in British industry was very different from that in the United States. Except in transportation and communication, the managerial class was tiny and the managerial enterprise was only beginning to make its appearance. In many firms owners still managed. Others had become large enough to have salaried managers in the middle and lower levels, but the owners still made top level strategic and policy decisions. Management consultants, courses, journals and associations were almost unknown.

The differences between the two countries with respect to large manufacturing enterprises can be most clearly demonstrated by examining the organisation of the 50 largest industrial enterprises in Britain in 1919, a list of which has been compiled by Margaret Ackrill (Table

1).[10] A comparison of the structure of and control in these companies with those of the largest in 1948 indicates that many of these differences continued at least until after World War II.

In 1919 the largest industrials in Britain, like those in the United States, were clustered in a few industries; 43 of the 50 were in food and drink, textiles, chemicals, metal making and fabricating, machinery, armaments and transportation equipment. The remaining firms were in those industries where the large firm had appeared in the United States – tobacco, rubber, electrical machinery, cement and paper. (In Britain the newspaper chains owned and operated extensive newsprint manufacturing facilities, which in the United States were operated by paper companies.) However, where the Americans had three or four large firms in each of these industries, the British had only one. None of the 50 were in the labour-intensive industries making apparel, lumber, furniture, leather or scientific instruments.

TABLE 1 50 Largest Manufacturing Companies in the UK in 1919

Rank	Name	Estimated Market Value (£m)
Group 19: *Armaments and ordnance*		
4	Vickers	19·5
11	Armstrong-Whitworth	12·2
38	Birmingham Small Arms	4·6
Group 20: *Food, Drink and Like Products*		
2	Lever Bros.	23·0
5	Guinness	19·0
19	Watney Combe Reid	6·9
25	Maypole Dairy	6·2
31	Bass Ratcliffe Gretton	5·3
34	Buchanan-Dewar	5·2
42	Distillers Company	4·3
43	Liebigs Extract of Meat	4·3
44	J. Lyons	4·3
Group 21: *Tobacco*		
3	Imperial Tobacco	22·9
Group 22: *Textile Mill Products*		
1	J. and P. Coats	45·0
8	Courtaulds (rayon)	16·0
12	Fine Spinners and Doublers	9·1
20	Bleachers Association	6·7
24	Calico Printers Association	6·4
27	Bradford Dyers Association	6·1
33	English Sewing Cotton	5·0
39	Horrockes Crewdson	4·5
41	Linen Thread Co.	4·4

Rank	Name	*Estimated Market Value ($£m$)*
Group 23: *Apparel and Related Products* (None)		
Group 24: *Lumber and Other Wood Products* (None)		
Group 25: *Furniture* (None)		
Group 26: *Paper and Allied Products* (None)		
Group 27: *Publishing and Printing*		
39	E. Hulton and Co.	6·0
45	Amalgamated Press	4·2
46	Associated Newspapers-Daily Mail Trust	4·4
Group 28: *Chemicals*		
6	Brunner Mond	18·7
7	Nobel Industries	16·3
15	Reckitt and Sons	8·8
17	British Dyestuffs	8·1
28	United Alkali	6·1
35	Boots Pure Drug	5·0
40	Borax Consolidated	4·4
Group 29: *Petroleum Products* (see text)		
Group 30: *Rubber*		
14	Dunlop Rubber	8·9
Group 31: *Leather and its Products* (None)		
Group 32: *Stone, Clay and Glass*		
13	Associated Portland Cement Manufacturers	9·1
Groups 33 and 34: *Primary Metals and Metal Fabricating*		
10	United Steel	13·2
16	Guest Keen and Nettlefolds	8·2
21	Consett Iron	6·6
23	Dorman Long	6·5
26	Richard Thomas	6·2
30	Mond Nickel	5·5
36	Stewart and Lloyds	5·0
47	Ebbw Vale	4·1
49	John Lysaght	3·9
Group 35: *Machinery, except Electrical*		
22	Babcock and Wilcox (former US subsidiary)	6·5
32	Hadfields	5·3
48	Platt Brothers	4·0
Group 36: *Electrical Machinery*		
50	English Electric	3·8
Group 37: *Transportation Equipment*		
9	Metropolitan Carriage Wagon and Finance	14·4

Rank	Name	Estimated Market Value (£m)
18	John Brown (Shipbuilding)	7·7
37	Cammell Laird (Shipbuilding)	4·8

Group 38: *Instruments and Related Products* (None)

Group 39: *Miscellaneous Manufacturers* (None)

The basic difference between the two countries was that the UK had more armament and textile enterprises than the US and far fewer machinery and petroleum firms. There were no companies in the United States comparable to Vickers or Armstrong-Whitworth, which produced a broad line of armaments and the materials used in their fabrication. In Britain, too, the largest shipbuilders, such as John Brown and Cammell Laird, were really armament firms building more naval than commercial ships. Since textiles had played such a fundamental role in the industrialising of Britain, the appearance of a number of textile companies on the list of the largest British enterprises in 1919 is hardly surprising.

The reason no oil companies appear on Table I is that the British-owned or partly-owned oil companies did not have refineries in the United Kingdom. Anglo-Persian Oil, in which the British government held just over 50 per cent of the shares, completed its refinery at Abadan in 1913 and sold its output to the British Navy. Burmah Oil carried out all its activities in the Far East, selling its refined products primarily in India. And at the outbreak of World War I Royal Dutch Shell, which was 40 per cent British owned, had only just begun to compete vigorously with Standard Oil (New Jersey) and Socony (formerly Standard Oil, New York), in the European markets. In 1910, before the breakup of Standard Oil, that company held 75 per cent of the European market for kerosene. The European Petroleum Union, controlled by the Rothchilds, Nobels and the Deutsche Bank, furnished all but 5 per cent of the rest. In 1919 Standard Oil (New Jersey) still supplied two-thirds of the British market.[11] In Britain then the oil business was, in 1919, an overseas, imperial venture which required the employing of few managers at home. Except for Royal Dutch Shell, no firm had a large integrated organisation producing for major markets in advanced industrial economies. By contrast 31 American companies already had by 1917 assets of over $20 million. All but seven of these were integrated enterprises distributing their products in American and European markets.

Even more striking was the difference in the number of firms producing standardised machinery in volume in the two countries. In 1917 there were 24 machinery companies in the United States with assets of $20 million or more. If electrical and transportation equipment firms (excluding shipbuilding) are included, the number was 53. In Britain there were only a handful of machinery firms of this size and only one of these produced standardised equipment in volume. The giant oil and machinery firms which were so central to the rise of big business and managerial enterprise in the United States were by the end of World War I only beginning to appear in the UK.

The differences between large British and American firms in their structure and ownership were even more striking than the differences in the type of industries in which they operated. Only in the food and in the chemical and drug industries were there similarities. Lever Brothers was a world-wide integrated enterprise similar to Procter and Gamble, American Cotton Oil and Southern Cotton Oil. Reckitt and Sons (listed under chemicals) appears to have been comparable to the starch producing and selling units of Corn Products Refining Company. Guinness with its national marketing and distribution organisation was similar to Anheuser Busch; and Liebigs was much the same as one of the smaller American meat packers.[12] Maypole and Lyons differed from American food firms in that they began as retailers and integrated backwards into the purchasing and processing of foodstuffs, but they operated in much the same manner as the butter, poultry and eggs divisions of Swift and Armour. None, however, had built huge organisations with hundreds of full-time salaried managers like those of Swift and Armour which made it possible for those two firms to distribute perishable meat from the five to six million cattle slaughtered each year, as well as millions of dollars worth of butter, eggs, fertiliser, soap, hides, and other by-products. The entrepreneurs – Lever, Reckitt, Carlisle and Gunther at Liebigs, Watson at Maypole – controlled the companies they had built. So also did the Guinness descendants. Management at the top of these entrepreneurial enterprises continued to be that of the owners. The other brewing companies on the list were also integrated, having their own buying organisation and controlling their outlets – the tied public houses. They remained regional, family-owned and family-managed enterprises.

In chemicals, those firms which had become integrated were also entrepreneurial. Roscoe Mond, at Brunner Mond, and Jesse Boot, at Boots Pure Drug, and their close associates remained responsible for the growth and current organisation of their enterprises.[13] They ruled with a strong hand. Neither, as yet, had worked out a departmental structure comparable to that used by leading American chemical firms.

Of the other chemical and related companies on the 1919 list, British Dyestuffs was just getting under way; while United Alkali, Borax Consolidated and also Associated Portland Cement remained federations of small firms. After completing the mergers that created them, these enterprises did not adopt the strategy of the successful American mergers. They did not rationalise the production facilities of the constituent enterprises, nor centralise their administration, nor build extensive buying and purchasing organisations.

Of all such federations, the largest and most sophisticated before the World War I was Nobel Dynamite Trust Company Limited. It had been, in fact, a European rather than just a British enterprise.[14] When it was organised in 1886, it included four German dynamite firms and Nobel's Explosives Company Ltd of Glasgow which was as large as the four German firms combined. Because the Trust was formed by an exchange of stock, it was legally a single enterprise. It did not become, however, centrally administered. Operationally, it remained a federation. Four professional managers – two in Britain and two in Germany – handled the day-to-day operations of the enterprise, whose stock was in the hands of Alfred Nobel and a few associates. These managers and representatives of the boards of the operating units met regularly with the representatives of the 'Powder Firms', an association of British and German makers of propellants for military weapons, at a formally established 'Council of Delegates'. They set prices, production schedules, allocated profits, and determined capital expenditures. Decisions made in the Council or on the board of the Trust were by a simple majority vote. Neither the Trust nor the Council had a permanent general office manned by a set of full-time general executives assisted by an advisory or financial staff. There were no research, purchasing or sales departments.

The contrast of the organisation and operation of the Dynamite Trust to the comparable merger in the United States is striking. In 1902 and 1903, three du Pont cousins completed a merger of companies that produced about 70 per cent of the black powder and dynamite and all of the smokeless (propellant) powder made in the United States.[15] They immediately consolidated production facilities, centralised the administration of their plants in three operating departments (one for each major product), built an international sales organisation manned by salaried managers, set up an extensive Essential Materials or purchasing department to obtain and control raw materials, formed a Development Department to administer research laboratories and to advise on long-term strategy and the allocation of resources, and organised a central financial department. They then dissolved the legal vestiges of nearly all the companies that had come into the merger. The Du Pont Powder Company provides a classic example of the centralised, functionally departmentalised structure as the Nobel Dynamite Trust does of a tight cartel.

Such federations (they were almost always federations of family firms) existed in consumer goods as well as in producer goods, and they usually had a simpler organisation than the Dynamite Trust. Imperial Tobacco, the largest and best known federation in the consumer trades, provides a good example. A merger of 13 firms, Imperial was formed in 1901 in response to the threat of invasion of the British market by the American Tobacco Company.[16] Although the holding company did set up a central purchasing agency from which each subsidiary could buy its supplies, these 'branches', as they were called, continued to handle their own production and sales. The central office of the holding company, consisting of senior partners of the branches, did little more than set prices, review annually the activities of the subsidiaries and allocate funds on the basis of this review. There was no office or executive responsible for long-term strategy and for short-term coordination of throughput.

Again the contrast to the American counterpart is revealing. Well before 1900, the American Tobacco Company's large central office at 111 Fifth Avenue in New York housed the headquarters of its production department which supervised all manufacturing activities, its leaf department which stored and cured as well as purchased tobacco, and its sales department which handled advertising and distribution on a global scale.[17] The central office had developed procedures to coordinate the flow of materials that produced and distributed four to five billion cigarettes a year and comparable amounts of other tobacco products. There, too, James Buchanan Duke and his associates planned and carried out their grand strategy.

In 1919, the two leading British producers of spirits, Distillers Company and Buchanan-Dewar, were administered in much the same way as Imperial Tobacco. So, too, apparently were the majority of the large textile firms. The Fine Spinners and Doublers Association, the Calico Printers' Association and Bradford Dyers' Association were all, as their names indicate, federations of small, single-function family firms which only handled one basic set of processes involved in textile manufacturing. English Sewing Cotton and Linen Thread were much the same.[18] Only J. & P. Coats, another merger of thread makers, had set up, under the leadership of O. P. Phillipi, a marketing organisation. Significantly that organisation also marketed the product of its major competitor, English Sewing Cotton. Because these federations handled only a single manufacturing process, their buying, selling and the coordination of throughput was of the simplest nature and required little in the way of managerial skills. On the other hand, two textile enterprises on the 1919 list – Horrockes Crewdson, cloth makers, and Courtaulds, producers of new synthetic fibres – did become vertically integrated, had more complex management needs, and created centrally administered, enterpreneurial enterprises similar to those in foods and chemicals.[19]

In the metal making and metal working industries most of the large companies were also federations of family firms. Although there were occasional horizontal combinations similar to those in the textile industry, the largest number were vertically integrated federations. Metal makers – Guest Keen and Nettlefolds, Stewart and Lloyds, and Dorman Long – obtained control of coal and ore mines and moved forward into fabricating and engineering.[20] The armament makers and shipbuilders, such as Vickers, Armstrong-Whitworth and John Brown, moved backwards into the making of steel and armour plate. In fact, the British metal making and metal working enterprises were integrated to a greater degree than those of the United States. There, except for United States Steel and Bethlehem, the metal makers did not yet produce fabricated and other finished products; and shipbuilders, machinery makers and other metal fabricators did not manufacture their own metal. Yet the British firms failed to create a centralised administrative structure to manage their scattered properties similar to those set up by Bethlehem, Jones & Laughlin, and Republic in the early years of the century. They had no central purchasing, sales, research, or even financial departments. Coordination of flows and the allocation of resources was done by representatives of the operating subsidiaries in committee or council or on the board of the parent company.

The most significant differences in the organisation of large firms in the US and those in the UK in 1919 came in the machinery and transport equipment industries. In Britain only one enterprise in the list of the largest 50 firms was comparable in its activities and organisation to the large American machinery companies making sewing machines, office machinery (typewriters, cash registers, mimeograph machines, calculators, and the like), agricultural machinery (harvesters, thrashers, ploughs and tractors), shoe machinery, pumps, elevators, printing presses, and those making a wide variety of electrical equipment and machines. Only Babcock and Wilcox had built comparable international sales networks to provide demonstration, installation, service and repair, consumer credit and other specialised marketing services. And that firm had its start as a subsidiary of the American company of that same name. By World War I, these American machinery firms all dominated or even had a monopoly of the British market for their specific products.

The machinery makers, besides Babcock and Wilcox, on the 1919 list included the Platt Brothers, builders of textile machinery to order, and Metropolitan Carriage and Wagon, long-established producers of railway, street railway and subway cars and equipment.[21] Neither had large international marketing organisations. English Electric, a recent merger of four regional manufacturers, only began to build an extensive marketing network in the 1930s. Birmingham Small Arms, still primarily an armament firm, had begun to manufacture bicycles but appears to have marketed them largely through jobbers. In Britain in 1919, the machinery companies were still primarily single function manufacturing enterprises.

As this review emphasises, the large industrial enterprises in Britain at the end of the First World War were either integrated, centrally administered entrepreneurial companies or federations of family (or entrepreneurial) enterprises which were legally but not administratively combined within a holding company. As a result there were very few large central offices manned by professional managers and served by extensive staffs. At the top, owners managed and managers owned. The integrated firms in consumer goods had a small number of middle managers to coordinate high volume flows of goods from the suppliers of raw materials to the retailers or ultimate consumers. Federations using the holding company form, however, did not require such middle managers and only rarely did they employ salaried senior executives at the top level. So the organisational framework did not exist in the UK, as it did in the US, in which to develop the new techniques of modern management. In 1919 few British firms used systematic budgeting, forecasting, or the use of statistical and accounting procedures to ensure a steady flow of information from the operating departments to the central office on output, sales, purchases and rate of internal investments. With few middle and almost no top-salaried, non-owning, career managers working in British enterprise, it is hardly surprising that specialised management associations, journals, and education had not appeared by 1919.

In the two inter-war decades, big business in British industry began to become more similar to that in the United States. But change came slowly. The large enterprises came to cluster more in the same industries as those in the US and to adopt more similar organisational structures and administrative procedures. By 1948, as a list of the 50 largest manufacturing companies taken from a list of the 100 largest companies quoted on the London Stock Exchange, prepared by the National Institute of Economic and Social Research indicates (Table 2), the number of food companies among the top 50 had increased and textile companies decreased. The most successful of the textile firms were the integrated synthetic fibre producers – Courtauld and British Celanese. Although the number of chemical companies were fewer because of the merger of four of the largest in 1926 into Imperial Chemical Industries, the industry was growing fast. In petroleum Royal Dutch Shell and Anglo-Iranian (the successor to Anglo-Persian) had become giant enterprises (even though they were not placed on the National Institute list). Anglo-Iranian remained primarily a producing, shipping and refining company. After 1930 it sold a substantial share of its refined products through Royal Dutch Shell whose world-wide- integrated operations had become in volume and geographical spread second only to Jersey Standard. During the inter-war years modern mass producing and mass marketing machinery companies with extended marketing organisations had appeared in the automobile and electrical machinery industries. But they still had not yet reached large size in the manufacturing of other types of standardised machinery. There the dominance of American firms continued.

TABLE 2   50 Largest Quoted Manufacturing Companies in the UK in 1948

Rank	Name	Net Assets (£m)
Group 19: *Armaments and Ordnance*		
6	Vickers (also in Groups 35 and 37)	56·7
Group 20: *Food, Drink and Like Products*		
1	Unilever	148·1
5	Distillers Company	62·9
20	Rank, Hovis	26·1
25	British Cocoa & Chocolate	23·8
30	Ind Coope & Allsopp	21·1
32	Watney Combe Reid & Co.	20·2
36	Bass, Ratcliff & Gretton	18·6
38	Guinness, Son & Co.	18·2
41	J. Lyons & Co.	17·4
42	Tate & Lyle	16·9
45	Walker Cain	16·2
49	Charrington & Co.	15·6
53	United Dairies	14·5
55	Home & Colonial Stores	13·5
Group 21: *Tobacco*		
3	Imperial Tobacco	117·6
Group 22: *Textile Mill Products*		
4	Courtaulds (rayon)	62·9
8	J. and P. Coats	45·7
37	Fine Spinners & Doublers	18·2
43	British Celanese (rayon)	16·6
57	Calico Printers Association	13·1
Group 23: *Apparel and Related Products*		
50	Burton (Montague)	15·3
Group 24: *Lumber and Other Wood Products* (None)		
Group 25: *Furniture* (None)		
Group 26: *Paper and Allied Products*		
22	Bowater Paper Co.	24·8

Rank	Name	Net Assets (£m)
	Group 27: *Publishing and Printing*	
31	Kemsley Newspaper	20·3
44	Amalgamated Press	16·5
	Group 28: *Chemicals*	
2	Imperial Chemical Industries	143·1
39	Beecham Group	18·2
59	Boots Pure Drug Co.	12·7
	Group 29: *Petroleum Products* (see text)	
	Group 30: *Rubber*	
7	Dunlop Rubber	47·6
	Group 31: *Leather and its Products* (None)	
	Group 32: *Stone, Clay and Glass*	
27	Associated Portland Cement Mfg.	22·0
28	Turner & Newall	21·9
	Group 33 and 34: *Primary Metals and Metal Fabricating*	
11	Stewart & Lloyds	38·8
12	Tube Investments	28·9
14	Richard Thomas & Baldwin	27·6
16	Steel Company of Wales	27·5
21	United Steel Co.	25·1
40	Dorman, Long & Co.	17·5
48	British Aluminium Co.	15·7
51	John Summers & Sons	15·2
52	Colvilles	14·5
	Group 35: *Machinery, except Electrical*	
10	Guest Keen & Nettlefolds (also 34)	38·8
46	John Brown & Co. (also 34 and 37)	16·1
	Group 36: *Electrical Machinery*	
15	General Electric Co.	27·6
17	Associated Electrical Industries	27·3
24	British Insulated Callender's Cables	23·8
60	English Electric	12·6
	Group 37: *Transportation Equipment*	
19	Ford Motor Co.	26·5
33	Morris, Austin Motors (merger occurred in 1952)	20·2
58	Hawker Siddeley Group	12·8
	Group 38: *Instruments and Related Products* (None)	
	Group 39: *Miscellaneous Manufacturing*	
54	British Match Corp.	13·5

Rank		Name	Net Assets (£m)
Non-Manufacturing			
Entertainment	9	Odeon Theatres	42·1
Retail	13	Debenhams	28·3
Retail	18	Woolworth & Co.	27·3
Wholesale	23	Powell Duffryn	24·6
Service	26	Union International Co.	23·1
Retail	29	Great Universal Stores	21·9
Entertainment	34	Associated British Picture Co.	19·0
Service	35	British Electric Traction Co.	18·6
Retail	47	Marks & Spencer	15·9
Service	56	Cory (Wm) & Sons	13·5

In the inter-war years the integrated entrepreneurial enterprises began to pay closer attention to organisation and administration. Dunlop Rubber, for example, installed 'a comprehensive system of internal audit, control, and forecasting', and more carefully defined the lines of authority and responsibility.[22] In fact, as Dunlop diversified out of tyres, it developed a modified multidivisional structure. Comparable moves to improve organisation which resulted usually in a more carefully defined functional structure, occurred in such integrated entrepreneurial enterprises as Brunner Mond (before it became part of ICI in 1926), British Celanese, Maypole, Bowater Paper, Reckitt, Boots, Courtaulds, Austin, and Morris.[23] Although the organisation at Anglo-Persian remained a relatively simple functional structure, Royal Dutch Shell had developed a complex organisation with integrated national subsidiaries as well as large functional departments operating out of two separate central offices, one in London and the other in The Hague.

In the inter-war years a few holding companies and the federations began to adopt the centralised functionally departmentalised structure. The most important of such reorganisations took place in 1920 at Nobel Industries (the successor to the Dynamite Trust) when Harry McGowan and his associates completely transformed the organisation of their holding company. They explicitly imitated the structure then used by the Du Pont Company, sending executives to Wilmington to study its organisation.[24] They centralised production and distribution under the Operating and Sales Department (the metal group based in Birmingham retained its autonomy) set up central purchasing and development departments, and established a top office called the Central Executive Department. The Nobel reorganisation may have helped to make the functionally departmentalised form better known in Britain. In any case, by the 1930s that form of organisation was becoming quite widely used in Britain.

Nevertheless, during the inter-war years large British enterprises grew primarily by merger and acquisition rather than by internal expansion. Very few of the new mergers and only a small number of the existing holding companies followed the Nobel example. Associated Portland Cement, General Electric, English Electric, and the United Steel Companies moved towards a functional organisation but not as explicitly and systematically as had Nobel Industries. The other holding companies continued as loosely controlled federations with a general office similar to that of Imperial Tobacco.[25]

If these mergers failed to centralise in the manner of Du Pont or Nobel, neither did they attempt, as General Motors did in 1921, to rationalise the activities of their subsidiaries and to build a large general office to coordinate, monitor and plan for the subsidiaries. The large food companies – Ranks, United Dairies and Spillers – appear to have been run along much the same lines as Home and Colonial stores, which has been described by Peter Mathias in his *Retailing Revolution*.[26] That enterprise had become loosely federated with three other integrated food companies – Maypole Dairy, Meadow Dairy, and Lipton Tea, when in 1929, they set up a joint purchasing and warehousing agency. The four did not become legally joined in a formal holding company until 1946. Spillers did reorganise its subsidiaries into regional groups but appears to have continued to operate its general office on the Imperial Tobacco model. This was also the case for the large metal-making and metal-working federations, such as Guest Keen and Nettlefolds and Hawker Siddeley. As they added firms to their groups, they made no attempt to enlarge the size and activities of their top office. Only Royal Dutch Shell in petroleum, Vickers in armaments, metal-making and machinery, and Turner and Newall in asbestos carefully and systematically regrouped their subsidiaries and improved their financial and statistical controls.[27] Their general offices, however, remained more those of a holding company than of a multidivisional enterprise, having only two or three general executives and no large general staff.[28] Vickers and, apparently, Turner and Newall relied on boards and committees consisting of managers from the operating subsidiaries to coordinate activities and to allocate resources.

The only two firms on the 1948 list to develop a multidivisional structure comparable to that set up by General Motors and Du Pont after World War I were Britain's two largest industrial enterprises, Unilever and Imperial Chemical Industries. Unilever, a merger completed in 1929 of Lever Brothers and two Dutch margarine firms, became one of the very first truly managerial enterprises in Britain. During the 1930s its chairman, D'Arcy Cooper, concentrated more on consolidating and rationalising the operating subsidiaries than on building its general office. By 1948, however, Unilever had as many general executives, as large a general staff, and as sophisticated set of controls and administrative procedures as any multidivisional enterprise in the United States.[29]

After the formation of Imperial Chemical Industries, a merger in 1926 of Nobel Industries, Brunner Mond, British Dyestuffs and United Alkali, Harry McGowan once again paid close attention to organisational matters. In defining a post-merger structure, he looked both at ICI's own experience and those of American firms, particularly General Motors, on whose board he served, and Du Pont, which had in 1921 set up its multidivisional structure. After a period of increasing centralisation, he and his associates consolidated operations into eight autonomous divisions or 'groups' defined along product lines.[30] The general office staff was large and, as at General Motors, divided into a general advisory staff and a financial staff. In purchasing and particularly in sales, the staff offices had much more authority and line responsibilities than did those at General Motors. So the operating groups were less autonomous than those in the American company. The general executives in the top office included the chairman, president and eight full-time executives who had no operating responsibilities in the subsidiaries they administered. These ten executives made up the General Purposes (originally Executive) Committee. Three of the full-time executives with the president, and chairman and the Treasurer formed the Finance Committee. These top managers controlled and planned through budgets, forecasting and performance measurements similar to those used at General Motors and Du Pont. Although still more centralised than these American companies – a centralisation that was enhanced by McGowan's autocratic rule – ICI's structure, in Leslie Hannah's words, 'clearly approximated to the paradigm of the multidivisional corporation.'[31] The new structure proved itself before and during the war. But it had few imitators before 1950.

After the war, as the British economy reconverted to a peace-time basis and then began to grow rapidly, British industrial enterprises expanded. As before, they grew more by merger than by internal growth. In the 1950s and 1960s, however, the motive for merger was different. It was more to expand and to diversify into new markets rather than to control competition in existing ones. Quite naturally British firms continued to rely on the holding company as an administrative as well as legal instrument for controlling the enlarged enterprise. They soon realised, however, that such an administrative structure did not permit them to take advantages of scale economies and other advantages of size. Nor did it provide the facilities needed to control, evaluate and plan for the subsidiaries. At the same time, several administratively centralised enterprises which had begun to diversify, such as Courtaulds and English Electric, were having problems in operating their new activities through their functionally departmentalised structure.[32] So in the 1960s large British industrial enterprises increasingly turned to adopting some variation of the multidivisional form. And as ICI had done earlier, they often looked to the American experience for guidance, relying heavily on American management consultants. In fact, a single American consulting firm, McKinsey & Company, played a central role in the reorganisation of major British companies in the food, tobacco, chemical, pharmaceutical, oil, paper, metals, metal fabricating machinery, engineering, and electrical industries.[33]

Thus the contrasts between the organisation and operation of large British and American industrial enterprise in the 1970s can be quite easily explained by the difference in its historical development in the two countries. In the United States the multidivisional form was adopted by large, usually centralised, managerial enterprise as they moved into new geographic and product markets. When they began to diversify, these companies were already, and often had been for decades, managerial enterprises. They were administered almost entirely by professional, career managers, trained in the methods and procedures developed in the early years of the century to administer American big businesses.

In Britain, on the other hand, many large enterprises never had had a formal, carefully articulated structure until they adopted, on the advice of McKinsey & Company, the multidivisional form. Many were still holding companies, federations of long-established family firms. Family members supervised plant and offices and represented their unit on the holding company's board. Even in the large centralised firms, founders and their families still managed at the top in a highly personal way. After the war, however, the days of family and personal management were numbered . The coordination of high volume throughput and the evaluation of and planning for capital intensive, technologically complex, industrial activity, required the employment of an increasing number of full-time, career managers who had no family connection with owners of the enterprise. At the same time, the capital needs of expansion scattered ownership. As a result, few families or small groups of associates were able to continue to control legally their enterprises. So in the 1960s and 1970s the managerial enterprise began to replace personal and entrepreneurial enterprise as rapidly as it had 50 years earlier in the United States. And as the managerial class grew to meet the needs of such enterprises, so too did the number of specialised management consultants, courses, journals and associations – the essential paraphernalia of a new professional class.

IV

This historical explanation of the differences that occurred in the development and use of the multidivisional structure and other techniques and procedures of modern management in the UK and the US in the 1970s does raise one basic question. And it seems proper to conclude this paper by making a stab at answering it in a most tentative way. Why, then, did the managerial enterprise and the managerial class appear so much later in Britain than they did in the US? Why as late as 1950 were there in Britain so few of the giant, integrated, centralised managerial enterprises in which the art and science of modern management had first been developed in the US? The answer may lie in the difference between the two countries in the size and nature of their domestic market, in the development and application of certain technologies, and finally in differing laws and legal constraints.

Of those three factors, the market was surely the most significant. By 1880 the American domestic market was larger than that of Britain. The population of the US was 50·2 million and that of the UK 35·1 million. National income stood at $7·2 million in the US to $5·2 million in the UK. Of greater importance, the American domestic market was growing much faster than that of Britain. By 1900 American population and national income was almost double that of the UK and by 1920 almost triple.[34] This fast-growing market appears to have been homogeneous. The income distribution was less skewed in the US and, except possibly on the East Coast, distinctive regional tastes had not had time to develop. The newness of the market also meant that institutional arrangements had had less time to become rigid and that the established middle men were less entrenched.

This fast-growing, relatively homogeneous mass market provided the incentive to create the modern integrated, centrally administered industrial enterprise in the United States in the years after 1880. The opportunity to exploit the economies of a high volume throughput was an underlying reason for building nation-wide sales, purchasing and raw materials departments and for creating a managerial hierarchy to coordinate the high-speed flow of materials through the processes of production and distribution from the supplies of raw materials to the ultimate customer. Once the enterprise had put together an integrated organisation in the United States, it took little effort to expand it overseas. Since the high volume of output for the American market lowered unit costs, the American enterprise overseas had an advantage over any British or European competitor based on a smaller and less dynamic market. As a result, American firms became much larger than those of Britain. The capitalisation of Armour and Swift was 10 to 15 times that of Liebig and Maypole, and International Harvester more

than 10 times that of Babcock and Wilcox, the largest British manufacturer of standardised machinery.

The differences in the two countries in the application of technology
reflect the differences in the market. The Americans manufactured
standardised machines in volume and invented or adapted mass-
production machinery and other equipment long before the British
did. They did so more because of the opportunities of the market than
from the need to cope with a shortage of labour.[35] A labour shortage
might help to account for the beginnings of what became known as
'the American system of manufactures' in the metal-working industries; but it can hardly be given the credit for the simultaneous adoption of continuous process and large-batch equipment and machinery
in so many different industries during the decade of the 1880s. Nor
can it be credited with the development of standardised mass produced
machinery that required specialised marketing services to be sold in
volume. And it was in just such industries that the large integrated
multinational enterprise first flourished in the US.

Though less important than markets, contrasting legal practices
made a further difference. The passage of the Sherman Anti-Trust Act
and its interpretation by the federal courts surely hastened the coming
of the large, centralised managerial enterprise in the US and the lack
of such legislation delayed its growth in the UK. Not only did cartels
of small family firms become illegal in the US, but the holding companies that replaced such cartels were also suspect. By 1900 American
corporation lawyers were advising their clients to transform loosely
held holding companies into centralised operating ones. American law
thus provided a positive pressure for federations of small family firms
to turn themselves into large functionally departmentalised managerial
enterprises. In Britain, however, comparable associations, such as the
Nobel Dynamite Trust, Imperial Tobacco, the Calico Printers, the
Bleachers Association, and other textile holding companies, and similar
federations in foods, chemicals, armaments, metal making and metal
working, remained perfectly legal. Under no legal pressure to consolidate, these combinations of autonomous firms made little attempt to
benefit from the economies of speed by rationalising facilities and by
employing salaried career managers. Cartel agreements controlling
price and production in both the domestic and international markets
permitted small, weaker firms to survive, whereas in the United States
they were usually merged or acquired by the larger integrated enterprises. In this way, the lack of strong anti-monopoly laws certainly
extended the life of many family and entrepreneurial enterprises in
Great Britain.

In the years after World War II, markets, technology and laws
changed. In Britain both the domestic and overseas markets expanded

rapidly, particularly for mass produced, standardised consumers goods and producers goods. To take advantage of these markets, food, chemical, petroleum, rubber, and metal firms adopted advanced continuous process and large batch production techniques. The British also began to produce automobile, office, agricultural, electrical and other machinery by the most modern assembly line methods; and to set up their own sales organisations needed to distribute and market these products. After the war, too, competition increased. Many American and a smaller number of other foreign multinationals entered the British and Commonwealth markets. The passage of the Monopolies and Restrictive Practices Acts of 1948, 1956 and 1965, by making cartelisation more difficult, increased pressure for more efficient management as well as more efficient facilities. The family firm and then the entrepreneurial ones were transformed into or gave way to managerial enterprises. As they did so the executives in charge adopted what was considered the best current practice. If a firm was at all diversified or operated in distant geographical areas, this meant the installation of some variation of the multidivisional form of organisation. By 1970 the structure of large business enterprise in Britain and the structure of the industries in which they operated had come to resemble their American counterparts. By 1980 the resemblance may be even more striking, at least in the remaining private sectors of the economy.

NOTES

1 Derek F. Channon, *The Strategy and Structure of British Enterprise* (Boston, 1973) p. 73. It was 86 per cent in US, p. 86.
2 For US this information is in Alfred D. Chandler Jr, 'The Structure of American Industry in the Twentieth Century', *Business History Review*, XLIII (1969) 254–97; for Britain the same pattern is suggested by the two tables of 50 largest enterprises in UK in 1919 and 1948. Margaret Ackrill prepared the 1919 list for Leslie Hannah's study, *The Rise of the Corporate Economy*, to be published shortly by Methuen. The 1948 list was published by the National Institute of Economic and Social Research as Appendix C of *Company Income and Finance, 1949–1953* (London, 1956).
3 Channon, *British Enterprise*, ch. 7.
4 Channon, *British Enterprise*, p. 69.
5 Channon, *British Enterprise*, ch. 3.
6 Alfred D. Chandler Jr, *Strategy and Structure* (Cambridge, Mass., 1962) ch. 3 for General Motors and ch. 2 for Du Pont.
7 This survey will be printed in tabular form and analysed in my forthcoming study tentatively titled, 'The Visible Hand: The Rise of Modern Business Enterprise in the United States'. The information on large-scale enterprise in the United States comes from this study.
8 Mira Wilkins, *The Emergence of Multinational Enterprise* (Cambridge, Mass., 1970) pp. 212–16.
9 A. D. H. Kaplan, *Big Enterprise in a Competitive System* (Washington, 1954) pp. 145–8.

10   They appear in Leslie Hannah's forthcoming *The Rise of the Corporate Economy*.

11   Harold F. Williamson et al., *The American Petroleum Industry: The Age of Energy, 1899–1959* (Evanston, Ill., 1963) p. 525, and George S. Gibb and Evelyn H. Knowlton, *The Resurgent Years, 1911–1927* (New York, 1956) pp. 201–3. From 1899 to 1914 Jersey Standard supplied close to three-fifths to two-thirds of the British market. According to Williamson, 'Royal Dutch Shell began about 1910 to move into the European market on an impressive scale' (pp. 259–60). Kenneth Beaton, *Enterprise in Oil* (New York, 1957) ch. 2 provides a useful summary of the history of Royal Dutch Shell based on F. C. Garretson's massive, *The History of Royal Dutch Shell* (Leiden, 1953). The Anglo-Persian story is given in Henry Longhurst, *Adventure in Oil* (London, 1959) chs. 3–5.

12   Information on the companies listed in this paragraph comes from Channon, *British Enterprise*, pp. 96–7, 167–9, 191–2; Charles Wilson, *The History of Unilever* (London, 1957) I, chs. 5–7, 10; II, chs. 10–12 and Peter Mathias, *Retailing Revolution* (London, 1967) chs. 9, 11.

13   For Brunner, Mond, see W. J. Reader, *Imperial Chemical Industries* (London, 1970) ch. 10; and for Boots, Stanley Chapman, 'Strategy and Structure at Boots the Chemists', ch. 5 of this work; also Channon, *British Enterprise*, p. 122, and Peter L. Payne, 'The Emergence of the Large-Scale Company in Great Britain, 1870–1914', *Economic History Review*, xx (1967) 535–6.

14   Reader, *ICI*, chs. 5, 7 (esp. pp. 131–5), and pp. 179–83.

15   Alfred D. Chandler Jr and Stephen Salsbury, *Pierre S. du Pont and the Making of the Modern Corporation* (New York, 1971) chs. 3 and 4.

16   B. W. E. Alford, *W. D. & H. O. Wills* (London, 1973) pp. 309–14, 330–3.

17   The operation and structure of American Tobacco will be described in my forthcoming study of the rise of large-scale business enterprise in the United States.

18   The information in Payne, 'Emergence of the Large-Scale Company', pp. 527–30, suggests that these textile companies were formed to control competition. Payne indicates they in time became centralised bureaucracies, but cites no specific evidence on internal organisation. The buying and selling units and statistical departments in these non-integrated industries could be used as much to control competition as to increase productivity and decrease costs.

19   D. C. Coleman, *Courtaulds* (Oxford, 1969) chs. 5, 6.

20   Channon, *British Enterprise*, pp. 151–5, Leslie Hannah, an unpublished article entitled 'Management Structure', and J. D. Scott, *Vickers, A History* (London, 1962) chs. 5–6, 9.

21   Channon, *British Enterprise*, pp. 135–6, and Hannah, 'Management Structure', has information on these companies. Scott, *Vickers*, points out that the Metropolitan Company purchased with Vickers in 1917 the British Westinghouse Electric and Manufacturing Company, and in 1919 Metropolitan was itself purchased by Vickers (pp. 140–2).

22   Leslie Hannah, 'Managerial Innovation and the Rise of the Large-Scale Company in Inter-war Britain', *Economic History Review*, xxvii (1974) 259, and 'Management Structure'.

23   As indicated in books by Reader, Coleman, Mathias and Channon and articles by Hannah cited above. Channon, *British Enterprise*, pp. 114–18 is good on the strategy and structure of the British oil companies.

24   Reader, *ICI*, pp. 389–94. The committee on organisation, Reader notes, 'had been greatly impressed' by their visit to the Du Pont Company in 1919. They reported: 'The movement towards large commercial combination originated in the United States . . . and the policy of large American amalgamations is crystalling out into complete merger, in which the separate management and personnel of the individual units disappear, even if the units themselves retain their nominal

existence, and a single executive and operating staff is created, in which the entire control is centralised.' (p. 390)

25 Channon, *British Enterprise*, pp. 122, 135–6, and Hannah, 'Management Structure'.

26 Mathias, *Retailing Revolution*, pp. 265–72, 367–72, Hannah, 'Management Structure'.

27 Scott, *Vickers*, ch. 15. Three functional 'subsidiary boards or committees' were set up: an industrial board (responsible for the management of the firm's industrial companies), an armament and shipbuilding board, and a finance board. The latter was to check costs and allocate resources (p. 159).

28 As pointed out earlier Channon found only four companies in his 1950 sample with multidivisional structures. He lists Turner and Newall as a holding company.

29 Wilson, *Unilever*, II, 309–13, Charles H. Wilson, *Unilever, 1945–1965* (London, 1968) ch. 2.

30 Hannah, 'Managerial Innovation', pp. 262–8, William J. Reader, *Imperial Chemical Industries – A History*, II (London, 1975) ch. 8.

31 Hannah, 'Managerial Innovation', p. 264.

32 Arthur Knight, *Private Enterprise and Public Intervention: The Courtaulds Experience* (London, 1974) pp. 70–1; Channon, *British Enterprise*, p. 136.

33 Channon, *British Enterprise*, pp. 103, 110, 115, 127, 134–7, 141, 143–5, 155, 166, 168, 170, 172, 179, 183, 187, 192.

34 W. S. and E. S. Woytinsky, *Trends and Outlooks in World Population and Production* (New York, 1953) pp. 383–5, also Simon Kuznets, *Economic Growth of Nations* (Cambridge, Mass., 1971) pp. 38–40.

35 H. J. Habakkuk, *American and British Technology in the Nineteenth Century* (Cambridge, England, 1967) sees advances in American technology almost wholly as a response to labour scarcity. Possibly this is because he focuses on the period before 1860.

2 The Chandler Thesis— Some General Observations

BERNARD W. E. ALFORD

Over the past twenty-five years there has been a steady accumulation of historical case studies of British companies which, in themselves, have shown an increasing level of sophistication of analysis; but this has not been matched by related efforts at building up a more general explanation of the process of change in business organisation and development. It may be that one reason for this is that the tradition of the heroic (or notorious) entrepreneur has exercised a strong influence on business historians. Moreover, there has been a somewhat uncritical reliance on certain concepts drawn from formal economic theory. The classical theory of the firm has been a favourite hunting ground; and although its assumptions have been steadily, and by now almost completely, undermined by empirical investigation, it is significant – and regrettable – that business historians have not played a major role in this process.[1] Yet the outlines of an alternative, independent and, dare it be said, potentially very profitable line of approach was indicated some years ago by two important books: E. T. Penrose, *The Theory of the Growth of the Firm* (1959) and A. D. Chandler, *Strategy and Structure* (1962).[2] Very recently, however, there have been signs – of which this symposium is one – of a growing interest among business historians in developing the approaches of Penrose and Chandler in the light of accumulating historical evidence. It is in this spirit that the following observations on the Chandler thesis are put forward; and although they may well be open to criticism as factless theorising, at least it is hoped that they will be accepted as a genuine attempt to stimulate further enquiry.[3]

I

Chandler has provided an impressive amount of evidence to demonstrate how general market (i.e. demand) and technological factors together constitute the stimulus for changes in business organisation and development. At the same time entrepreneurship remains a major element in his analysis through its responsibility for devising strategic and structural responses to match and take advantage of a changing market/technological environment. In particular this role can be brought into sharp focus when these external factors precipitate a major crisis in a company. Furthermore, in examining entrepreneurship Chandler draws a clear distinction between executives – or entrepreneurs at the top – who determine strategic objectives and who are responsible for the company structure through which they are to be achieved, and managers who are responsible for the day-to-day operation of a company. And in accordance with this, structure usually follows strategy though the response may be delayed and/or inefficient depending on the quality of entrepreneurship.[4]

The operation of market/technological factors will be considered at a later stage; for the moment attention will be concentrated on internal business organisation and, to begin with, on the relationship between executives and managers.[5] Now clearly, business histories provide a great deal of evidence of this division of function, but the question which arises is whether in the dynamics of entrepreneurial and managerial activities the division is so clear cut. To draw a medical analogy: the business historian needs to question whether he can derive the physiology of a business from its morphology. The crux of this problem is that of understanding how various levels within a business relate to one another over time. In some cases it is possible to get a fairly clear insight into this process. For example, the study of the Imperial Tobacco Company below illustrates how, in a company operating under a loose form of holding arrangement, the relationship between the subsidiary branches and the controlling body was crucial.[6] In this case, in conjunction with other factors, the bargaining strength of individual branches was such as to inhibit the executive committee from adopting a comprehensive strategy for the company as a whole; or, in other words, those who were formally designated managers were able to exercise considerable influence on overall strategy. Another example is provided by Kocka's work on Siemens, traditionally regarded as an archetypal family business of the late nineteenth century.[7] In fact Kocka shows that although Werner Siemens believed himself to be in complete control of the firm, throughout the last 20 years or so of his life the company's strategy was the outcome of a complex management structure of which Werner Siemens was largely a figurehead. And recent work on Rio Tinto Zinc would also appear to confirm the general proposition being advanced here.[8]

It could be argued, of course, that this feature of business development is limited to a certain stage of organisation : a stage of fragmentation during which *personal* or *entrepreneurial* enterprises are evolving into the *managerial* form of either the centralised or multi-divisional company.[9] But even if this qualification were accepted it would remain true that, historically at least, these stages involved long periods and many firms. However, what may be termed 'diffused entrepreneurship' is almost certainly a widespread feature of large managerial companies. Unfortunately in the British case there has been very little study of such companies (in particular of the multi-divisional type), probably mainly because they have not been a major part of British business until recent years.[10] Nevertheless, there is sufficient evidence to bear out the general point, though further progress in this direction will be difficult since the nature of business records imposes on the historian constraints similar to those affecting top executives. An obvious aspect of this phenomenon is in the study of the control of information.

Managers may well be able to exercise a significant influence on strategic decisions through their responsibilities for generating and regulating the flow of information within a company. Now, of course, the degree of this influence depends on the competence of top executives to demand the sort of information they require for making strategic decisions; but even this is only one aspect of the problem since, as Chandler has shown, in the main policies are based on accumulations of information rather than on what might be called short-term procurements.[11] Indeed, the nature of modern technology and market research almost necessarily requires this. Close attention by business historians to the manner in which information is collected and transmitted in large companies is therefore essential. In the British context a useful paradigm is provided by the civil service in which, it is widely accepted, by careful control of information and advice given to a minister, senior civil servants are able to exercise considerable powers of policy-making; and business historians who have some acquaintance with the functioning of large multi-divisional companies will no doubt recognise strong parallels with the civil service. Those who claim that civil servants do not exercise such control use such magic phrases as 'the experienced civil servant is able to anticipate the minister's wishes' or 'know the minister's mind'.[12] Furthermore, such management structures constitute bureaucracies which generate incentives to gain control over sources of information as an important means of establishing and defending status and role within an organisation.[13]

Control of information can be closely bound up with the complexity and scale of technical change. There is the problem of whether executives are able to make a comprehensive appraisal of the commercial potential of a new technical development. However carefully the claims of a technical department are checked – and there are obvious limits to this because of problems of secrecy – inevitably, heavy reliance has to be placed on internal experts whose goals might not be entirely in tune with those of the company as seen from the top. Moreover, if a project fails it is not easy to attach blame to its originators – unless it is a spectacular technical failure – since many hands are involved in turning invention into innovation. Sometimes, indeed, managers may seek to overcome resistance to certain projects at the top by representing them as technical imperatives. One example of this from the pre-Second World War period is provided by Reader in his account of ICI; although on the face of it McGowan exercised dictatorial control over the company he admitted to knowing little about technical matters and was, therefore, usually willing to assent to projects wrapped up in technical language; and even though at any given time McGowan imposed overall limits on expenditure, in many cases these limits would have been substantially pre-determined by previous technical commitments. Furthermore this illustrates how a snapshot view of a company's command structure may not adequately reflect the actual process of decision-making. Another variant of the gambit of managers using the complexity of technical information to obscure the true intent of proposals being made to higher authority, has been discovered by Payne. In order to overcome the high resistance of family trusts which controlled certain Scottish steel firms, managers disguised quite substantial programmes of innovations to appear as essential repairs to existing plant.[14]

This problem was intensified in certain British industries in the early twentieth century – for example in motor cars and electric power generation – because of the high status enjoyed by certain levels of technical management, which had become deeply established over a long period. In consequence 'the engineer' was able to exercise such control over top executives that sometimes matters of commercial viability were inadequately considered, with serious financial consequences.[15] More generally, the greater the range and/or complexity of goods produced (and this includes the number of markets served) the more dispersed the determinants of a company's strategy are likely to be. And for business historians this involves giving detailed attention to matters of pricing, credit facilities, sales organisation, relationships with customers – ostensibly mundane, mechanical matters but which may, nevertheless, be inter-laced with a variety of objectives which determine crucial inter-relationships between different levels of a company.[16] Moreover, insofar as these objectives involve vested interests in maintaining the existing structure of a company, a stage could be reached at which, in effect, structure was determining strategy. The possibility of this reverse relationship is considered more fully a little later.

Recently Chandler has put forward a hypothesis which lends support to the main line of argument which has been developed here : '. . . the general office [i.e. head office] does not really control the divisions, for the information on which it acts still comes largely from within and therefore senior executives rely primarily on information generated by the day-to-day operations of the divisions'.[17] One reason for this procedure, Chandler suggests, is that top executives have most likely been recruited from divisions and are thereby sympathetic to the objectives and procedures of divisional management. Thus top executives '. . . tend to be uncomfortable . . . with proposals of the general staff or outside consultants to make strategic moves into areas where their divisions are not yet operating. So in reality, it is the more aggressive division managers who determine strategy, that is, the investment decisions . . . Rarely do [top executives] take action to remedy the situation [i.e. declining performance] by removing managers or discontinuing lines'.[18] Chandler does not go quite as far as to argue, as we have done, that the making of strategic policy is frequently and necessarily diffused and may even be originated from levels below that of divisional manager. Moreover, our argument implies that the more dispersed the entrepreneurial function the less likelihood there will be of a coherent growth strategy.[19]

Before leaving this aspect of the discussion it is interesting to reflect on whether Japanese experience provides suggestive evidence in support of our analysis relating, essentially, to company organisation in Western Europe and North America. In a recent stimulating article Yamamura has argued that the somewhat distinctive characteristics of Japanese culture (as seen through Western eyes) have directly affected patterns of company structure and management practice in Japan.[20] In particular he lays stress on the loyalty shown to the *uchi*, or enterprise,[21] and on the *ringi* system of decision-making which '. . . is a system by which any change in routines, tactics, and even strategies of a firm is originated by those persons who are directly concerned with the change, and the final decision is made at the top level after an elaborate examination of the proposal which results in acceptance or rejection by consensus at every echelon of the managerial structure'.[22] In relation to this Yamamura goes on to highlight the remarkable success of Japanese economic performance since the Second World War, or, as Chandler expresses it in commenting on Yamamura's paper : 'No nation appears to have been culturally better equipped to handle the managerial demands of modern technologically advanced urban economies than the Japanese.'[23] Could it be, in effect, that large-scale multi-divisional companies in the West operate with varying degrees of the *ringi* system combined with generally far less developed senses of loyalty to the *uchi*?

More broadly, the foregoing observations imply the impossibility of generalising about the degree of what has been termed 'diffused entrepreneurship'. In some cases and/or at some times the competence and effectiveness of a small group of entrepreneurs – even of one man – in determining business strategy may be very great indeed; and there may be occasions when such entrepreneurs possess sufficient power to act irrationally, in the sense of disregarding available information and the assumed strategy of a company, in order either simply to take a gamble or to precipitate the business into disaster so as to satisfy some personal whim or spite. Yet there is little evidence of the latter form of behaviour in modern business. At the same time, moreover, whatever the overall role of entrepreneurship in business performance, the role of top executives is almost certainly somewhat less than might be gauged from much business history. Discussion of grand diplomacy and of major crises involving so-called key individuals should be treated, if not with scepticism, then with great caution. Similarly the apparent precision of flow diagrams of company structure should be approached with wariness lest form is mistaken for reality;[24] and analyses of the pyschology and motives of so-called leading businessmen, however fascinating, should not be allowed to cloud an evaluation of their true role in a company's development.[25]

II

As has been noted, a major strength of Chandler's approach is its emphasis on general market and technological factors as they interact with functional relationships within large companies. And in a recent paper he has underlined this by stressing the bunching in timing of the emergence of large firms in various industries in the UK and the USA, for example.[26] One might even go further than this – at the risk of being charged with indulging in uncritical, counterfactual history – by hypothesising that the general development of such industries as, say, soap and tobacco in the UK in the nineteenth century would not have been significantly different without William Lever or the Wills brothers. Yet while the broad trends of business development may be fairly clear there are obvious differences in the manner and degree of change which occurs and it is necessary to consider whether this calls for further refinements in the strategy/structure approach. A useful way to begin probing this is to ask whether the degree of market power exercised by a firm is of any importance in conditioning changes in strategy and structure, since this concentrates attention on the very point of connection between external factors and internal organisation.

The account of the development of the Imperial Tobacco Company below provides an interesting case study of this connection.[27] ITCo's very limited reaction to the effect of changing market conditions on its major branch, Wills, in the 1930s was in large measure due to its overall market strength; though, as has been shown, the effects of this on the viability of the company were not serious. This example prompts broader comparisons, however, since although from the early decades of the twentieth century onwards many leading firms in a variety of industries have exercised oligopoly power the precise degree and nature of it has differed considerably both as between firms and over time. For example, if such power were heavily concentrated in a given company and based on large-scale capital requirements, the ownership of patent rights to crucial manufacturing processes, or tariff protection, this could lead to delayed (or to no) strategic reaction to quite major changes in general market conditions, in turn producing slower growth of the company. Because of its market power and therefore ability to squeeze other firms by various means, its profits might well remain substantial; while all the while the underlying position of the firm could be weakening, making it increasingly vulnerable to, say, international competition or further changes in domestic market conditions, so that it could be forced into permanent decline or, even, immediate collapse. Those companies involved in the merger movement in Britain at the end of the last century and firms in the industries protected by tariffs in the 1930s can be cited as cases in which this factor might be found, on further investigation, to have been of considerable significance in determining their lack of success in making strategic and structural adjustments to broad market and technical changes.[28]

Such failures could be attributed to the poor talents of the entrepreneurs at the top of the companies in question. But this is only one way of looking at the problem : it does not explain why those particular entrepreneurs were directing affairs for so long; yet this is the crucial factor in terms of the dynamics of strategic and structural change and, incidentally, one to which more attention should be paid in discussions about the quality of entrepreneurship in Britain generally.[29] It is at this point that the degree of market power of a company can well be the major factor in preserving an existing entrepreneurial structure; executives find it easy to use this power to enforce various short-run defensive arrangements, most probably at the expense of other firms. Thus a strategic response which would sustain or improve the company's position over the longer run is thwarted, even though the 'new men' who are required are to be found within the company's hierachy. Correspondingly this might be taken as suggesting that the potential supply of entrepreneurial talent with the ability to perceive the need for and nature of strategic changes is less of a problem, and therefore less significant, in determining whether such changes are made than is the influence of external market structure on internal entrepreneurial mobility and thereby on the quality of entrepreneurial response.[30]

Chandler deals with a related condition in his discussion of the effects of family control, but this is seen as an obstacle to change at a particular stage of development, whereas the point here is that there is a *continuing* and *varying* relationship between strategy, structure, and market power which can be of primary importance.[31] Nevertheless, in a broader sense generation change may well exercise a recurrent but somewhat irregular and unpredictable effect. UK business histories relating to the period before the Second World War illustrate how the demise of family succession was usually followed by career succession; natural wastage rather than board-room revolution – a somewhat more recent innovation – became the final arbiter of entrepreneurial incompetence.

What can be viewed as a variant of the argument concerning the effect of market power has been advanced by Mathias, notwithstanding that his focus is on problems which develop in relation to an increase in the scale of business so that 'the variables which collectively make up the balance of forces determining the frontiers of a business are not easily formulated in terms which have predictive value, or even much regularity of incidence. The determination of a man or a committee can push out the frontiers of a business, where the context gives room for manoeuvre – and great fluidity clearly exists across a wide spectrum of business . . . But the context itself can exert powerful conditioning influences'.[32] In part technology is such an influence but so also is '. . . the logic of power relationships between firms in different, related industries; between centres of power in retailing and manufacturing'.[33] While one might doubt whether the range of possible outcomes is as random as Mathias suggests, the crucial importance to strategy and structure of these power relations, which, it can be contended, depend ultimately on a firm's market power, is clear.[34]

Does this line of analysis lead to the proposition that structure can, and frequently does, determine strategy? Such a proposition is, of course, in direct contrast to Chandler's original thesis in which structure follows strategy even though the efficiency of the response in terms of timing and suitability may well fall short of the optimum. There seem to be strong grounds for viewing the relationship as symbiotic rather than causal. In the case of ITCo, for example, for a long period structure determined strategy quite strongly because of the semi-independent nature of branches: in overall terms Imperial had under-employed resources in the Penrose sense, particularly of finance, yet the strength of individual branch interests inhibited a broader strategic policy.[35] The argument can also be illustrated in relation to suggestions that some large companies in the interwar years in the UK did not need multi-divisional organisation.[36] For the problem with this view is its implied assumptions about the growth potential of such firms in terms of their resources and their potential for using them more productively through diversification or more extensive integration. Indeed this is a matter of crucial importance when considering the process of the restructuring of industry – or lack of it – in the interwar years. In short, if potential resources were available then failure to employ them might well have been a case of existing structures inhibiting new strategies; and in this context the whole issue of existing industrial location and infrastructure assumes major significance.[37] This raises, further, the interesting question of whether such structural log-jams could be broken only by some external agency such as the government or some private financial-cum-industrial consortium.

Another facet of this relationship has been highlighted by Mathias and further emphasised by Supple : '. . . the goal of the institution, of the business, may have to be adapted to the organisation, rather than the organisation of the business always having to be adapted to the goals'.[38] Problems arising in relation to distribution and to forward integration in shoemaking and grocery retailing are cited as clear examples of this. A similar process can be seen at work in two other areas. First, in the field of multi-national companies it is often impossible to categorise firms as either centralised or multi-divisional since the inter-dependancy of strategy and structure makes a company a mutant of both forms.[39] Secondly, if a company is reorganised on a multi-divisional basis this may generate external economies for at least some of the divisions which can only be reaped – thereby allowing the division to function at its most profitable – by further changing the strategy of the company at least in respect of these divisions but, more probably, in a more thoroughgoing fashion.[40]

There seems little doubt that detailed examination of other businesses would reveal further examples of the symbiosis of strategy and structure : a process of development through adjustment and adaptation, often quite slow, but in time leading to major cumulative changes. This in no way denies the importance of dramatic, or radical, changes in market-cum-technological factors, as Chandler has described for certain leading American firms in the early decades of this century. Nevertheless, even where periods of particularly concentrated changes are concerned the question arises as to the precise meaning of the term strategy.

What can be seen as strategic changes *ex post* might not have been conceived as such *ex ante*. For example, as Supple has observed, growth in the scale of enterprise may 'just happen' in response to problems as they arise and, therefore, it is not the outcome of the pursuit of growth as such.[41] This is probably too sweeping since businessmen usually act in accordance with certain objectives; though these objectives are probably more complex and variable than business historians often care to admit, and they certainly may not constitute a strategy. And in this

context uncritical borrowing from economic theory is often most evident since the historian may too readily assume that business behaviour
is dominated by such objectives as profit maximisation or growth
whereas, for example, a company's strategy may be the integral of a
series of relatively short-term tactics designed, say, to maintain a constant income to its owners, or to ensure maximum job security for its
managers. And because in such cases strategy is a resultant and not a
planned course of action, it may well lead a firm into quite unexpected
areas.

The merger movement of the turn of the century was in many ways
a series of 'happenings'; and it also raises the issue of the form of
growth followed by a firm – whether it was by means of takeover, amalgamation, or internally financed diversification. The study of Imperial
– a classic case of the merger movement – indicates how the manner of
its formation had a long-term effect on its strategy; and it is interesting
to speculate on the possible alternative development of the company
had the Wills family more clearly understood the strength of their
firm and adopted an independent strategic response to the challenge
of the American Tobacco Company.[42]

The merger movement prompts some mention of the role of lawyers
and, more especially, accountants in the formulation of strategy and
structure. The relationship between the accountancy profession and
demands from business for improved financial procedures is the subject
of debate, not least through want of evidence.[43] However, business
historians working on the pre-Second World War period would probably agree that it is not so much a question of companies suffering
a shortage of professional financial advice as one of the nature of the
basic principles of accounting which determined the quality or, more
accurately, the appropriateness of the advice proffered. For example,
the reorganisation of the British steel industry between the wars seems
to have been bedevilled by zealous accountants proffering putative
solutions which appeared satisfactory in narrow financial terms but
which made far less sense in relation to technical and commercial
requirements.[44] And the activities of Treasury accountants in the post-
1945 nationalisation programme can be cited as another similar example – though, of course, it must be admitted, Treasury officials are
always in a class of their own.[45]

One other element of internal structure which warrants special
attention concerns the attitudes and organisation of labour. Analytically,
however, this presents a problem since in some ways this factor operates
as an integral and active element in company structure, whilst in other
ways it has to be considered along with other external, exogenous, variables which will be discussed shortly. Moreover, many business
historians will have experience of the difficulties involved in working in

this area in terms of getting hold of evidence, especially for the period before the First World War. Nevertheless there is sufficient information relating to, say, some of the declining industries in the UK between the wars such as coal and shipbuilding or to a so-called new industry such as motor-cars, to indicate how features like demarcation and the high specificity of skills were powerful determinants of company structures and, in particular, active restraints on diversification strategies.[46] Certainly, however, this area requires intensive investigation.

III

Having considered the Chandler typology mainly in relation to the internal operations of large companies, the remainder of the discussion will concentrate on what have already been defined as external factors. For Chandler, of course, market-cum-technological factors are paramount in this respect and he specifically downgrades 'anti-trust laws, taxation, labour and welfare legislation'.[47] However, even while accepting market-cum-technological factors as ultimately necessary conditions of changes in business organisation and development, they do not necessarily determine immediately the timing and nature of these changes; and the manner in which their effect is thus muted, augmented, or even suppressed, by the intervention of other, secondary factors is of primary importance to attempts at explaining differences between companies, industries and, ultimately, economies. Indeed, a number of countries are defined as industrialised and, therefore, there is a high degree of congruity between them in terms of market and technological factors; but when compared with one another in terms of economic performance they differ very considerably and, it can be suggested, a significant part of these differences arises from variations in the nature of external influences affecting patterns of business development. Of course, to some extent – and in some instances it may be substantially so – such variations may be explained by more detailed analysis of market-cum-technological factors : in such terms as size, age structure and growth of population; distribution of income; diffusion of technology. Yet, the business historian must needs cast his net widely, and not take as given a whole range of conditions and then simply examine the response of individual businesses or businessmen to them. This is the only way of discovering whether and, if so, to what extent such secondary factors *directly* determine business strategy. In order to illustrate this five such factors will be considered very briefly. They are drawn from evidence relating to a very few companies, which in itself suggests that close analysis of other firms would probably make it a fairly easy exercise to extend the list by quite a lot.

The first of these factors is the nature of the law. This is well illustrated by Wills' development in the latter part of the nineteenth century, as it was strongly determined by the introduction of new regulations dealing with the quality of tobacco goods and, more powerfully, by the patent system.[48] The operation of these factors was crucial in conditioning the impact on the industry of changes in demand and of a fundamental technical breakthrough, in a manner which accelerated the oligopolistic development of the industry through the resultant strategic and structural changes in tobacco firms. The entrepreneurial success of the Wills brothers has to be measured in terms of their ability to ensure that it was their firm which benefited from these conditions rather than one of a number of others snapping at their heels; and serendipity was very kind to the Wills brothers. More generally, legal factors were almost certainly an element in the slow rate at which the multi-divisional form of organisation spread in this country as compared with the USA.[49]

Taxation is the second factor. Here again tobacco provides a good illustration. The heavy excise tax on tobacco leaf resulted in high proportionate and absolute capital requirements and almost completely determined pricing policies. Before the war this served to reinforce growing concentration in the production and marketing of cigarettes, which resulted fundamentally from technical change. In the succeeding interwar period, however, the change in consumption of tobacco goods from being predominantly of pipe tobaccos to being predominantly of cigarettes caused the tax system to become a more independently powerful factor; through its effect on capital requirements it served as a bastion to Imperial's market position enabling the company to deal with potential competitors without having to pursue a vigorous counter-strategy for which, as a precondition, there would have to have been a radical change in its existing, loose holding company structure.[50] Another good example is provided by Rio Tinto Zinc.[51] Between 1900 and 1906, 1920 and 1931, and 1936 and 1939 its strategy was a direct response to taxation policies of the Spanish government, while market factors were of very secondary importance. More generally, in recent years the incidence of company taxation in the UK has probably had a major influence on business strategy; the sorts of things involved include the distribution of investment between domestic and foreign branches; the building up of conglomerates; the direct pull of devices such as tax holidays offered by certain countries.

The impact of two world wars constitutes a third and fairly obvious factor in the British case. The manner in which ITCo was forced to adopt a strong centralised system of organisation in place of its existing loose holding-company arrangement is almost certainly just one of a number of similar examples of war forcing a major shake-up of company structure.[52] Moreover, the economic consequences of the war, in terms of postwar restrictions and regulations, exercised a continuing and powerful control over business strategies. And these effects were not just short-term. For example, the enforced demands on certain major industries such as railways and steel during both wars virtually dictated subsequent strategic alternatives;[53] or, again, the enforced sale of foreign subsidiaries by certain companies during the Second World War must have directly affected possible competitive strategies once peace-time conditions returned.[54]

Government intervention in business, which has been growing throughout this century but which, in most countries, has been immeasurably increased since the Second World War, is another factor to be considered. The range of aims pursued by government has become bewilderingly wide – certainly this is so in the UK – but in this context it will be sufficient to comment on just two facets of this development. First, in the post-1945 period the government showed increasing concern over monopolies and monopoly practices, and this led to the establishment of the Monopolies and Restrictive Practices Commission in 1948 and to a further tightening up of this legislation in 1956. ITCo is an example *par excellence* of the consequences of this, though unfortunately it is the only large monopolistic company for which detailed evidence is available. The sheer size and monopoly power of ITCo was obvious and from the 1940s onwards, therefore, its executive committee measured its strategy against what it considered would be judged to be in the public interest – or, perhaps more accurately, not against the public interest. One obvious consequence of this was that the company made no attempt in the 1950s to restore profits on tobacco goods to anything approaching pre-war levels; and, in turn, this was an important element in causing it to adopt a more vigorous policy of diversification in order to secure new sources of profit.[55] Further evidence of the effect of this factor is provided by Knight in his very interesting discussion of the relationship between Courtaulds and the government in the period since the early sixties. For example he comments : 'In managing the Lancashire situation that consciousness [of government attitudes] was not only present but it was a dominant element in leading Courtauld's into their change of policy.'[56]

The second facet of government interference worth looking at is nationalisation. Evidence on this in the British case is still thin though there are indications, for example in the case of steel, of how nationalisation proposals stimulated counter strategies among the companies concerned.[57] This factor has also been commented on recently by Laux in relation to French business strategy in the post-1945 period, by suggesting how the stimulus to and pattern of diversification policies may well have been a response to fears of state take-over.[58]

The final factor in this discussion concerns production/supply possibilities. An excellent example of this is provided by the problem of the declining quality of ore supplies for a mining company such as Rio Tinto Zinc.[59] Such a development may cause a company to diversify and re-structure in order to secure new and more profitable ore supplies; and in conjunction with, or alternatively to this it may adopt a strategy of transferring a proportion (or the bulk) of its resources into a different range of activities. Additionally, international mining companies are among the best examples of firms whose strategies are extremely sensitive to political elements. Another, very topical, example in this category is the effect of OPEC's cartel oil policy on the strategy of the large international oil companies; on the one hand the companies' strategy on the marketing of oil is virtually dictated by the 'supply conditions', while on the other hand the companies are busily diversifying into a whole range of activities in order to limit their future dependence for profits on oil.[60]

It is worth adding that of the five external factors which have been considered the last two – political factors and production/supply possibilities – are those most likely to be completely independent of market-cum-technological factors.

The value of the strategy/structure approach to the analysis of the development of business organisation is established but, at the same time, it has to be recognised as a typology and, as such, like all historical typologies its greatest merit is in defining and elaborating concepts which might then be developed more fully as means to understanding more clearly the process of change[61] Thus some ways in which the Chandler approach might be developed have been tentatively suggested. In particular, it has been argued, it is necessary to define entrepreneurship more widely while judging its role more cautiously, and to view the relationship between strategy and structure as symbiotic and not causal. Furthermore, the need to examine in more detail a wide range of external factors has been equally stressed; while nevertheless accepting that market-cum-technological factors are ultimately the dominant external progenitors of changes in strategy and structure. Such refinements are especially necessary if business history is to adopt the potentially rewarding approach of comparative analysis, right up to the international level.[62] Clearly this involves difficulties of measurement and of assessment of efficiency, not least because of the complex nexus of business behaviour and business performance. For this reason business historians should think less in terms of the monograph history of a firm and more in terms of a number of histories examining different aspects of a firm's development. At least, a careful consideration of the objectives of business history which symposia such as this encourage, may lead to strategic changes which, together with appropriate structural reorganisation, could prove a most rewarding intellectual enterprise.

NOTES

1 See P. J. Devine, *An Introduction to Industrial Economics* (Allen & Unwin, 1974) pp. 108–292, for a recent survey of the current state of the theory of the firm. See also John H. Dunning (ed.), *Economic Analysis and the Multinational Enterprise* (Allen & Unwin, 1974). This book includes a very useful bibliography.

2 Penrose (Oxford, 1959), Chandler (MIT Press, Cambridge Massachusetts, 1962) – the latter book is cited hereafter as *Strategy and Structure*.

3 The wide-ranging and speculative nature of this paper reflects my brief from the editor.

4 In addition to *Strategy and Structure*, see Alfred D. Chandler, 'The Development of Modern Management Structure in the US and UK', pp. 23–51 above.

5 'The general executive of the large corporation is then as crucial and identifiable a figure in mid-twentieth century economy as Adam Smith's capitalist was in the late eighteenth century, and Jean Baptiste Say's entrepreneur in the early nineteenth.' *Strategy and Structure*, p. 314.

6 See Bernard W. E. Alford, 'Strategy and Structure in the UK Tobacco Industry', pp. 73–84 below.

7 See J. Kocka, 'Family and Bureaucracy in German Industrial Management, 1850–1914 . . .', *Business History Review*, xlv (1971) 133–56.

8 I am grateful to Mr Charles E. Harvey for this information. Mr Harvey is completing a detailed study of Rio Tinto Zinc covering the period up to 1939.

9 These terms are developed in more detail in Alfred D. Chandler Jr and Herman Daems, 'The Rise of Managerial Capitalism and its Impact on Investment Strategy in the Western World and Japan', in Herman Daems and Herman van der Wee (eds), *The Rise of Managerial Capitalism* (Martinus Nijhoff, The Hague and Leuven University Press, Belgium, 1974) pp. 1–34 but particularly pp. 5–6.

10 A general examination covering this period has been made by D. F. Channon, *The Strategy and Structure of British Enterprise* (Macmillan, 1973); see also Derek F. Channon, 'Corporate Evolution in the Service Industries', pp. 213–34 below.

11 See for example Alfred D. Chandler Jr, 'Structure of Investment Decisions in the United States' in Daems and van der Wee, op. cit., pp. 35–53; *Strategy and Structure*, pp. 311–14. The importance of information flows is also well brought out by Arthur Knight, *Private Enterprise and Public Intervention: The Courtaulds Experience* (Allen & Unwin, 1974) pp. 76–83. However, Knight also seems to imply that top management and, most particularly, the chairman, were in complete control of this flow. For myself, I feel that this opinion requires a great deal of supporting detailed evidence to be convincing.

12 See R. G. S. Brown, *The Administrative Process in Britain* (Methuen, 1970), for a very useful discussion of this and related issues. See also A. Dunsire, *Administration: The Word and The Science* (Martin Robertson, 1975) pp. 153–79. This book gives a comprehensive survey of both the theoretical and case-study literature in this field, though the jargon is a little forbidding. A great deal of information on this is also contained in Sir Norman Chester, *The Nationalisation of British Industry 1945–51* (HMSO, 1975) though since the author is content to describe events at great length the full impact of the civil servants role is not brought out. Cf. *Strategy and Structure*, p. 322 where Chandler discounts parallels between business and government organisation.

13 A study of some of the literature in this field would seem to me to be of value to business historians. A useful introductory survey is provided by Peter M. Blau and W. Richard Scott, *Formal Organisations: A Comparative Approach* (Routledge and Kegan Paul, 1963).

14 W. J. Reader, *Imperial Chemical Industries – a History*, II (London: Oxford University Press, 1975) pp. 143–4. I am grateful to Professor Payne for allowing me to cite the example relating to Scottish steel firms.

15 Evidence of this is provided by P. W. S. Andrews and Elizabeth Brunner, *The Life of Lord Nuffield* (Oxford, 1955) pp. 181–231; however, one has to read between the lines in order to divine the over-riding role of the engineers whereas it is brought out more clearly in Graham Turner, *The Car Makers* (Eyre & Spottiswoode, 1963) pp. 177–82. Our knowledge of this major industry is still, however, sadly deficient. See also D. Andrew Wilson, 'The Strategy of Sales Expansion in the British Electricity Supply Industry between the Wars', pp. 203–12 below.

16 For example the sort of things I have in mind are surveyed in R. M. Cyert and J. G. March, *A Behavioural Theory of the Firm* (Prentice-Hall, 1963); H. Igor Ansoff (ed.), *Business Strategy* (Penguin, 1969).

17 Alfred D. Chandler Jr, 'The Multi-Unit Enterprise: A Historical and International Comparative Analysis and Summary', in Harold F. Williamson (ed.), *Evolution of International Management Structures* (University of Delaware Press, Newark, 1975) pp. 251–2.

18 Loc. cit.

19 It will be noted how the approach being developed here is somewhat different to Penrose loc. cit., where major emphasis is given to 'management resources'. The line of criticism of Penrose which, given space, would be developed here would be that Penrose's concepts are too generalised; though she herself pointed to the potential value of business history in this connection.

21 Kozo Yamamura, 'A Compromise with Culture: The Historical Evolution of the Management Structure of Large Japanese Firms' in Harold F. Williamson, op. cit., pp. 158–85.

21 'The word *uchi* means "house", but can be used to refer to any unit, large or small, to which the speaker belongs.' Yamamura, op. cit., p. 183, n. 7.

22 Ibid., p. 162.

23 Alfred D. Chandler Jr, 'The Multi-Unit Enterprise . . .', op. cit., p. 247.

24 Cf. the comments here with W. J. Reader, *Imperial Chemical Industries*, pp. 133–44.

25 Close analysis of individual businessmen is a major feature of the approach of the business press to company performance, and if the talents of successful entrepreneurs are as unique and important as is usually claimed the outlook for most companies would seem to be grim. Happily the frequency of such profiles gives grounds for optimism and suspicion that successful companies sometimes produce successful company chairmen. For an up-to-date example see the profile of Lord Kearton in *The Sunday Times*, 3 August 1975, p. 33; see also note 30 below.

26 Chandler, 'The Development of Modern Management Structures in the US and UK', pp. 23–51 above.

27 pp. 73–84.

28 An examination of the available evidence seems to bear this out. Cf. Evelyn Hubbard, 'American "trusts" and English combinations', *Economic Journal*, XII (1902) 159–76; H. W. Macrosty, 'Business Aspects of British Trusts', *Economic Journal*, XII (1902) pp 347–66; and *The Trust Movement in British Industry* (Longman, 1907); P. Fitzgerald, *Industrial Combination in England* (Pitman, 1927); P. L. Payne, 'The Emergence of the Large-Scale Company in Great Britain, 1870–1914', *Economic History Review*, 2nd ser., XX (1967); Arthur Fletcher Lucas, *Industrial Reconstruction and the Control of Competition – The British Experiments*

(Longmans, Green & Co., 1937); H. V. Hodson, *Slump and Recovery 1929–1937* (London: Oxford University Press, 1938).

29   For example, much of the debate on the alleged decline in entrepreneurship in late nineteenth century Britain centres on how inefficient entrepreneurs depressed business performance, instead of on how these individuals managed to exercise a bad influence on their firms for so long. If more attention were paid to the dynamics of entrepreneurial change it would be necessary to consider carefully to what extent the quality of entrepreneurship was dependent on factors affecting the mobility, as against the potential supply, of entrepreneurs.

30   A slight variant of this is exemplified by Knight, op. cit., pp. 33–6, 76–83, where he discusses the accession of Kearton to the chairmanship of Courtaulds. Knight stresses the particular qualities of Kearton in relation to the subsequent success of the company in beating off the ICI takeover bid. But could it not be argued that the more significant factor in this respect was the manner in which the nature of the bid generated managerial mobility in Courtaulds involving a number of men who were available within the company? In general, Knight's analysis appears somewhat ambivalent in terms of the significance of top management as against 'other factors'. See note 56.

31   *Strategy and Structure*, pp. 380–1.

32   Peter Mathias, 'Conflicts of Function in the Rise of Big Business; The British Experience' in Harold F. Williamson, op. cit., p. 56.

33   Ibid.

34   In his comments on Mathias's paper Barry Supple suggests some ways in which possible outcomes could be systematised, loc. cit., p. 63.

35   Alford, 'Strategy and Structure in the UK Tobacco Industry', below pp. 73–84. Chandler comes near to describing a similar situation in relation to multi-function enterprises in *Strategy and Structure*, p. 296, but it is viewed as a transitory phase.

36   Cf. Leslie Hannah, 'Strategy and Structure in the Manufacturing Sector', pp. 184–202 below, in which he cites firms producing semi-finished products for a few industrial consumers.

37   See Duncan Burn, *The Economic History of Steelmaking 1867–1939* (Cambridge University Press, Cambridge, 1961) pp. 441–3 and generally pp. 393–515; John Vaizey, *The History of British Steel* (Weidenfeld & Nicolson, 1974) pp. 20–87. See N. K. Buxton, 'Entrepreneurial Efficiency in the British Coal Industry between the Wars', *Economic History Review*, 2nd ser., xxiii (1970); B. W. E. Alford, *Depression and Recovery? British Economic Growth, 1918–1939* (Macmillan, 1972) pp. 45–56. This view is also taken by Anthony Slaven in respect of John Brown & Co., a major Scottish shipbuilder. I am grateful to Dr Slaven for allowing me to cite his, as yet, unpublished work on this company.

38   Supple, op. cit., p. 60.

39   See the comments of Mira Wilkins on this problem in Harold F. Williamson (ed.), op. cit., pp. 217–24.

40   This case is very well developed by Peter Mathias, op. cit., pp. 51–5.

41   Supple, op. cit., p. 60. See also B. W. E. Alford, *W. D. & H. O. Wills and the Development of the U.K. Tobacco Industry, 1786–1965* (Methuen, 1973), pp. 247–77 for a detailed analysis of the major 'happening' of the so-called amalgamation movement.

42   See Alford, 'Strategy and Structure in the UK Tobacco Industry', below pp. 73–84; Alford, *W. D. & H. O. Wills . . .*, loc. cit.

43   See Mathias, op. cit., pp. 44–7, for a brief survey of this aspect.

44   Vaizey, op. cit., pp. 20–87. Professor Peter Payne has also done some fascinating work on this in relation to the Scottish steel industry over the period 1923–36. I am grateful to him for allowing me to draw attention to it.

45 See Sir Norman Chester, op. cit., especially pp. 383–456, 1009–25.

46 See James Hinton, *The First Shop Steward's Movement* (Allen & Unwin, 1973) pp. 56–100 – generally, Hinton shows how the strength of labour on, what were in effect strategic policies, was in part a function of the existing structure of a firm. Dr Slaven's work on John Brown & Co. also indicates the effect of specificity of skills on limiting possible strategies.

47 Of course it is important to bear in mind that Chandler is dealing with the USA whereas this discussion is based mainly on UK experience.

48 For detailed analysis of this see Alford, *W. D. & H. O. Wills.*, op. cit. chs. 5, 7, 10.

49 i.e. various defensive monopolistic and restrictive practices helped to protect existing structures; and unlike the USA they did not fall foul of the law – indeed, in the 1930s the government actively encouraged such arrangements in certain major industries. See Leslie Hannah, 'Business Development and Economic Structure in Britain since 1880', pp. 1–19 above; Alfred D. Chandler, 'The Development of Modern Management Structure . . .', pp. 23–51 above. The best account of the situation in Britain is still A. F. Lucas, op. cit.

50 See Alford, *W. D. & H. O. Wills . . .*, passim, and Bernard W. E. Alford, pp. 73–84 below.

51 I am grateful to Mr Charles E. Harvey for this information.

52 See Alford, pp. 77–8, 81 below.

53 For general accounts of these developments based on a range of sources see Alford, *Depression and Recovery? . . .*, and Sidney Pollard, *The Development of the British Economy 1914–1950* (Arnold, 1962).

54 A good example of this is Courtaulds' sale of AVC to the Americans – D. C. Coleman, *Courtaulds: An Economic and Social History* (Oxford: Clarendon Press, 1969), II, 460–91. Professor Coleman will no doubt deal with the full consequences of this in his foreshadowed volume III.

55 See Alford, p. 82 below; The Monopolies Commission, *Report on the Supply of Cigarettes and Tobacco etc.*, (Cmd. 218, 1961).

56 Knight, op. cit., pp. 67–8, 97–215. Once again, however, Knight makes no attempt to evaluate such a factor against other elements determining strategy.

57 Sir Norman Chester, op. cit., pp. 149–83; Vaizey, op. cit., pp. 118–49.

58 James M. Laux, 'Managerial Structures in France', in Williamson, op. cit., p. 112.

59 Again I am grateful to Mr Charles E. Harvey for drawing my attention to this point.

60 See Anthony Sampson, *The Seven Sisters: The Great Oil Companies and the World They Made* (Hodder and Stoughton, 1975). A somewhat racy account but, nevertheless, a revealing one.

61 I am less than optimistic, however, about the possibilities of relating the performance of individual firms to general economic performance over time – even if one concentrates on what have been termed 'core firms'. The theoretical problems appear extremely complex, not least in terms of defining appropriate measures for individual business performance and its effects. Somewhat related, though more general, issues of this nature are dealt with by Peter Temin, 'General Equilibrium Models in Economic History', *Journal of Economic History*, XXXI/1, 58–75.

62 Comparisons can be made between British firms and American subsidiaries with American management operating in this country, in order to emphasise the significance of the superior performance of American management in comparison with British. But one of the difficulties with this kind of analysis would seem to be the problem of discovering to what extent this superior performance reflects external economies to the parent firm. Such things as development costs, experi-

ments in manning requirements, and marketing experience, spring to mind. Cf. John H. Dunning (with two case studies by W. G. Jensen), *The Role of American Investment in the British Economy* (PEP Broadsheet, 507, 1969), esp. pp. 130–9. Moreover, some of the evidence cited here could be taken as further examples of structure inhibiting strategic change.

Part Two
CASE STUDIES

CASE STUDIES

3 Strategy and Structure in the UK Tobacco Industry

BERNARD W. E. ALFORD

This paper covers the development of the Imperial Tobacco Co. (of Great Britain and Ireland) Ltd (ITCo) over the period from 1901 to the early 1960s. My analysis is divided into two parts: a brief description of the main changes in the company's organisation and a comparison of Imperial's development with the Chandler typology.[1]

I

The ITCo was formed in 1901 during the 'tobacco war' which involved an attempt by the American Tobacco Company to establish a dominant hold over the UK market for cigarettes and tobaccos.[2] The original company was made up of thirteen previously independent firms; in 1902 these firms were joined by four more, and Ogden's of Liverpool was acquired later in the same year. In addition Imperial acquired Mardon, Son and Hall Ltd and Salmon and Gluckstein.[3] A former senior executive of Imperial described the attitude of the constituent branches of the new company as '. . . not unlike that of the 13 states of America, who, when the federal constitution was first adopted by the United States, gave the central government as little authority as possible and retained as much as they could in their own hands'.[4] Nevertheless, in 1903 the Organising Committee, which had coordinated the formation of ITCo and directed the subsequent campaign against the ATCo, was reconstituted as the Executive Committee for the company.[5]

Following the conclusion of the 'war' certain functions were centralised for the company as a whole – in part this was a residual from the 'war'. Thus, the purchase of leaf, cigarette paper, cartridge paper, and general materials, were all controlled by head office departments. Moreover, all technical information had to be pooled through the Engineer's Department even though certain developments might originate within individual branches. Other departments were developed including those of Chief Accountant and Solicitor. The main department was that of Secretary which was divided into various sections and it was responsible for general administration on behalf of the company as a whole, it provided the secretariat for the Executive Committee, and it was the agency through which the Executive Committee and branches communicated with one another. Yet in terms of organisation and managerial responsibility these changes were relatively limited, and the whole range of activities concerned with selling, advertising, costing, pricing, and finance, remained largely under individual branch control.

A limited effort to grapple with certain aspects of these branch functions was made in 1903 when the Executive Committee took up a suggestion from Wills' management that all branches should conform to Wills' system of dissection sheets, which had originally been devised in 1886 and then gradually elaborated over the 1890s. These analyses broke down trading accounts into minute detail, showing how individual items of cost and revenue had changed in comparison with the previous year, and gave a detailed record of the sales performance of each brand of cigarettes and tobaccos. At least the extension of this method facilitated fairly detailed statistical comparisons between branches, but in no way did it amount to any kind of procedure for coordinating sales policies. A move in this direction was made in 1904 with the establishment of District Committees, whereby branches were organised into regional groups centred on Bristol, London, Liverpool, and Glasgow. The idea behind this was that branch managements could come together and discuss matters of common interest and, in particular, iron out selling problems and elements of unfair competition within regional areas.[6] The system was not a success. Branch managements had little enthusiasm for it and there was no clearly defined relationship between the Districts and the Executive Committee; anyway, branches had interests in all regions. Therefore the Committees discussed only peripheral and fairly trivial matters, while on important issues branches continued to deal directly with the Executive Committee.

In an effort to secure closer control over and coordination between branches, in 1905 the Executive Committee introduced a system of annual reports from branches. These provided data for forecasts for the coming year and, hence, claims for capital and marketing expenditure. Each report thus incorporated a detailed analysis of sales, costs, and gross and net profits; and because of the level of the excise duty in relation to cigarette and tobacco prices, amounts were calculated very finely (to three decimal places of a penny). Attached to the general analysis was an appendix in which 39 separate heads of revenue and expenditure were analysed in detail; in addition to statistics this section contained the branch management's views, explanations, suggestions and requests concerning all aspects of its trade – in short, the argument supporting its budget claims for next year. Indeed, the branch manager actually read the general sections of the report to the Executive Committee and he was then cross-examined on them.

From the outset the Executive Committee had taken every opportunity to standardise prices and terms between branches. In 1906 this became the specific responsibility of a newly established Prices Section which was also charged with the responsibility of fixing prices and terms on any new brand sanctioned by the Executive Committee. By 1914 there was, in consequence, a high degree of standardisation between branches in this area.

Within a few years of the establishment of Imperial, therefore, a number of innovations in organisation had been made; in addition since 1902 Imperial had operated a bonus scheme for customers on behalf of all branches.[7] For all this, however, over the first 25 years of the company's existence the Executive Committee did not operate anything approaching a detailed, centralised, comprehensive policy for the company; and there were two main reasons for this : there were no significant changes in market trends and Wills remained the dominant branch of Imperial. A sensitive indicator of this stability is provided by Wills' expenditure on advertising : it fell from 0·7d per lb. in 1907 (already a very low figure) to 0·1d per lb. in 1918. Control over branch budgets therefore amounted to little more than sanctioning proportionate increases in expenditure to match growth in demand, which was particularly sharp in the case of cigarettes. Even the First World War brought little extension of central control since War Office contracts were easily administered.[8]

District Committees were finally wound up in 1926 and even though they had been of little significance since their inception it was felt necessary to replace them by a Joint Branch Committee. This committee was composed of branch managers who met with representatives of the Executive Committee to discuss various aspects of the trade. Yet the precise relationship between the Joint and Executive Committees, and branch policy, was not clearly specified. Not surprisingly, the new Joint Committee soon proved ineffective.

Within branches a fairly clearly formalised departmental structure was evolved. The Selling Department was central and, in effect, all other departments were subordinate to it. Advertising, Travellers, Distribution, and Sales came under its direct control while Manufacturing and Accounts were indirectly subject to it. Manufacturing offered little scope for branch initiative, as has been noted, while Accounts covered largely routine work and prepared data for the annual report.

By the mid 1920s Wills' golden age was just beginning to wane. Competition was growing, and one of the most interesting aspects of this was the steady expansion of the Player branch. In addition, other firms outside Imperial – in particular Godfrey Phillips, Carreras, J. Wix & Sons, Gallaher – were beginning to make some headway in the cigarette market.[9] The fundamental reason for this was that the character of demand for tobacco goods was undergoing a major change : as cigarettes came to make up the bulk of tobacco consumption smokers' preferences began to turn less on the choice between cigarettes and pipe tobaccos and more on the choice between cigarette brands; and as the axis shifted so an opportunity opened up for firms to break into the cigarette market which had for so long been dominated by Wills.[10] At the same time the general rise in real wages enabled smokers to switch to more expensive cigarette brands in which Wills' national advantage over its competitors was less than in low-priced brands.

The expansion of the Player branch began to alter the balance of forces within Imperial; moreover, Player's success illustrates the loose and fairly diverse nature of Imperial's organisation nearly thirty years after its formation. Three factors stand out as explaining Player's success : as a branch of Imperial it had natural advantages over outside firms in having easy access to ample finance and the best technical information and resources; its Player's Medium brand proved ideally tuned to the growing demand for a more expensive cigarette;[11] its selling organisation was vigorous and effective in its efforts to take full advantage of the market opportunity. This was particularly true of Player's travellers who had not, over the years, enjoyed the easy market dominance of their counterparts in Wills and as a result were more energetic and cooperative in their dealings with retailers.

By 1930 competition was intensifying sharply as coupon trading spread. Between 1925 and 1930 coupon brands had increased their share of the market from 4 per cent to 16 per cent, and as a direct consequence Imperial's hold was weakening. This growing threat to the company's dominance caused the Executive Committee to take a more direct role in the formulation of branch sales policies, and one result of this was massive increases in branch advertising budgets, thus ushering in the modern era of big-budget advertising in the industry. Furthermore, Imperial introduced its own large and expensive advertising for all the company's leading cigarette and tobacco brands; and this involved expansion of its Advertising Department. When all this proved inadequate to stem the advance, in 1932 the Executive Committee decided to counter-attack by introducing a very heavily financed coupon brand of its own and it gave Wills the task of preparing and launching it because of its long experience with low-priced, large-selling brands.

The details of the 'coupon war' are not our concern here but the manner of its conclusion is significant to our analysis.[12] In late 1933 Imperial signed a treaty with most other major tobacco firms – known as the Martin Agreement – under which coupon trading was outlawed and arrangements made for compensating manufacturers who suffered sales losses as a result of the termination of coupon trading; to enforce these terms, including provisions for resale price maintenance, a Manufacturers' Committee was established.[13] So, just as the ITCo had been called into existence by an international trade war which ended in a treaty with the foreign invader, over thirty years later a domestic trade war caused Imperial to use its combined strength to force other British manufacturers to the conference table. Once the dust of coupon trading had settled, branch operations returned to much the same pattern as before, with the exception that price control and brand specifications were now tightly standardised, though this was little more than a feature of Imperial's new role as price leader for the industry. Nevertheless, in 1936 the Executive Committee again took direct action to counter what it considered to be an undue challenge to its market position : it instructed its Churchman branch to produce a cigarette to compete directly against a very successful intermediately-priced brand being produced by the Walters Tobacco Co. Ltd.[14] Apart from this, Player's continued growth resulted in it now virtually matching Wills in importance; moreover, a significant part of Player's success had, in terms of growth, been at Wills' expense.

Within the industry, however, Imperial was noticeably more active, as a company, in the 1930s than in the 1920s. In the main this activity was defensive : in 1932 it secretly acquired a controlling interest in Gallaher, one of its major competitors;[15] it took full advantage of its exclusive rights in patents owned by Molins Machine Co. Ltd;[16] it acquired a number of ancillary firms; and, as a sequel to the Churchman attack on the Walters Tobacco Co. Ltd, it acquired the Walters' business in 1938.[17]

With the onset of war in 1939, the government imposed a variety of controls on the industry, but it chose to operate indirectly through agencies established largely from within the industry. This inevitably meant that Imperial took major responsibility for operating various schemes for rationing supplies, particularly of leaf. Controls were continued, though with lessening degree, until 1955 when there was a return to free market conditions. Over the early 1950s, however, Imperial's market position began to slip a little; it recovered in 1954–5 because there was a shortage of cigarettes but once this was met the company's share began another, sharper decline so that, by value, its share of the market fell from 79 per cent in 1955 to 63 per cent in 1959. This decline was partly the result of heavy responsibilities carried by the company over the period 1939–55 : in bearing the brunt of rationing schemes it could less easily maintain the quality of its leading brands than smaller companies, and this enabled the latter to build up relatively favourable brand images for their products which had considerable effect when free trading conditions returned.[18]

More fundamentally, however, wartime conditions had altered the nature of the market for cigarettes which by 1945 accounted for 84 per cent of all tobacco consumption. A series of sharp increases in duty over the war years was capped by an enormous increase in 1947, to be followed by yet further, though smaller, increases in 1948 and 1956. Major price adjustments which these rises necessitated caused substantial shifts in patterns of cigarette consumption, and against this Imperial found itself under much sharper competitive attack than at any time since the coupon war.[19] Over the late 1950s and early 1960s, therefore, the Executive Committee both initiated and effected changes in the organisation of the company.

During the war it had been necessary to strengthen head office organisation and over the post-war period this process was continued so that by the late 1950s there were fifteen head office departments. A notable feature of this development was the expansion of the Research Department which became the largest of all and was given wide terms of reference in the field of research and development for the company as a whole. Together, these departments formed a general staff for the Executive Committee, which was now composed of the company's chairman, deputy chairman and three other directors. The Executive Committee met weekly and meetings usually occupied two full days in each week; it was, of course, formally subject to the general control of the Board.

Major changes in structure occurred within branches. There was rationalisation of smaller branches through amalgamation;[20] but Wills and Player dominated the company, and it was in these that the major changes occurred. Initially reforms were in the direction of decentralising responsibility for selling as a means of achieving greater flexibility in handling different sections of the trade in response to competition, but after a short period this was replaced by a totally different approach. Selling lost its previous central role and, instead, became part of a general marketing strategy which aimed to integrate all branch functions in accordance with clearly formulated market objectives. To implement what was, for Imperial's branches, the completely new concept of marketing, required changes in personnel as well as in structure. In the case of Wills, for example, a new management team appointed by the Executive Committee, and which for the first time included recruitment from outside the company, reorganised the main functions of the branch. The organisation of selling and advertising was completely recast and, more importantly, superimposed on these departments and on more routine operations were three product-group teams which covered the main sections of the trade. Marketing and sales policy were coordinated by a newly appointed general marketing manager; and this included close coordination with the general factory manager who was responsible for production. The final policy-making bodies at branch level were the Management Committees which in 1964 were renamed Boards of Management. This last change followed on from a general reorganisation of Imperial in which a tobacco division was created to deal with all the company's interests in this field.

To complete the picture of the company's development up to 1965, it is necessary to add that the general reorganisation of 1964 created divisions for the various business interests that had been acquired over the years and prepared the way for further diversification. The underlying significance of this will be discussed shortly though, it is to be noted, in 1965 the tobacco division accounted for by far the greater part of Imperial's total net profit. The new divisions were as follows : paper and board – Robert Fletcher & Son Ltd (1935),[21] St Annes Board Mill Co. Ltd (1921); distributive trade – Finlay & Company Ltd (1963), Robert Sinclair Ltd (1930); general trade – Anselm Holdings (London) Ltd (1964),[22] Bernat Klein Ltd (1962),[23] Bewley Properties Ltd (1964),[24] The British Nicotine Company Ltd (1906), Educational and Scientific Developments Ltd (1964),[25] Golden Wonder Crisp Co. Ltd (1961). In addition mention must be made of Mardon International Ltd (1962) which was jointly owned with the British American Tobacco Co. Ltd, and of Imperial Investments Ltd to which the group's minority holdings in a number of companies were transferred in 1965.

II

If we look, first of all, at the period up to 1939 then in Chandler's terms Imperial was a hybrid cross between a holding company and a weak strain of the multi-divisional type of organisation. The resultant form produced a considerable degree of duplication of functions especially in relation to the company's smaller branches. And although there were clear channels of command from the Executive Committee to the branches they were of limited compass. At the same time, however, it has to be born in mind that over the first half of this earlier period Wills' dominance of the tobacco market, and hence of the company, meant that there was no pressing need for fundamental reorganisation. Correspondingly, when Player began to increase its market share this not only compensated for Wills' relative decline but also maintained the growth in Imperial's overall market dominance. Indeed, the changing balance within Imperial has to be seen as a benefit to be weighed against the direct costs of tolerating a considerable measure of duplicated functions. In an industry where, in comparison with many others, performance depended disproportionately on the selling/marketing end of the business, this form of organisation had much to commend it.

It has been noted how the 'coupon war' and the continued relative growth of Player made for greater centralised control of the company through the Executive Committee, but how there was little substantial change in organisation before 1939. The consequences of the 'coupon war' related more to the long-term structure of the industry as it affected all tobacco firms, rather than to Imperial's internal structure. Moreover, the ability of the company to restore its market hegemony by limited action – even though it was very costly in the short-run – meant that detailed examination of its own internal operation was not called for. Furthermore, the existence of the excise duty on tobacco produced a certain level of business efficiency independently of company structure. For one thing, the duty provided a ready and very sensitive measure of a firm's market share – the kind of comparative information which was often extremely hard to come by in many other industries, and the inability or unwillingness of firms to gauge their comparative performance could have serious consequences for their overall position. For another thing the duty made it necessary to produce precise statistical information – particularly of costs – and this provided the basis for sound, if narrow, budgetary control.

Apart from the statistical discipline of the excise tax there were certain other factors which combined to simplify management tasks in a manner which obviated problems of duplication between branches : the highly standardised nature of the product and the proportionately very low cost of technical innovation meant that investment plans were not complicated;[26] there was a high degree of capital security; standardised production and fast stock turn produced a plentiful cash flow. And, for Imperial, underlying these advantages was the security it enjoyed from its extremely strong oligopoly position and the tribute of very high profits which went with this.

None of this must be taken to deny that there were weaknesses and shortcomings in Imperial. The major problems in this respect arose within the Wills' branch. In general there was no recruitment of management from outside the company and in Wills' case this exacerbated the failure to deal with creeping weakness in its performance in sections of the market in the 1930s. By nature of their internal recruitment, training and experience Wills' management persisted in the application of traditional methods which were no longer appropriate. Yet these failings were in no sense serious in immediate terms even for the branch; it still held a large share of the market and made handsome profits. From the Executive Committee's point of view there was no compulsion to change Wills' branch management or innovate in marketing methods and organisation, since Wills' relative loss was Player's gain. Hence the Committee made no major effort to over-ride the interests of its major branches by devising a broad strategy for the company as a whole which could well have led it into much greater activity outside tobacco.

During the wartime period Imperial's management structure became more akin to the centralised, functionally departmentalised type. This period was followed by one of increasing marketing difficulties which contrasted strongly with Imperial's pre-war experience. Coincidentally, these years also saw the accession of a new generation of executives to control of the Executive Committee, and it seems probable that this made an important contribution to the quality of the company's eventual response to these difficulties. It would appear that not only were the new leaders of the company men of considerable business ability who were able to operate free from the Wills' family control, they had also gained close-hand experience of the detailed working of the company and of the tobacco industry as a result of promoting and operating various war and post-war rationing schemes within the industry. Under their direction the central departments at head office were reorganised and strengthened. And as a result of the increased flow of commercial intelligence which this produced – relating both to the tobacco industry and to any other industries in which the company might wish to take an interest – the Executive Committee began to exercise a more active, strategic function in relation to the company as a whole.

The changes at head office together with structural reorganisation within branches resulted in a modified multi-divisional form for the company; modified in the sense that although there was some specialist production in small branches the two major branches, Player and Wills, which accounted for over 90 per cent of Imperial's turnover in the mid 1950s, continued to produce and sell the full range of product groups. There were two reasons why in a large tobacco company this did not lead to costly inefficiency : there was an extremely high degree of standardisation in the production of cigarettes of all product groups, since in this respect the differences between the three product groups were mainly of size and packaging; and the overriding importance of marketing – particularly in relation to branding, advertising, and selling – meant that there could well be advantages in spreading the company's operations over two well-established branches. Support for this is provided by the fact that by the end of the 1960s the traditional strengths of Player and Wills were completely reversed – the former came to dominate the market for small, low-priced brands whereas the latter assumed leadership of larger, more expensive brands.

A further reason for this form of overlap between the two main branches was the Executive Committee's belief in competition between branches as a means of promoting management efficiency and more vigorous overall performance.[27] It is worth noting, also, how this 'competitive' structure was a factor which the Monopolies Commission considered to have some value as safeguarding the public interest.[28] Indeed, more directly, since the war years, in making strategic decisions the Executive Committee has paid close attention to government attitudes towards the industry and what it has considered to be its public responsibility, and this has undoubtedly conditioned the company's structure.

The establishment of divisions in 1964 made the multi-divisional form more thoroughgoing and this has been considerably reinforced and enlarged in recent years. This new strategy clearly turned on a number of considerations : in comparison with the lush years before the war Imperial's profit rates would be limited to a good average in relation to manufacturing industry generally (particularly in the light of the Monopolies Commission Report) and, therefore, it would be wise to search for new sources of profit; the matter of smoking and health cast real doubt over the long-term prospects of the industry; and there was evidence to suggest that smoking was a declining fashion among younger age groups. In relation to these issues Imperial had the obvious advantages of a strong cash flow position and ample capital resources, and the Executive Committee believed that the company was well supplied with management resources having particular strengths in the marketing of perishable consumer goods.[29] Hence the policy of diversification, particularly into the food and drink industry, which has been the dominant feature of Imperial's growth over recent years.

This broad survey of Imperial's development over this century in many respects confirms Chandler's typology of the evolution of large-scale business organisations. Yet a close examination of the actual process of this development suggests that it is probably necessary to widen the framework within which changes in strategy and structure are analysed to include more than the variables of general market-cum-technological factors. In particular, the development of Imperial indicates the need to pay attention to the issue of the degree and nature of market power exercised by a firm and, even, of whether this can produce situations in which structure determines strategy. But these and other related issues are best considered separately.[30]

NOTES

1 This paper draws heavily on my detailed knowledge of the W. D. & H. O. Wills branch of Imperial, though I have taken account of respects in which it was not representative of the company as a whole.

2 See B. W. E. Alford, *W. D. & H. O. Wills and the Development of the U.K. Tobacco Industry, 1786–1965* (London, 1973) pp. 251, 254, 259–60, 264–97, 304, 363.

3 The former did a great deal of printing and carton manufacture for the company and the latter owned a large chain of retail tobacconists and had pursued a very vigorous price-cutting policy in the trade since the 1890s – see B. W. E. Alford, op. cit., especially chapter 9.

4 Sir Wilfrid Anson (deputy chairman of the company from 1948 to 1958) in R. S. Edwards and H. Townsend, *Business Enterprise: Its Growth and Organisation* (London, 1961) pp. 65–6.

5 This committee was the brainchild of H. H. (Harry) Wills who drew his partners' attention to the problem of general managerial control in a large company.

6 For example it arranged schedules whereby travellers from the various branches did not clash in their visits to retailers.

7 See Alford, op. cit., pp. 264, 266–7, 320, 325, 345; The Monopolies Commission, *Report on the Supply of Cigarettes and Tobacco and of Cigarette and Tobacco Machinery* (Cmd. 218, 1961) pp. 82–7. This scheme was originally introduced as part of the 'tobacco war' campaign.

8 Branches produced goods for distribution mainly through the British American Tobacco Company Ltd which, according to the 1902 agreement between Imperial and the American Tobacco Company, handled both companies' brands outside the UK and the USA.

9 See Monopolies Commission, op. cit., pp. 18–23, 55–67.

10 For a more detailed analysis of this see Alford, op. cit., p. 334.

11 According to marketing men in the industry today, movement into new sectors of the market caused by such outside influences as income or duty changes is far more important than advertising in determining the popularity of brand classes; advertising is more effective in persuading smokers to smoke particular brands within brand classes. There seems every reason to believe that the same was true for this period. More generally the close correlation between changes in average real incomes and total consumption is widely accepted as a direct causal relationship.

12 For details see Alford, op. cit., pp. 349–53.

13 Full details of these arrangements are given in the Monopolies Commission, op. cit., pp. 20–1.

14 Ibid., pp. 21–2, 187–8.

15 Ibid., pp. 21, 59–60. This was in order to counter an alleged threat of acquisition by the American Tobacco Company. However, Imperial never interfered in the management of Gallaher.

16 Ibid., especially, pp. 109–11; and more generally, pp. 102–21.

17 An action criticised by the Monopolies Commission, op. cit., pp. 187–8.

18 Carreras' 'Senior Service' brand is a good example of this. In addition Carreras had acquired exclusive rights to a technique known as the 'dense end' device which packed the tobacco at the ends of a cigarette more firmly than throughout, and this gave the impression of the cigarette being larger than directly competing brands.

19 Gallaher, in which Imperial still had a substantial interest, was Imperial's most successful competitor – its share of the market, by value, rose from 19 per cent in 1956 to 29 per cent in 1959.

20   By 1959 the Mitchell, Smith and Macdonald branches had been amalgamated with Wills; the Hignett, Clarke, Faulkner, Adkin, and Davies branches were part of the Ogden branch; and Franklyn, Davey & Co. had been merged with the Ringer (formerly Edwards, Ringer & Bigg) branch; the remaining branches were Player, Lambert & Butler, and Churchman. For some years the Executive Committee had resisted rationalisation – even to the extent of not dropping loss-making brands – for fear that trade would be transferred to competitors and that because of possible economies of scale competitors' gains might prove greater than Imperial's losses thus progressively strengthening their overall competitive position.

21   Manufacturer of cigarette paper and a variety of other papers. In this and following cases the date in brackets refers to the year in which Imperial acquired a majority holding, or complete control of the company in question; in a number of cases it had held minority interests for a number of years previously.

22   Manufacturer of plastic products used extensively in the motor industry and for civil engineering and domestic appliances and equipment.

23   Specialises in high-quality knitting wools and yarns and couture fabrics of original design.

24   Responsible for matters relating to the leasing and renting of Bewley and other shop properties.

25   Specialises in the production and promotion of educational and instructional services and systems.

26   This feature is dealt with extensively in my book.

27   However, it is not clear how one measures this effect in an objective manner. Within the company it is certainly true that the Executive Committee and the major branches paid considerable attention to comparative sales performances.

28   Nevertheless, the Commission was extremely guarded in its views and considered '. . . internal competition . . . at best a poor substitute for real competition . . .'. Yet the impression given by the report is that branch system had given some protection to the public in a way in which an outright efficient monopoly would not have done; see Monopolies Commission, op. cit., pp. 203–7.

29   In this respect there is a stronger rationale in Imperial's diversification policy than is sometimes allowed. Although it is clear from subsequent results that the company might well have over-estimated the quality of its existing resources in this respect. cf. Derek F. Channon, *The Strategy and Structure of British Enterprise* (London, 1973) pp. 99, 100–1, 102, 103.

30   See my article pp. 52–70 above.

4 A Family Firm becomes a Public Company: Changes at Pilkington Brothers Limited in the Interwar Years*

T. C. BARKER

My title is strictly – and intentionally – incorrect. Pilkington had ceased to be a partnership in 1894. The company then formed never offered any of its shares to the general public until 1970. Yet I have chosen this title because, from the management point of view, Pilkington Brothers Limited continued to manifest the features of a family firm until 1931 when, unable to stand the strain any longer, a major reorganisation occurred which took the company in one great leap a considerable way along the road towards its ultimate Chandlerian destination of head office and operating divisions.

The persistence of the simplest sort of administration for so long is remarkable, for by 1920 the business was already nearly a century old and of a size to lay claim to a place among the 50 largest manufacturing companies in the UK. It had outlived all its British competitors but one, Chances of Spon Lane, Smethwick, which no longer operated in the same league and was soon destined to fall into Pilkington's grasp. In 1920 Pilkington had shares, debentures and reserves worth £4,905,000, of which £4,229,000 represented fixed assets. These included three factories at St Helens, Lancashire, and a fourth being built at Doncaster, a factory in Canada (not doing well and shortly to be closed) and one at Maubeuge in France. The business was integrated forwards into the market via a series of warehouses throughout Britain, a chain of them across Canada and one in Buenos Aires; and backwards to its raw materials with interests in coalmines and sandfields. But, as a private company, its balance sheets were its directors' affair and since its shares were not quoted on the Stock Exchange nobody took much

* This paper is based upon a fuller, annotated treatment of this subject in a new and updated history of the company which will be published in 1976 to mark its 150th anniversary.

D

interest in it. This explains its absence from the published list of the 50 largest companies in 1919. In any case, Pilkington in those days did not like self-advertisement. It operated in an industry full of technical secrets. It sold its glass to the trade who knew all about its size and importance without having to be told.

Pilkington was then able to operate a simple administrative system, despite its size, because of its geographical concentration (its head office and all its major works were at St Helens) and because almost all its output consisted of three types of flat glass sold to a comparatively small number of customers in the building and furniture trades. These were :

1. Polished plate glass, usually $\frac{1}{4}''$ thick, sold for larger and more prestigious windows and for silvering as mirrors. This type of glass had to be laboriously ground and polished. It was an expensive product and brought in a good profit between the wars.
2. Sheet glass, a thinner type used for general glazing. This was much cheaper than plate and constituted the bulk of Pilkington's output. Six times as much sheet as plate glass was produced, but in the interwar period the product was much less profitable.
3. Rolled plate glass. More accurately described by its earlier name, rough plate glass, this was an even cheaper product used for the roofs of railway stations, factories and market halls and for horticultural purposes where translucency rather than transparency was all that was needed. It could be impressed with a pattern and in this form was in growing demand for bathroom and lavatory windows.

Unlike its opposite number in America, the Pittsburgh Plate Glass Company, Pilkington had never diversified its activities into paint. Nor did it have the interest in chemicals which the French-based giant, St Gobain, had.

In the 1920s Pilkington's head office still consisted essentially of a small building which had been used since 1887. Although it had been extended just before 1914, the heart of this ecclesiastical edifice – it had been designed by a Manchester architect who specialised in churches – was a large general office in which orders were processed. Leading immediately off it, through heavy oak doors, were the rather dark and austere, though spacious and panelled, offices of the directors. Through a diamond pane of glass in each of these doors, the family heads of the business could be seen at work. Their comings and goings, as they entered or left their sanctums by way of the general office, were known to all.

Here the directors kept control of the day-to-day working of the business through a network of managers who, if they operated away from St Helens, sent in a stream of returns and maintained a regular correspondence. Some of these deputies were of great importance, especially the works managers, for the science of glassmaking was still not entirely understood and the experience of these men counted for a great deal in keeping production costs down. A check on manufacturing costs had been maintained on a works basis since at least the 1880s. In 1913 a central cost department (one man in charge of two clerks) was set up, equipped with a Hollerith machine (Pilkington was Hollerith's second oldest customer). Care was taken that these people did not compare notes with those who had access to the sales figures. Profits were a private matter for the attention of the directors alone and a small, discreet circle of trusted retainers who prepared the necessary documents and, having been instructed to do so by the directors, took action on confidential matters. The company's registered office was in Liverpool, twelve miles away.

The running of a business with a sales turnover of over £3½m in the better years of the 1920s in such a highly centralised way called not only for very able lieutenants but also for directors of ability and physical strength as well as dedication to duty. Historians have tended to assume too readily that such people were lacking in family businesses of the third generation for, they argue, the grandsons of the founders, brought up to enjoy wealth and demanding a more leisurely way of life, could not possibly provide the drive needed to sustain growth even if, by some fluke, they happened to possess the ability to do so. This argument, however, fails to take account of the fact that birth-rates were still high until the last quarter of the nineteenth century. Only after the mid-1870s did the national birth-rate begin to fall. In the 1890s older-established firms still had plenty of candidates to choose from, and these men, entering businesses then, were at the height of their powers in the 1920s.

In the Pilkington case, the four partners of the second generation had, between them, fathered 35 children, all but two of whom survived infancy, and 20 of them were males. What is more, because they had not all married about the same time, there was a helpful mixture of directors of various ages as the proved members of the third generation gradually took over control. The two of them who exercised most power in the 1920s were the chairman, Richard Austin Pilkington (b. 1871) and his brother Alfred Cecil (b. 1875). Both had been educated at Shrewsbury and Christ Church, the latter reading Natural Sciences. Despite this wide choice of eligible males, however, unexpected illness which struck down one of the more promising in the 1890s, and the Boer War which also took its toll, caused the family to cast its net even wider. In so doing it brought in the man who was to play the leading role in the company's transformation of 1931 .

This was Edward Herbert Cozens-Hardy (b. 1873), who was a consultant electrical engineer by profession, having served a pupillage with Brush after a formal education at Rugby School and a spell at the Royal Technical College, London. As a partner from 1898 in the firm of electrical engineers, O'Gorman and Cozens-Hardy, his advice was sought by Pilkington about some electrification which was then taking place at one of its works. In 1903 he married R. A. Pilkington's sister and in 1908 he was given a place on the Board. His father, an eminent lawyer and eventually Master of the Rolls, was created the first Baron Cozens-Hardy in 1914 and he himself eventually succeeded to the title in 1924.

A second non-Pilkington who married into the family, though more remotely, and also became a director, was a no less remarkable man. Ronald Morce Weeks (b. 1890), eventually to become Deputy Chief of the Imperial General Staff, chairman of Vickers and a director of a host of other companies, came to St Helens in 1912 straight from Cambridge through the University Appointments Board in response to one of Pilkington's early attempts to recruit promising graduates. He distinguished himself in the army during the First World War and shortly after his return to St Helens, in 1920, he was put in charge of the company's plate glassworks there. Two years later he married the daughter of a daughter of a second generation Pilkington partner. This qualified him as a member of the family and in 1928 he became a Pilkington director.

In the 1920s Pilkington needed all the family talent and new blood it could get for, despite its being sole producer of plate glass and of machine-made sheet, competition was intense in free-trade Britain. Glassmaking was moving fast from a craft industry to modern continuous production. This came first in rolled plate manufacture and here Pilkington kept up with its rivals. It did even better in polished plate, for during the 1920s, following the example of the Ford Motor Company at Detroit, with which it collaborated, the company developed a method of flowing a ribbon of high quality, rough cast glass which was then ground and polished, one pane at a time, under a large number of grinding and polishing heads, a Pilkington invention. In sheet glass, however, Pilkington lagged behind, while its competitors in Belgium, enjoying cheap water transport to Britain, a devalued Belgian franc and access to the British market unimpeded by tariffs, were prepared to develop two new continuous processes, the Fourcault and the American-invented Libbey-Owens. Pilkington pinned its faith in quality rather than quantity and still made its sheet glass either by hand blowing and flattening or by a half-way, intermittent method which involved machine blowing and hand flattening. In the mid-20s it made a major mistake in deciding to put down more of these machines. As a result, by the end of the decade, when the continentals had improved the quality of their Fourcault and Libbey-Owens glass, Pilkington was on the verge of abandoning sheet glass manufacture altogether and concentrating on the two other sorts which remained profitable.

This was not a good performance when the market for flat glass was growing impressively. More glass was needed for building as greater efforts were made, with government encouragement, to make good the post-war shortage and then advance to slum clearance. More houses were built in Britain in 1925 (175,000) than ever before, and in the following years, right through the depression, the total never fell below 200,000. A great new market for glass was opening up, too, as more and other vehicles came on the road. There had been under 200,000 cars licensed in Britain in 1920. By 1930 there were over 1,000,000 and many of these were saloon models with more glass in them than the open tourers had. In these favourable market conditions, Pilkington should have been doing well despite the onset of the world depression. In fact, mainly because of the plight of its sheet glass, its half-yearly profits fell from the second half of 1929. In the six months ended 31 March 1931 it lost nearly £89,000. Change and reorganisation followed swiftly.

In 1929 Cecil Pilkington (54), who had been the senior director in charge of the manufacturing side of the business, had made an arrangement to restrict his time at the works to Monday morning – Thursday afternoon so that he could spend the week-ends at a house he had bought just outside Oxford. In 1931 he retired there. Austin Pilkington also resigned as an active director. An Executive Committee was then formed, with Cozens-Hardy as chairman, and the opportunity was taken to introduce to it two of the company's trusted confidants, its solicitor and its secretary, as non-share-qualified directors. From time to time the Executive Committee was joined by the other directors (including Austin and Cecil Pilkington) as a full Board to discuss matters of broader policy. The non-executive directors were also looked upon as elder statesmen whose advice and help could be sought at any time.

In July 1931 Cozens-Hardy explained the thinking behind these changes :

The problem, as I see it, is to evolve from our present somewhat haphazard way of working, a scheme of organisation which (i) will retain the close personal touch with the work and with the employees which has been characteristic of the firm (ii) will ensure continuity of policy (iii) will fit in with the personalities now concerned and be adaptable to probable future requirements.

Under present arrangements the Board collectively and through its Chairman concerns itself in a great many matters of comparative detail which, in view of the size to which the business has grown, tend to absorb a large part of its time, leaving too little time for proper consideration of broad questions of policy. It is believed that more effective use can be made of the services of Directors and Staff if a scheme is evolved under which responsibility for definite parts of the work is put on individual shoulders, whilst leaving control of all important matters of policy in the hands of the full Board.

The Executive Committee was at first only six in number and each was put in charge of a particular part of the company's activities, Cozens-Hardy himself being responsible for 'the financial department, accounts, costs and cash'. The Committee was not slow to enquire into every aspect of the company's working.

Bedaux engineers advised on time and motion in works and warehouses (Pilkington in the end settled for its own time and motion men) and the National Institute of Industrial Psychology was called in to report on the working of the general office. It soon produced an interim report which was diplomatic but devastating. To quote parts of it :

The Firm, in view of its old establishment, has certain deep-rooted principles upon which its policy is founded. These principles, amounting almost to traditions, should be left intact as much as possible. A fine spirit prevails throughout the organisation, such as can be found only in the older family businesses and which it is most important to foster. At the same time, it should not be allowed to interfere with the growth and future prosperity of the Firm.

The existing routines work well and smoothly in nearly all departments, and achieve the results that are expected of them. They are, however, cumbersome and in many cases costly. We feel that they could be expedited by a thorough analysis of the present methods, and by the introduction of more modern systems and a greater amount of inter-departmental co-ordination.

We do not imply that the present routines are fundamentally wrong, but during recent years office machinery has been installed, and to obtain the best results from it new routines must be devised to suit the altered conditions.

It has obviously been the policy of the Board to introduce machinery into the offices wherever it appeared that beneficial results might be obtained. There is, however, a tendency for the machines to be forgotten except by the manager who is responsible for their use. Moreover, the operators do not receive any proper training in the use of their machines . . .

The Managers collectively do not form the Management. They are fully engaged with the responsibilities of their own respective departments, and there is no great amount of co-ordination between them. In general, they appear to perform their routine functions very satisfactorily; but the majority are men who have spent their lives in the service of the Firm, and many of them have spent a number of years in the same department, either as Managers or previously as clerks. A certain amount of stagnation is the natural outcome. The various departments are practically watertight, and there are few managers who have a knowledge of the details of any department other than their own.

Later NIIP reports spelt out these criticisms in detail. Each works had different ordering arrangements and there was much unnecessary copying in longhand amounting, it was calculated, to 2400 hours per week, the equivalent of the work of 58 clerks. A Methods Committee and multicopy typewriters were recommended and the former was at work by the middle of 1933. A trainee scheme for executives was also introduced that year after consideration had been given to similar schemes working at Rowntrees, Standard Telephones, Unilever and ICI. The trainees consisted of bright men from the Pilkington ranks and promising university graduates. In the meantime the training of each family 'youth . . . on trial with a view to an ultimate directorship' was also systematised. Regular reports were sent in by managers of the departments in which these men were working, not all of them by any means complimentary. One candidate, having soldiered on for six years, was allowed a final testing period but then advised to find a job elsewhere. Others emerged successfully from their ordeal and came on to the Board as sub-directors. They included the present Lord Pilkington whose five-year probation ended in 1932.

These efforts to streamline the business were clear evidence of a wish to move towards a more up-to-date company structure. So, too, was the setting up of a Personnel Department in 1934 to be concerned, *inter alia*, with staff selection. The Board noted, however, that 'appointment for the higher positions must continue to be under the control of the Directors, and Departmental Managers must have full say in regard to their staff'. Progress was also made in an effort to mobilise and concentrate the company's technical and scientific personnel. These men had previously been scattered around the various works and were concerned mainly with analytical tests. Works managers had little time for research, which had a nasty habit of reducing their present output performance in the vague hope of improving their output in the future. In 1933 however, a Technical Committee was formed which met every two months. It was soon ordering foreign journals and thinking of opportunities for cost-saving innovation. Three years later a Technical Development Department was formed under its direction and the decision taken to build a central research laboratory. The Director of the Scientific Instrument Research Association was hired to take charge of it at the princely salary of £2000 a year – almost as much as a senior works manager then received – though his task, apart from concentrating some of the company's scientists in one place and recruiting others, was not clearly understood, as may be seen from the wording of a report to the Board on the subject :

> The Directors were of the opinion that the establishment of Research Laboratories will prove to be of very great value to the Company, although the benefits may be neither immediate nor easily identifiable.

The strengthening of the Technical Committee in 1936 was part of a further reorganisation which involved the creation of a Finance Committee and a Sales Committee. Among the functions of the former was the direction of the financial policy of Pilkington Brothers Limited and its subsidiary companies. It was chaired by Cozens-Hardy and it included two of the Company's accountants as well as three other members of the Executive Committee. The brief of the Sales Committee was 'to consider market prospects, commercial agreements and prices, and to deal with sales questions and points of policy'. It was also to secure collaboration with the various works on production, sales budgets, qualities and despatches. One export market and one depot (with the depot manager present) was to be scrutinised at each meeting.

By this time the Company's activities had become more diversified. More safety glass was fitted into cars from the later 1920s, and from the beginning of 1932 it became compulsory in windscreens. Pilkington joined Triplex in 1929 to form a subsidiary, Triplex (Northern) Limited, which opened a safety glass factory at St Helens in the spring of 1930. There toughened, as well as laminated, glass was soon being made, thus finding a new outlet for plate glass as well as sheet. From the latter Pilkington again made a profit after the company had, in the nick of time, obtained a licence to work a new and improved continuous sheet glassmaking process developed at the end of the 1920s by the Pittsburgh Plate Glass Company. It was being operated commercially at St Helens from the end of 1931. Safety glass processing plants were later opened in South Africa at Port Elizabeth (1935) and in Australia at Adelaide (1936) and Geelong (1937). Pilkington also had interests in Duplate of Canada. Sheet Glass Limited which had struggled to make Fourcault glass at Queenborough on the Isle of Sheppey, was bought in 1933, and in 1936 an agreement was reached to purchase the old rival, Chance Brothers. With this acquisition went an interest in the new but growing glass fibre industry. In 1938 Pilkington became the largest shareholder in glassworks at Llavollol in the Argentine and opened a sheet glassworks at Pontypool in South Wales to forestall a possible foreign competitor. These developments at home and abroad put increasing pressure on office accommodation at St Helens. A new extension, curvaceous and most unecclesiastical in style, added to the existing 50-year old building at the end of the decade, signified the new order of things.

Since 1945 the development of Fibreglass, Pilkington's venture into optical glass, its acquisition of Triplex, and its new factories and alliances abroad, often connected with its remarkable new invention of the 1950s, Float Glass, have resulted in further significant changes in the company's structure. In 1954, three separate committees were formed to manage its flat glass, worked glass and sales operations. Ten years later, the Group Executive controlled the organisation's operations through five divisional boards dealing with flat, pressed, optical and safety glass and glass fibres respectively. By the early 1970s, Pilkington Brothers Limited had 40 subsidiary and associated companies operating in 16 countries and its five divisions employed about 30,000 people (to be compared with a labour force of about 12,600 in 1924 and about the same number at the end of 1945). The company's turnover, £3½m in the 1920s, was worth £135m in 1972. A spacious and splendid high tower of offices, opened in 1963, was soon not large enough to house all the office employees of the parent company and its subsidiaries at St Helens.

This case study of the development of Pilkington's raises some important points for the understanding of the historical performance of the British economy. The market value of companies like Pilkington, which until recently operated as family businesses and were not quoted on the Stock Exchange, is more difficult to estimate than is that of other business concerns. Although Pilkington was probably the largest of such companies it was by no means unique, and historians may therefore have overlooked the importance of family enterprise in the twentieth century.

Entrepreneurship in family companies, on the Pilkington showing, deserves more scrutiny. Did other family businesses have such a wide choice of talent open to them for so long for demographic reasons? In the fourth generation, of which the present Lord Pilkington is a member, the choice was in some ways even wider, despite the fall in the birth-rate, because there were the children of a greater range of forbears from whom to choose, including the distaff side. Did other family businesses interpret 'family' so liberally as Pilkington and did they impose such a rigorous apprenticeship on the candidates who came forward for the top managerial positions?

Although most family businesses do not, whilst remaining under family control, attain a size which creates problems of management which are insoluble within the traditional framework, some, like Pilkingtons, do encounter problems of strategy and structure closely akin to those met by larger corporations in which ownership is divorced from control. The Pilkington family were slow to alter the nineteenth century partnership structure as the business grew, but the changes of 1931 which gave the new Executive Committee the task of forward planning as well as day-to-day control represented one important step forward, and the setting up of the three committees in 1936 another. The interpretation of these changes poses more difficult problems. Was anything more to be expected, given the size of the market for Pilkington glass at that time? If, for the sake of argument, the structure of 1931 had been imposed in 1920 would diversification have occurred sooner? Alternatively, was development in the 1930s in any way the result of the new structure of 1931? Or would these changes have come about anyway given technical innovation and managerial ability? If so, structural change should be seen as the removal of a brake on progress and nothing more.

5 Strategy and Structure at Boots the Chemists*

STANLEY CHAPMAN

Chandler's *Strategy and Structure* centres on an intensive study of four United States multi-divisional companies that rapidly outpaced their competitors and established their pre-eminence in the period from the 1880s to the end of the First World War. Each was built by a super-salesman whose sense of market opportunity, combined with personality, stamina, and drive, created a huge new vertically integrated enterprise. The careers of these empire builders found a striking parallel, both as to chronology and entrepreneurial profile, in that of Jesse Boot (1849–1931), the creator of Boots the Chemists. From the inheritance of a small down-town herbalist's shop in Nottingham, Boot outpaced his competitors to build the biggest and most successful chain of company chemists' shops in Britain, supporting his principal interest in retailing with manufacturing, wholesaling and printing departments. The present-day Boots company, still based in Nottingham, can fairly be described as a multi-divisional corporation, but its pattern of development is so distinctly different from that of Chandler's four giants that it deserves separate consideration as a case-study. The exercise is also worthwhile because of Chandler's frank recognition that the mass-mechandising enterprises as a group warrant closer attention than he was able to devote to them.

There have been two important periods of structural re-organisation at Boots in the period from when the business was founded by Jesse's father in 1849 to the present time. The first of them followed Jesse's belated retirement in 1920, when the controlling interest in the business was acquired by the American drug store tycoon, Louis K. Liggett. The second emerged in the late 1960s as the consequence of a number of pressures, most important among which were the take-over of Boots'

---

* The first three sections of this paper are largely drawn from the author's *Jesse Boot of Boots the Chemists* (Hodder & Stoughton, 1974) and the last from the Monopolies Commission Reports. Additional information has been supplied by Dr G. I. Hobday (Chairman), Mr S. M. Peretz, Mr J. W. Seekings, and Dr T. A. Ratcliffe.

principal retail rivals, Timothy Whites & Taylors, and the strong growth of the Company's manufacturing and export operations. The context and nature of these two periods of organisational innovation form the subject matter of this paper. The connections between them and earlier American experience of company decentralisation and multi-divisional organisation will be of particular interest to readers of Chandler's book.

I

THE JESSE BOOT ERA, 1870–1920

The foundation of the structure of Boots was laid down by Jesse's father, John Boot I, insofar as his herbalist's shop in Nottingham manufactured some of its best-selling remedies on the premises and distributed them to country agents round the town, as well as selling them over the counter. John died in 1860, but the idea was kept alive by his widow and taken over by Jesse when he became of age in 1870. Moreover, John had been linked as an agent to a loose association of other 'medical botanists', a movement that had begun with Samuel Thomson in New England in the 1830s. As interest in medical botany waned, young Jesse searched for a new way of capturing the interest of ailing consumers and, after one or two abortive trials, found it in the well-advertised sale of cut-price patent medicines. The phenomenal success of his advertising campaign in the *Nottingham Daily Express* in 1877 led to the opening of new shops, first within the catchment area of his traditional country customers and the local newspaper circulation, and then along the network of the Midland Railway. Manufacturing capacity was stepped up to keep pace with retail sales, and wholesaling overflowed into a jumble of buildings near the Midland Station and adjoining the cheap labour area of Nottingham's densely-packed back-to-back terraces.

Other departments were added as need and opportunity arose. A hard-fought legal action, *Pharmaceutical Society of Great Britain* v. *London and Provincial Supply Association* (1880) confirmed that a limited liability company could employ pharmaceutical chemists, so Boot incorporated his small chain in 1883 and hired a young chemist-manager, the first of many to stand on his pay-roll. A break-down in health in 1885 led him to take a holiday and find a wife. Florence Rowe proved to be an independent-minded woman with considerable business ability, and introduced books, stationary, art, fancy goods, libraries, and cafés to numbers of the bigger shops. When the First World War cut Boot off from his main source of quality drugs in Germany, he seized the opportunity to establish his own department for the manufacture of fine chemicals. Enthusiasms for this or that new opportunity would fill his mind for weeks or months at a time, but his deepest and most continuous interest was in multiplying and refurbishing his shops and a retailing policy of 'cheapest is best'. To make his shops the biggest and most popular in every High Street, he formed a series of satellite service departments, most important among which were building, shop-fitting, printing, and sales promotions (special stunts). The extension of Boot's chain of shops to London and the south, and northwards to Yorkshire, Lancashire, and (most latterly) Scotland brought new depots and supporting factories, notably the photographic works at Brighton and Liverpool.

This vertically integrated organisation can be recognised as aspiring to a self-sufficient manufacturing, wholesaling, and retailing organisation, but in practice it was a series of *ad hoc* growths, built round Boot's passion for opening shops, his wife's persistent demands for her portion, and their sporadic enthusiasms for other supporting enterprises. In other words, it was an untidy conglomerate of ill-fitting parts whose individual contribution to the business, in terms of profitability, was simply unknown. It lacked forward planning or blueprint, and had no central executives responsible for overall guidance of the business or continuous liaison with the branches. It was the single creation of one man and his wife, served by administrators who retained their offices only by deference to the Boot family. It was a successful enterprise in the sense that it was easily the largest chain and most aggressive selling organisation of the various company chemists that emerged during the last two decades of the nineteenth century, but overall profitability was low, and when Boot was forced by ill-health to sell out, his successors inherited a heavy burden of financial and organisational problems.

II

LIGGETT'S TAKEOVER AND THE AUTOCRACY OF JOHN BOOT II, 1920–54

Louis Kroh Liggett (1875–1946), the head of the leading United States drug store chain who bought the controlling interest in Boots in 1920, was far too heavily involved in his North American activities to spend much time in Britain. He lent his most able executive, George M. Gales of Boston, to Boots to set reorganisation in motion, and appointed the head of his Liverpool depot, W. C. Church, to head the newly formed Manufacturing Executive. Otherwise, the reorganisation of Boots was left to a group of managers who were sent to Liggett's offices in Boston and St Louis to be educated in the new organisational precepts. The managers included Jesse's only son John Boot II (1889–

1954), and his contemporary J. E. Greenwood, a Cambridge graduate, lawyer, accountant, and war-time guards officer, who had been brought into the business in 1919 when Jesse was desperate for successors. Most of the other managers who were sent to America were Jesse Boot's administrators who had come up the long hard way, and had already served the business thirty years or more. Though long inured to taking orders without question, they looked forward to emancipation with pleasure; in particular, H. B. Holthouse (head of manufacturing), whose technical expertise had given him some autonomy, and T. S. Ratcliffe (merchandise controller) whose 1913 trip to the USA to learn some techniques of cost accounting had given him a welcome measure of personal independence, hoped for more opportunities to express their ambitions within the Company.

Realistically, there was no real alternative to running Boots through a number of committees as Jesse Boot had not trained anyone to succeed him; indeed there was no general manager after 1913 when Jesse's deputy and right hand man from the early years (Albert Thompson) died in harness. Jesse regarded his only son John as a failure (his school, college, and wartime record failed to impress anyone), and he never succeeded in finding an acceptable successor to Thompson. So the new American owners appointed two committees, a Manufacturing Executive headed by Church, and a Retail Executive chaired by John Boot, to run the organisation. The two executives synchronised their activities in a Company Executive which formally reported to Boston, USA. The manufacturing and wholesale side appears to have been the biggest muddle, and some of the most severe headaches were delegated to sub-committees, including mechandise (stock control), prices, and formulae committees. The latter was established to set down and regularise the 'recipes' that Jesse's men had collected from far and wide over the years and which mainly existed in furtive notebooks or the secret recesses of their minds, and the attempt to pool information produced deep resentments springing from inter-departmental jealousies. The greatest satisfaction at this period derived from departmental managers taking genuine responsibility for their sections for the first time.

The extension of Boot's retail empire had been Jesse's main concern, with the various other functions playing supporting roles, so the 600 or so shops were in general in better shape than the wholesale and manufacturing side of the business. The main problem was that as Jesse's health had declined, and as he had become preoccupied with the development of fine chemicals during the war years, the shops had been less and less frequently visited, so that the managers inevitably went their own ways. This lax control of the branches was terminated by establishing a new system of liaison with head office through nine

Territorial General Managers, helped by Assistant TGMs and Supernumary (or acting) TGMs. Moreover, the new Directors were also assigned to regions and encouraged to make frequent tours of the shops and develop inter-regional rivalries. The number of TGMs has been increased from time to time, but the basic structure is still based on that established in 1920. The appointment of a General Sales Manager opened the way for direct communication between the TGMs and the Company's buyers.

When Boots had settled down to the new management and adjusted itself to Liggett's stringent economies in stock, wages, salaries, and retail property, the existence of two executives was found to be cumbersome. So after three-and-a-half years' experience the two bodies were formally amalgamated, with Church and John Boot as joint managing directors. Gales had returned to Boston after only a few months in Nottingham in the latter half of 1920, so that John Boot, who knew the business so much better than Church, can be seen to be steadily gaining control. He and his mother and sisters resented father's sale of the business and were ready to do whatever was necessary to regain personal control. John won an early victory, in 1920, when he succeeded in blocking the appointment of directors from two rival concerns, and in 1923 he was able to persuade Liggett to sell a quarter of his shareholding in Britain.

As the post-war economies were relaxed, young Boot resumed his father's empire-building activity, buying up chemists' shops in localities where Boots' representation was thin. He remained loyal to his father's basic policy that 'cheapest is best', but strove to improve Boots image by raising the quality of the merchandise sold and the standards of service. In 1927 he took up his father's plan to build a new factory complex on a virgin site at Beeston (three miles west of Nottingham) and appointed a Research Director, a post that had been vacant since 1919. These initiatives, and others of lesser moment, took John Boot to the head of the Company, and when Jesse's 'old guard' retired one by one in the late 1920s and early 1930s, he had no serious rivals in the organisation, apart from Greenwood. Consequently when Liggett went bankrupt in 1932 and his controlling interest in Boots had to be sold off, there were only two contenders for the succession. By good fortune rather than financial skill, John Boot linked himself with a syndicate who won financial control, in 1933. Two years earlier he had inherited his father's recently-conferred title, Lord Trent; to this patrimony was now joined father's personal authority in the business. For the next twenty years (1933–53) he was to be the one undisputed authority at Boots.

The period of American control left important organisational features in the Company, particularly a committee structure and the TGM system, but after 1933 it was always understood that these existed to serve and advise Trent (as we may now call him), and he could accept or override their advice as he chose. The Executive became an assembly of departmental managers who laid information before the Chairman for his decisions. The most important working committee proved to be the one originally set up to plan and supervise the development of the new site at Beeston, the Works Planning Committee, and here again it was tacitly understood that Trent could consult or override the committee as he thought fit. He was just as likely to seek advice from a small group of favourites, very often the Earl of Selbourne (a non-executive brought in by Trent), J. P. Savage (a former Expense Controller who showed exceptional skill at oiling the wheels), Dr P. C. Brett (medical adviser) and John Boyd (the Edinburgh TGM). Trent never owned Boots as his father had done, but such were the forces of continuity in the firm that, despite a dozen years of American ownership, the family authority was practically unimpaired so late as 1954. Figure One attempts to summarise the structure of the business during the period of Trent's personal rule.

III

THE ORIGINS OF DEVOLUTION AND MULTI-DIVISIONAL STRUCTURE

No autocracy can be complete, and Trent's endeavour to obtain full personal control of the Company was bound to go by default at some point or other. In this matter, as in so many others, his actions echoed those of his father a generation earlier. Jesse had been unable to rule Holthouse (production manager) because of his technical expertise, and Holthouse's successor, B. A. Bull, maintained the independence of his department. When the Beeston factory was opened in 1933, processes that had been scattered through a whole range of buildings were brought together and the principle of 'functional' (as opposed to 'line') management was recognised. Responsibility was divided between four younger managers in charge of manufacturing, packaging, warehousing, and quality control, all under Bull's general direction.

A further interesting development took place in 1940, when Trent agreed to serve as Regional Commissioner for Civil Defence, and so had to depute day-to-day control of the business during the five years of war. During this period, the business was effectively run by J. P. Savage, who had won Trent's confidence by his administrative ability and diplomatic skill, and had been his personal assistant since 1936. Savage had a gift for elucidating a problem so that his listener felt he had discovered the solution, a rare talent that won Trent's favour.

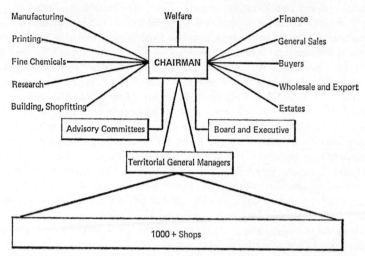

Figure 1 Structure of the Boots Company during the Chairmanship of Lord Trent, 1933–54

When Trent returned from war service he found Savage's guidance indispensable, and other executives, realising this, and often finding it difficult to anticipate the Chairman's mind, made a routine of consulting Savage whenever they wanted to launch new ideas.

In 1954, when ill-health forced Trent to retire, Savage was the only possible successor. His period as Chairman and Managing Director (1954–61) is an important preface to the organisational changes that followed soon after. The executives of the period are unanimous that he encouraged them to discuss their problems freely with him, and that for the first time the Executive became a genuine forum for exchange of information and ideas, decisions being taken on a majority vote. Savage had come of a working-class background and risen to the top from being an office boy; consequently he took no stand on inherited authority as such. On the contrary, he was a great debunker of all pretentiousness, so that rising executives had to make their claims on merit. Taken at so recent a period, such a change may seem modest enough to outsiders, but the novelty of open discussion made some contemporaries think of the period as the beginning of a new era at Boots.

The end of the Second World War, like the First, brought financial problems to Boots. Stock was out of control, profit margins thin or non-existent, and shops run down; the printworks had been destroyed in an air raid and there was a serious shortage of manufacturing capacity. It was the kind of 'sizeable crisis' that (following Chandler) we should expect to see precipitating change. Trent responded by appointing a new finance director to succeed Greenwood, a modest initiative, but one that was to have far-reaching but for the time being largely unforseen consequences. The man appointed was F. A. Cockfield (now Sir Arthur Cockfield), 36-year-old Director of Statistics and Intelligence to the Board of Inland Revenue. Within a few months, Savage succeeded Trent as Chairman and Managing Director, and Cockfield began introducing the concepts of cost accounting in easy stages. His aim was not only to locate unprofitable operations and so establish the Company on a sound financial basis, but also to introduce a concept of management in which the various departments of the business would acquire a much greater degree of autonomy but be financially responsible to the Executive. Cockfield's ideas on devolution and profit accountability were not a novelty at the period, but were only beginning to be adopted by the biggest and most progressive British firms; indeed the pioneer texts, so far as accountants are concerned, did not appear until a decade later – John Argenti's *Corporate Planning* (1968) and David Solomans' *Divisional Performance: Measurement and Control* (1965). In pressing his principles in the Executive, Cockfield drew assurance from the experience of several forerunners in devolution and planning, particularly ICI, whose Chairman, Sir Paul Chambers, had been his chief at the Inland Revenue.

When Savage retired in 1961 his office was divided; Cockfield succeeding as Managing Director and Willoughby Norman (Trent's son-in-law) as Chairman, so the work of devolution continued. It reached a crescendo in 1966 with a thorough investigation of the Company's structure and functioning by Peat, Marwick & Co., the management consultants. The Peat Report was not, in Cockfield's words, 'the light on the road to Damascus', so much as an outside assessment of conclusions towards which the Executive had now been working for several years, partly directed by their observations of other companies, partly by the rise of new functions. Some of the recommendations of Peat Marwick were adopted, others declined.

The first step in divisionalisation was to distinguish between the operations of manufacturing and non-retail marketing on the one hand and retail distribution on the other. Cockfield created a Pharmaceutical and Fine Chemical Division, but it was not yet 'relatively autonomous' in the Chandler sense, for he still held firmly to the need for centralised control through the Executive Committee, which continued to be the sole management authority controlling all Boots' operations, retail and non-retail. In other words, this 'Division' was created primarily for accounting purposes, so that the profitability of the Company's various activities could be more accurately measured.

Cockfield left Boots in 1967 to return to government service, and was succeeded as managing director by Dr Gordon Hobday, who had worked his way up the Company from the research department. The next year, Boots bought out its only major rival in the retail company chemists' business, Timothy Whites & Taylors, and initiated a major programme to digest this acquisition. They changed shops with no local Boots rival to the Boots insignia, and converted shops where there was already a Boots branch to retail houseware, so creating a second and distinct line of retail enterprise, named Timothy Whites. This busy period coincided with a continuing growth of manufacturing and the fulfilment of Cockfield's financial reorganisation, which both suggested and created the opportunity for more substantial devolution.

The elements of the new structure are set out in Figure Two. Jesse Boot and his son were essentially shop-keepers, so that manufacturing had been regarded as an ancillary activity, and the Cinderella when it came to investment. Retailing and Manufacturing were now separated into distinct divisions, respectively named Boots the Chemists and Boots Pure Drug. Timothy Whites became a separate division, and Boots International was formed to take charge of the Company's growing operations abroad. The old Executive Committee was abolished and a great deal of autonomy was granted to the new divisional boards. Cockfield's Pharmaceutical and Fine Chemical Division was divided between Boots Pure Drug and Boots International.

The fourth division of the reorganised Company, Boots International, had long roots in the history of the business, but was a fairly recent success story. A Wholesale Department was established shortly after the Liggetts' takeover to supply Boots' products to Rexall retail chemists (i.e. members of Liggett's British co-operative). Trent had no continuous interest in it, but it achieved sporadic importance from the influence that different members of the Executive were able to exert on him. Liggett dreamed of a Boots that would cover the British Empire, and after the control of the Company was repatriated, Colonel Braithwaite, a London stockbroker who became one of Trent's first non-executive directors, pressed for retail chains in India, Australia, New Zealand, and other empire countries. After the war, Boots' new research director, Sir Jack Drummond, foresaw a growing market for manufactured goods in Africa, and tried to lead research and exporting in this direction. These ventures were only a limited success, partly, no doubt, because they were sporadic, but more particularly because of the concerted opposition of retail chemists in Australia and New Zealand to Boots, while, on the manufacturing side, Boots' products frankly lacked sufficient originality to make the cost of overseas sales promotions worthwhile. Wholesale depots were established in several countries round the world (India, Australia, New Zealand, South Africa, Kenya, etc.)

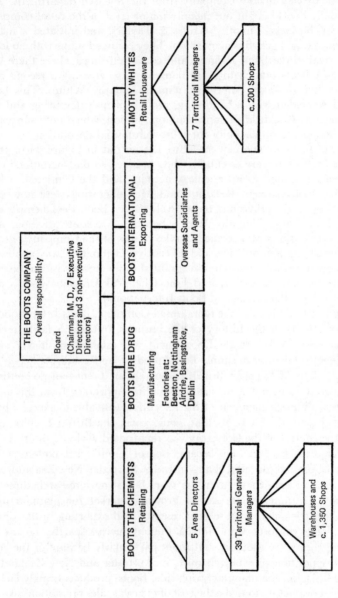

Figure 2   Divisional Structure of Boots established in 1970

but the scale of business was modest, and the organisation ancillary to the Company's main interest in retailing in the domestic market.

The status of the Wholesale and Export Department was transformed by the arrival of the first major success of Boots' Research Department, a valuable discovery for the treatment of rheumatoid arthritis and osteoarthritis called 'Brufen'. The new drug has found an extensive international market and has been the starting point for a rapid growth of the overseas organisation, the beginning of which broadly co-incided with the busy period of absorption of Timothy Whites & Taylors.

IV

MONOPOLY COMMISSION RESTRICTIONS ON BOOTS' GROWTH, 1972–3

This review of Boots' recent history harmonises with Chandler's view that the market was of the greatest importance to changing strategy and structure. But the effect of British government control can be much greater than anything which fell within his purview in the American economy, to judge from Boots' experience in the last two or three years. The Company achieved some of their most spectacular advances by takeovers, but their most recent attempts to create new divisions by this process have been frustrated by the Monopolies Commission.

The incentives for further diversification at Boots can readily be understood in the light of the Company's historical experience. The Company has traditionally concentrated on retailing, but further growth in this area, both for Boots and Timothy Whites houseware chain, is limited by the shortage of good central sites, while the economics of retailing on a national scale have directed the closure of 'neighbourhood' shops with a limited turnover. The law in most EEC countries prohibits company chemist retailing as developed in Britain. The most promising sector for future expansion appears to be the international market for pharmaceutical products, but Boots' research and development, and its overseas selling organisation, though growing rapidly, are still dwarfed by the retail side. Clearly a more 'balanced' organisation could be achieved more quickly by acquisitions to give the parent company, on the one hand, a much bigger research and manufacturing interest, and on the other, a base for extension of retailing, both by extending into departmental store retailing and opening shops abroad.

The outcome is familiar to all newspaper readers. In 1972, Boots competed with Beecham for control of Glaxo Laboratories, the British pharmaceutical manufacturers, but the public battle was stopped by the government's referral to the Monopolies Commission, which recommended that neither merger should be permitted. The following year, Boots tried to take over the House of Fraser, a London-based group of Departmental and chain stores with a small interest on the Continent. It was thought that a merger of Boots and Frasers would provide a suitable base for the establishment of departmental shops on the Continent. Despite some hostility from newspaper commentators and shareholders, who felt that further diversification might not be good for Boots, the deal would have gone through if it had not been referred to the Monopolies Commission, and if the investing world had not suddenly fallen apart following the oil crisis at the end of 1973. Fraser would not agree to renegotiate on price, and the Stock Exchange Panel decided in his favour, so that by the time the Commission reported, their adverse decision was of little more than academic interest. However, the important point in the present context is that, for the time being at least, the 'public interest', as interpreted by the Monopolies Commission, has frustrated the formation of further Boots divisions. Government regulation has had a decisive effect on the Company, though whether this restraint curtails the organisation for a long period of time remains to be seen.

V

CONCLUSIONS

The evidence surveyed in this paper can be summarised in this way:
1. The elements of vertical integration, manufacturing, wholesaling, and retailing, were present at the foundation of Boots first enterprise in Nottingham, and have remained a feature of the organisation ever since. The Company carried a long manufacturing and retail inventory from the pioneer years, but its rapid growth under Jesse Boot was largely based on the multiplication of popular cut-price neighbourhood stores. Shop management was by qualified chemists, as the Pharmacy Acts required, and the growth of secondary and technical education from the 1880s ensured easy recruitment of capable men. Autocratic central control was united to a clear and explicit recognition of the importance of the chemist-managers to the success of the growing number of shops.
2. At head offices, loyalty to Jesse Boot and his son proved to be unusually resistant to change. It not only survived two periods of acute financial difficulty (1920–22, 1948–52) but, even more remarkably, the sale of the Company in 1920 and 1933, and a dozen years of American control. The main reason is to be found in the team of deferential (often nonconformist) managers which Boot trained up in his ways, and the parochialism of his organisation. The consequence was that

the personal authority of the Chairman remained largely intact until Trent's retirement in 1954, and even then dissolved relatively slowly as Savage introduced genuine discussion, and a new generation of managers rose to prominence in the firm.

3. However, the divisional structure established in 1967 can be seen as the product of a long period of gestation, finding origins in the latitude enjoyed by some of the more technical departments (manufacturing, fine chemicals, research) in Jesse Boot's day and perhaps even more in Trent's. The years of American control had left a legacy of the Territorial General Manager system and a number of forward-looking advisory committees. The close of family rule marked the end of the Chairman's absolutism, but substantial delegation of authority to the departments and divisions still had to be learned. Writing of so recent a period, it is impossible to assess the relative importance of long-term influences with assurance, but it seems that the rapid post-war growth of Boots' organisation as a whole, and more particularly the manufacturing and wholesaling functions, were the most important considerations in the reorganisation of 1967. Certainly there was nothing comparable to the 'sizable crisis' that often dictated major reorganisation in Chandler's American companies.

6 Personality, Strategy and Structure: some Consequences of Strong Minds

W. J. READER

I

My view of business history has a strongly 'political' tinge to it. That is, I think that in looking at the way businesses develop, particularly those run by large corporations, one is looking at power politics in an economic landscape. Businessmen are often driven by motives which are by no means purely commercial. They seek power. They engage in rivalry. Their rivalries may be personal, or corporate, or both. The plans they make, though presented, for orthodoxy's sake, as being aimed purely at the maximisation of profits, often have quite other ends in view as well. It follows that in business history, as in political history, we are concerned with the interplay between men and events, and it is equally important to understand both. Indeed I would go so far as to say that without having a pretty good knowledge of the people you are dealing with, you are unlikely to form a sound judgement of the things that have happened in – or to – their companies and their industries.

This is largely because whenever strategy is being planned, or a decision is being taken, there are usually several options open, and it will depend very much on the personalities involved which one is chosen. A very powerful personality will impose a pattern on events just as surely in business as in politics. Or he will seek to impose one, and fail. Or he will succeed in a totally unexpected way, and everybody will believe him when he says that that was what he meant to do all along. All these things happen in business as they happen in other human activities. If we want to understand how business develops we must pay as much attention to its outstanding personalities as to matters of technology, finance, labour relations, or any of the other possible chapter headings in the book. And certainly personalities come powerfully into play in Professor Chandler's field of strategy and structure, as he and Professor Salsbury have demonstrated in their biography of Pierre S. du Pont : a major work which deserves to be at least as widely known as Alfred P. Sloan's autobiography *My Years with General Motors*.[1] Works like these are as important to the historian of business as biographies and memoirs of statesmen are to the political historian, and it is perhaps in this direction, among others, that we should look if we are seeking to widen the field of business history. I propose to discuss three men in detail and two briefly. The three whom I propose to discuss in detail are among the outstanding figures in British business in the last hundred years. One – the first Lord Leverhulme – could sustain a claim to be considered the most remarkable character who has ever played a part in British business, and he would certainly stand out more prominently in our national record if as much attention were paid by historians and biographers to business men as to politicians. What I have to say about Leverhulme is founded on the narrative in Volume I of Professor Wilson's *History of Unilever*. The conclusions I draw from the narrative, however, are entirely my own responsibility and are not to be attributed to Charles Wilson in any way. My account of the other two is based on my own work on ICI. To avoid a superabundance of footnotes, I have been sparing in my citations from Wilson's work and my own, but where no attribution is given for statements of fact it can be assumed that the source is either *The History of Unilever* or *Imperial Chemical Industries: a History*, chiefly the second volume, from which are reproduced, by permission, the diagrams illustrating ICI organisation. My three main characters are :

William Hesketh Lever, first Viscount Leverhulme of the Western Isles (1851–1925), founder and first Chairman of Lever Brothers Limited,

Alfred Moritz Mond, first Baron Melchett of Landford (1868–1930), co-founder and first Chairman of ICI,

Harry Duncan McGowan, first Baron McGowan of Ardeer (1874–1961), co-founder and second Chairman of ICI.

As a group for study, they have the advantage that each falls into a clearly defined category familiar to everyone who is concerned with the history of business or with social history. Lever is that central figure of the middle class : the self-made man who goes into business for himself and from small beginnings creates a very large enterprise indeed. Lord Melchett, perhaps better known as Sir Alfred Mond, represents the second generation in business, the founder's son, who is required simultaneously to advance his father's work and to make a position for himself. (He was the son of Dr Ludwig Mond FRS (1839–1909), co-

founder of Brunner, Mond & Co. Ltd, alkali manufacturers, which
was one of the four firms which merged to form ICI.) McGowan, a
'Scotsman on the make' if ever there was one, represents the professional
manager who, without capital or family interest, and without ever
being the owner of the businesses he works for, nevertheless rises to the
highest positions within them.

II

William Lever was the son of a moderately prosperous wholesale grocer
of Bolton, Lancashire.[2] He was born, that is to say, in the very heart
of the English middle class – the middle class which lived by trade and
had no pretensions to gentility – and he was brought up on the flood-
tide of Victorian middle-class success and optimism, when the first
murmurs of self-doubt were faint and far away and the ambition of
the 'honest artisan' was to be as much like his master as possible. For
the ambitious young man, in Lever's view, Samuel Smiles' *Self-Help*
was required reading. 'My advice to the young man of the present
generation', he said much later, 'is to act on the principles taught in
Smiles' philosophy. He will go further than his competitor who does
not.'[3] Lever acted on his own advice. He went into the family business
and in his early thirties had made enough money to contemplate retirement. Retirement, of course, was not really in his nature, but he was
by then becoming bored with wholesale grocery in provincial England,
having carried it about as far as it would go, and he was looking for
wider horizons, both commercial and geographical. He found them in
soap-making. He started making soap (as distinct from selling soap made
for him by other firms) in 1885 on capital of £27,000. By the turn of
the century Lever Brothers Limited was a public company with about
£3.4m capital employed. Besides the world's largest soapworks at Port
Sunlight in England, the firm owned factories in Australia, Canada,
Germany, Switzerland and USA and the total output was running at
some 70,000 tons a year. Lever's personal income by this time was of
the order of £80,000–£90,000 a year.[4]

Over the next twenty-five years, up to the date of Lever's death, the
growth and diversification of the business were enormous and very
widespread. Lever Brothers Limited turned into a multi-national conglomerate with capital employed of about £64m, engaging in activities
which were held under the same ownership less by commercial logic
than by the many-sided personality of the founder. On the soap-making
side Lever built up a group of companies, most of them wholly-owned,
which by 1925 controlled some 60 per cent of the soap trade in the
United Kingdom. (The remaining 40 per cent was chiefly in the hands
of one competitor – the Co-operative Wholesale Society.) Levers' out-

put of soap at home was in the region of 240,000 tons a year, as well as nearly 160,000 tons produced by Lever companies abroad.

On the raw material side, from 1901, Levers went in for coconut planting in the South Seas and then, on a very large scale indeed, for oil-palm planting in the Belgian Congo (Zaïre) where a convention negotiated in 1911 gave them an option on up to 750,000 hectares (1,852,000 acres) in widely separated areas of uncleared rain forest. The policy of controlling supplies of raw materials led Levers also, by stormy paths, into West African produce trading, and by 1925 they were the largest merchants on the Coast, having in 1920 absorbed one of their biggest rivals, the Niger Company, in a takeover so disastrously devised that it nearly broke them. As well as all this, Lever Brothers in 1925 were oil millers and margarine makers on a large scale. Somewhat less largely they were in disinfectants, chocolates, shipping, baby food. They were in ice cream and sausages too, as well as canned food and trawling, all because in 1922 they had become the owners of Mac Fisheries Limited, themselves owners of a nation-wide chain of fish shops.

What, you may ask, has retail fishmongery to do with soap? Not much, except through the personality of William Lever, and that is what we are coming back to. Listen to what he once said to a journalist :

> My happiness is my business. I can see finality for myself, an end, an absolute end; but none for my business. There one has room to breathe, to grow, to expand, and the possibilities are boundless. One can go to places like the Congo, and organize, organize, organize, well, very big things indeed. But I don't work at business only for the sake of money. I am not a lover of money as money and never have been. I work at business because business is life. It enables me to do things.[5]

A celebrity is not upon his oath in a newspaper interview. Nevertheless even if Lever had never given any other indication of his motives – and he was among the most articulate of men – the whole pattern of his life and the extraordinary development of the business he founded suggest that in this piece of self-revelation he was entirely sincere and that he understood pretty well what drove him : namely, a desire for power. If he had been born in a later generation or in a higher social class he would almost certainly have become a politician, and he might have been a very considerable one. As it was, he went into business and proceeded, as he put it, to 'organize, organize, organize, well, very big things indeed'. He used business, that is to say, as a vehicle for his ambitions and for his creative impulse, and in looking at the history of Lever Brothers during the founder's lifetime it is illuminating to distinguish between activities directed to purely commercial ends – to the maximisation of profit, if you like – and activities differently motivated in part or wholly.

The foundations of his success were solidly commercial. He was a brilliant marketing man. Along with others of his generation – Jesse Boot (1850–1931), for example, and Thomas Lipton (1850–1931) – he recognised the glittering opportunities that were opening up, in the last quarter of the nineteenth century, in the widespread rise in the nation's standard of living, especially among 'the class of fully paid labour in regular employ' which, in Charles Booth's words, 'contains the largest section of the people, and is thus, more than any other, representative of "the way we live now" '.[6] With this class of consumer firmly in view, he promoted his principal product – Sunlight Soap – by all the devices of brand marketing, including heavy national advertising, gift schemes, and a fixed price which was the same from one end of the country to the other. He was the first soapmaker to operate in this way, and he reaped his reward.

Success with soap gave him the 'room to breathe, to grow, to expand' which he sought. This he was the more readily able to do, in any way he thought good, because for the greater part of his career he kept about 80 per cent of the ordinary capital of Lever Brothers Limited in his own hands, giving him an unquestionable right, so long as the Preference dividends were paid – as they always were – to do what he liked with the business. Until very late in life he had no outside investments (apart from land and houses) of any consequence, and he regarded Lever Brothers as his own personal property, much as if it had been a small corner grocer's shop.

The most spectacular of Lever's ventures away from soapmaking were concentrated on tropical Africa, especially the Belgian Congo. There he undertook to carve plantations out of virgin jungle, to bring in the labour force to work them, and to provide roads, telecommunications, housing, schools, hospitals and medical services. If he had simply been concerned to invest capital profitably, or even to secure his supplies of palm oil, he could certainly have found easier, cheaper and quicker ways of doing it. Lever never made much pretence that his *Huileries du Congo Belge* were justified in any ordinary commercial sense. He made it plain that he was fascinated with the country and with what he could do there. He visited the Congo twice, once in 1912–13 and once just before he died, in 1924–25. He was over sixty when he made the first journey and nearly 74 at the time of the second. Certainly he made his journeys in state, but they were major, not to say foolhardy, undertakings for a man of his age, to be explained far more by the enthusiasm of a pioneer than by the prudence of a business man. 'We have got hold of something', he wrote in 1913, 'we can employ all our talents and energy upon for the next quarter century and still find plenty to do.'[7] No mention, it will be observed, of soap, raw materials, or return on capital employed : only 'plenty to do'.

Lever's other deviation, on a grand scale, from commercial rationality was his adventure in the Western Isles, undertaken from 1918 onward as a hobby for his retirement.[8] Put very briefly, what he set out to do was to pour money – his own money – into schemes intended to restore the economy of the Western Isles by applying capital and resources to the support of their fishing industry. It was entirely Lever's private venture and it would not have entered the history of Lever Brothers, except by way of a footnote, if it had succeeded. In fact, for reasons which need not detain us, it failed. It failed, moreover, just after Lever had been put to great expense, personally, in rescuing Lever Brothers from some of the troubles they had been plunged into by the disastrous takeover of the Niger Company. Lever decided, therefore, to recoup his outlay by selling to Lever Brothers the group of companies which he had set up to further his schemes in the Hebrides, and in 1922 he did so. Since he was in full command of the Ordinary shares, there was no one to say him nay.

In this way Lever Brothers Limited, soapmakers, plantation owners, West African merchants, oil millers, margarine makers and much else besides, became in addition to all the rest, and in defiance of any kind of commercial or technical logic, processors, merchants and retailers of various kinds of food, both preserved and fresh. It might be said, indeed, that Levers, and Unilever after them, slipped sideways into sausages, ice cream, Skippers, canned fruit, canned salmon, and Mac Fisheries shops – all because Lord Leverhulme had planned some modest occupation for his old age. I am not suggesting that all Lever's plans for expanding his interests had so strong an element of romantic power-seeking as the Congo adventure or the Western Isles project. Oil milling and margarine manufacture were perfectly logical activities for a large user of oils and fats. The advance into West African trading and into shipping were measures of industrial warfare : defensive manœuvres against the threat of monopoly in the supply and transport of soapmakers' raw materials.

Nevertheless, whatever Lever's motives, the net result for Lever Brothers Limited of his restless energy and overmastering will-power was to build up a large, sprawling, disparate and extremely idiosyncratic conglomeration of business activities, some in manufacturing, some in merchanting, some in tropical agriculture, some in retail trade. This, it might be thought, would set a very pretty problem in corporate organisation, but, as far as I know – and I think I have read more of Lever's papers (which are plentiful) than any other man alive – Organisation with a capital O was not a subject which interested the Old Man very much, and I doubt if he ever gave much thought to it in an abstract way. I have certainly never seen any indication that he paid any attention to the extremely sophisticated notions of the Germans, as typified by the idea of the *Interessen Gemeinschaft*, or to the kind of organisation which, towards the end of his life, was being devised on the other side of the Atlantic, and which has been so thoroughly investigated by Professor Chandler. He never even bothered to set up a holding company for Lever Brothers' manifold interests, and until the day he died Lever Brothers uneasily combined the functions of a manufacturing company and of the directing authority of a world-wide commercial organisation.

Lever Brothers Limited, when the founder died, owned a business comparable in size and complexity, perhaps, with Du Pont. It was still being run, nevertheless, as far as possible on the lines of a Victorian family business in the hands of its owner. So far as Lever had any fixed principles in the matter, they were that his soap companies, as one by one he acquired control of every soap company of any consequence in the United Kingdom, should continue to compete with each other, and that his own authority was absolute. In fact, as the price of rescue by Barclays Bank from the Niger Company disaster, he was compelled from 1921 onward to accept discreet control from Francis D'Arcy Cooper (1882–1941), who became his successor, but that was not apparent outside a very small circle and it was very tactfully exercised. There was, it is true, an imposing array of committees from the Board downwards, and a considerable bureaucracy, but in all essentials, when Lord Leverhulme died, Lever Brothers still awaited a managerial revolution.

III

In September 1925 the *IG Farbenindustrie AG* was formed to merge eight of the most important German chemical firms.[9] Their American and British contemporaries, who regarded them as the strongest, most versatile and most efficient chemical firms in the world, were much alarmed. The British response was rapid and dramatic. In the Autumn of 1926 the four largest British chemical firms, Brunner Mond & Co., Nobel Industries, the United Alkali Co. and the British Dyestuffs Corporation, merged to form Imperial Chemical Industries Ltd.[10] This was much the largest merger, up to that time, ever undertaken in the United Kingdom. Its co-authors were Sir Harry McGowan, who first put the idea forward, and Sir Alfred Mond, who became ICI's first Chairman.

Mond's parents were Jewish immigrants from Cassel in Germany. His father, Ludwig, united academic attainments in science with a good head for business – not a common combination – and in partnership with (Sir) John Brunner (1842–1919) he founded the highly successful alkali firm of Brunner, Mond & Co. Ltd, at Winnington near Northwich in Cheshire. Ludwig was formidable and overbearing: Alfred stood in awe of him. By 1880 or thereabouts Brunner Mond was making money fast, and Alfred Mond was brought up against a cultured, cosmopolitan background, strongly Continental and Jewish, rather than provincial English, in flavour. Nevertheless he had a conventional upper-middle-class education at Cheltenham and Cambridge (where he failed in the Natural Sciences Tripos) and all his life sought assimilation: a goal the more elusive because of a persistent trace of German accent in his speech.

As a young or youngish man he spent the years between 1894 and 1906 in Brunner, Mond's London office, but then he turned to Liberal politics where, as his biographer makes clear, his main ambitions lay.[11] He held office as First Commissioner of Works from 1916 to 1921 and as Minister of Health from 1921 to 1922, but any further prospects he may have had were destroyed by the fall of Lloyd George. He remained an MP until he was raised to the peerage in 1928, but for the last eight years of his life his main energies were directed into business. Mond went back into business reluctantly, as a second-best choice to politics, and not at first into the family firm, except as a non-executive Director. He was obliged to become full-time Chairman of Brunner, Mond after an action for fraudulent breach of contract was brought against the company by Lever Brothers. Mond was in no way implicated, but it destroyed the reigning Chairman, Roscoe Brunner. Therefore although he was a son of one of Brunner, Mond's founders, his pathway to the head of the business was hardly a conventional one.

In ICI the closest colleague of this wealthy, cultivated Jew, ex-Minister and Privy Councillor, was a Glasgow brass-fitter's son who had spent all his working life in the business which at the time of the ICI merger was known as Nobel Industries Limited. Harry Duncan McGowan joined Nobel's Explosives Company in Glasgow as an office-boy aged 15 in 1889. In 1926 he was Chairman and Managing Director of Nobel Industries, the holding company of a previous merger, largely negotiated by himself, which included every explosives company of any consequence in the United Kingdom and their subsidiaries and associates abroad, as well as a group of companies engaged in various ways in the non-ferrous metals trades. Nobel Industries had investments, too, in the motor and motor components trades, notably in General Motors Corporation of USA.

These two men of such dissimilar origins, upbringing and accomplishments worked surprisingly well together. McGowan, by nature anything but submissive or self-effacing, had an immense respect for Mond's public position and seems always to have been ready to defer to him. He conceded the Chairmanship gracefully, contenting himself with the title of President, though quite what he was to preside over, and with what rights and duties, was never made clear. The idea of setting up ICI had been McGowan's and he had pushed it through, at first against an alternative scheme of Mond's, with energetic determination. His main point won, it seems clear that he was prepared to see Mond take most of the initiative in getting ICI going, with himself just a barely perceptible half-pace in the rear.

The biggest problem in making a merger is not, as a rule, negotiating a basis for bringing it into being but the practical and psychological difficulty of making it work – of getting rid of the feelings of insecurity and resentment which almost every merger brings and of making the whole into more than the sum of the parts. Of this problem both Mond and McGowan were well aware. At the first meeting of ICI's management, before ICI came formally into existence, both insisted on the importance of sinking four old identities in one new one. 'I want us all', said McGowan, 'to forget our old Companies.'[12] ICI, although in law created by a merger of four co-equal companies, represented in fact a takeover by two strong businesses – Brunner, Mond and Nobel Industries – of two weak ones – United Alkali Company and British Dyestuffs Corporation. UAC was weak almost to the point of extinction, to which it would be carried much nearer by any thorough-going policy of rationalisation, which was partly what the merger was for. BDC, on the other hand, represented not only dyestuffs but the whole 'fine chemical' side of the industry, all extremely important in war. Hence there were strong motives for preserving and strengthening it, and indeed the need to provide capital for doing so had been one of the reasons, certainly on the Government side, for promoting the merger idea.

The task, then, which faced the founders of ICI was to get rid of obsolete and surplus capacity; to strengthen the activities of the new concern and to widen them beyond the scope of the old companies; and generally to make the chemical industry in Great Britain and the British Empire fit to stand up to competition from Germany and America. So far as rationalisation was concerned, there had already been very thorough rationalisation, over which McGowan had presided, on the explosives side of Nobel Industries. Brunner, Mond and the United Alkali Company, on the other hand, overlapped with each other a great deal in the heavy chemical industry, particularly in the manufacture of alkali and acids. ('Heavy' in this context refers to the scale of operations – production in hundreds of thousands of tons a year – not to the physical nature of the products.) Mond, who claimed to have invented the term 'rationalisation' in its industrial sense, had already taken a leading part in rationalising the Welsh anthracite-mining industry, and he intended to operate on the chemical industry in the same way, using the power which large scale organisation would bring. 'The trend of all modern industry', he wrote in 1927, 'is towards greater units, greater co-ordination for the more effective use of resources.'[13]

The imperial purpose of ICI, which in 1926 most people in this country – or, for that matter, in the Empire overseas – saw no reason to be ashamed of, was very strong. '[The] Company', announced the founders, 'has, of deliberate purpose, been given the title of "IMPERIAL CHEMICAL INDUSTRIES LIMITED". The British Empire is the greatest single economic unit in the world, one in which every patriotic member of the great British Commonwealth has a personal interest. By linking the title of the new Company to that unit, it is intended to lay emphasis upon the fact that the promotion of Imperial trading interests will command the special consideration and thought of those who will be responsible for directing this new Company.'[14] Mond himself went further. 'My ideal', he said in 1926, 'is to see . . . our great organisation controlling the production and sales of the whole chemical manufacture within the Empire.'[15]

Mond, in late middle age (he was 58), brought to ICI a mind at first schooled in science-based industry, under the strong German influence of his father, and then for fifteen years immersed in politics, latterly at ministerial level. His upbringing gave him a thoroughly German respect for academic attainments, particularly in science, and he escaped the English error of scorning the application of 'pure' science to commercial ends. His years with Brunner, Mond gave him a clear perception, very uncommon in British business of the day, of the industrial importance of scientific education up to the highest level : not for Alfred Mond the exaltation of 'practical experience' over 'book learning'. In business, what appealed to him above all else were new technical developments on the largest possible scale, and he had a dangerous confidence in his own technical judgement. As a politician, he liked projects with a strong infusion of patriotism and social purpose : as it might be, developing the resources of the Empire or, at home, helping to solve the problem of unemployment. In effect, he undoubtedly saw his position at the head of ICI as a continuation in business of the public career which in politics he had been forced to abandon.

McGowan, though not blind to the long view, the large prospect, or the public interest, was far more singleminded in business than Mond. Not for him the higher flights of national or Imperial politics, though industrial politics at the highest level, preferably conducted in a haze of cigar smoke and high living, were what he excelled at and exulted in. He was above all a negotiator, a maker of mergers and complex agreements, and his great skill lay in driving a bargain hard enough but not

E

too hard, so that all parties could feel satisfied. McGowan, too, had come under strong German influence, though of a kind very different from that which played on Mond. He had made his whole career in the Nobel business which, up to 1915, was part of the Anglo-German Nobel-Dynamite Trust.[16] The organisation of that business was very sophisticated, and McGowan was much better aware than most British business men of the possibilities and intricacies of holding companies, pooling agreements, and elaborate regulations for sharing markets. Nobel Industries, as McGowan brought it into ICI., was far more advanced in its organisation than Brunner, Mond (where they were only just getting round to the idea of a holding company) or, indeed, than most British businesses of the day.

The strongest influence on McGowan, though, was American. Throughout his career Nobels had been closely associated with Du Pont : a business which McGowan admired immensely. Moreover he was on good terms, personally, with members of the du Pont family, particularly Pierre S. du Pont (1870–1954).[17] In Harry McGowan's view, what was good for Du Pont was likely to be good for Nobels, and when he was looking for a good home for Nobels' surplus funds, towards the end of the Great War and in the early twenties, he followed Du Pont's lead into the motor industry. He did this partly by developing, with help from Du Pont, business in cellulose finishes and leathercloth; partly by directing the 'metals end' of Nobels into the manufacture of radiators, carburettors and motor-cycles; partly by causing Nobels to take large, though not controlling interests in Dunlop, Joseph Lucas and other components businesses.[18]

Nobels' most important investment in the motor industry, made at the instance of McGowan under the direct influence of Pierre S. du Pont and J. J. Raskob, was in General Motors.[19] The sum originally invested, in May 1920, was about £3.5m. Until GM stock crashed in the Depression the investment was immensely successful, and Mond was greatly impressed with McGowan's financial shrewdness in having made it. After the Depression the story was different, but Mond was dead by then. McGowan would never willingly allow the stock to be sold off entirely, although there were many dealings in it, and so, until it had to be sold to the British Government during the Second World War, ICI's reserves included a large holding in a foreign company which they did not control, the value of which varied from day to day with the movement of Stock Exchange values. It was a highly unconventional financial policy, as was frequently pointed out at the time, and it was entirely due to McGowan's personal influence.

These two dissimilar characters from dissimilar backgrounds, Mond and McGowan, had in common a highly autocratic temperament. Each expected unquestioned personal authority, neither was afraid to use it, and the early organisation of ICI was designed to centre round it. The awkward question of precedence between them was settled by appointing them joint Managing Directors, each with a five-year service agreement which gave them, 'subject to the control of the Board', direction and control of the Company's powers and duties. The Board's control was remote and shadowy, for the same agreements delegated to the Managing Directors 'all the powers of the Board'. Within ICI Mond and McGowan were supreme : joint autocrats over all others, including their colleagues on the Board (see Figure 1). The rest of the Executive Directors – there were at first only half a dozen of them, drawn equally from Brunner, Mond and Nobels – formed an Executive Committee and two, of whom one was Alfred Mond's son Henry, sat with the Chairman and President on a Finance Committee. The Directors' subordination was made quite plain : 'The ICI', wrote Mond, introducing ICI's first scheme of organisation in April 1927, 'have really entrusted the President . . . and myself with the powers of management of the concern; the Executive Committee operates under our supervision.'[20] Thus the Directors, as Directors, were put firmly in their place. As departmental managers, nevertheless, they were powerful. Each Director had under his hand one or more of ICI's central Departments – Technical, Development, Commercial and the rest – which were expressly intended to *control* the operations of subsidiary companies, not merely to give advice. Moreover he would be on the Boards of several of the subsidiaries, giving him the opportunity, if he had the time, to take a close interest in their affairs.

The independence of the subsidiaries was quite deliberately destroyed by a device taken over, as a good deal of ICI's administrative apparatus was, from Nobels. The Directors of the subsidiaries were required to resign and ICI was then put in as sole legal Director and Manager. There were then no independent Directors with a statutory right, and probably a duty, to query policies which they disagreed with. The subsidiaries' Boards were then reconstituted as Delegate Boards, manned by Delegate Directors. The device was very much to Mond's taste. It gave the ICI Board – meaning, in effect, himself and McGowan – 'absolute and rapid control over all the activities of the four constituent companies' and, of course, over their subsidiaries. This control must not be hampered by any compulsion to take the lower management into consultation. 'The whole picture of ICI', wrote Mond, 'has to be kept in view by those directing its affairs and . . . they cannot be asked to discuss matters of ICI policy with Boards of Directors who are not themselves ICI Directors, firstly because a great deal too much of ICI policy . . . would become disclosed . . . and secondly, the natural viewpoint of those who are merely Directors of Subsidiary Companies might quite legitimately be widely separated.'[21]

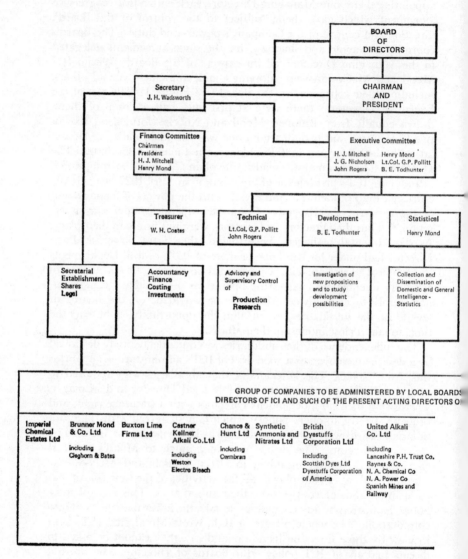

Figure 1   ICI Organisation Chart, April 1927

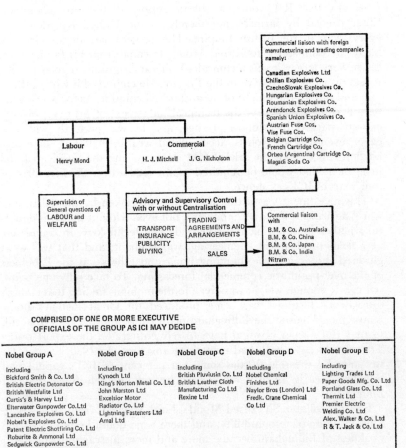

Commercial liaison with foreign manufacturing and trading companies namely:

Canadian Explosives Ltd
Chilian Explosives Co.
CzechoSlovak Explosives Co.
Hungarian Explosives Co.
Roumanian Explosives Co.
Arendonck Explosives Co.
Spanish Union Explosives Co.
Austrian Fuse Cos.
Vise Fuse Cos.
Belgian Cartridge Co.
French Cartridge Co.
Orbea (Argentina) Cartridge Co.
Magadi Soda Co

Labour

Henry Mond

Commercial

H. J. Mitchell   J. G. Nicholson

Supervision of General questions of LABOUR and WELFARE

Advisory and Supervisory Control with or without Centralisation

TRANSPORT
INSURANCE
PUBLICITY
BUYING

TRADING AGREEMENTS AND ARRANGEMENTS

SALES

Commercial liaison with

B.M. & Co. Australasia
B.M. & Co. China
B.M. & Co. Japan
B.M. & Co. India
Nitram

COMPRISED OF ONE OR MORE EXECUTIVE OFFICIALS OF THE GROUP AS ICI MAY DECIDE

Nobel Group A

including
Bickford Smith & Co. Ltd
British Electric Detonator Co
British Westfalite Ltd
Curtis's & Harvey Ltd
Elterwater Gunpowder Co. Ltd
Lancashire Explosives Co. Ltd
Nobel's Explosives Co. Ltd
Patent Electric Shotfiring Co. Ltd
Roburite & Ammonal Ltd
Sedgwick Gunpowder Co. Ltd
W. H. Wakefield & Co. Ltd
Eley Bros. Ltd

Nobel Group B

including
Kynoch Ltd
King's Norton Metal Co. Ltd
John Marston Ltd
Excelsior Motor
Radiator Co. Ltd
Lightning Fasteners Ltd
Amal Ltd

Nobel Group C

including
British Pluviusin Co. Ltd
British Leather Cloth
Manufacturing Co Ltd
Rexine Ltd

Nobel Group D

including
Nobel Chemical
Finishes Ltd
Naylor Bros (London) Ltd
Fredk. Crane Chemical
Co Ltd

Nobel Group E

including
Lighting Trades Ltd
Paper Goods Mfg. Co. Ltd
Portland Glass Co, Ltd
Thermit Ltd
Premier Electric
Welding Co. Ltd
Alex. Walker & Co. Ltd
R & T. Jack & Co. Ltd

Nobel (Australasia) Ltd.
African Explosives and Industries Ltd
Canadian Explosives Ltd
B.S.A.E. Co. Ltd

Under this highly centralised system, which concentrated authority in the hands of the two Managing Directors, ICI moved towards its first large investment decision : whether to go ahead with building fertiliser plant at Billingham on the basis of development work carried out before the merger in Brunner, Mond's business. From this development work, itself based on the Haber-Bosch process brought into operation in Germany before the Great War, there was emerging the possibility that ICI would be able to supply all the nitrogenous fertiliser needed by farmers, not merely in the United Kingdom, but everywhere in the British Empire. This project had all the elements likely to commend it to Alfred Mond. It came from his family firm; it was very large; it was technically brilliant; it promised good profits; it had overtones of service to the Empire. He embraced it with enthusiasm and put all the weight of his authority behind it. As for McGowan, he was content to accept the technical judgement of Brunner, Mond's experts, backed by Mond's prestige, and he was perfectly willing – eager, even – to see Nobels' accumulated wealth, including some proportion raised from the sale of GM stock, go into the massive capital investment that would be required : some £20m over the first three or four years of ICI's existence.

This investment was a disaster. It was overtaken by the collapse of world agriculture from 1929 onward, but even without that it is doubtful whether it would have succeeded. The technology, in completely new fields of chemical engineering, was brilliant, and that was what glittered in Mond's eye, blinding him – and others – to the flabbiness of the over-optimistic commercial forecasting. To take only one point, not nearly enough weight was given to the ominous finding that enough nitrogenous fertiliser was being produced for Great Britain's home requirements before the Billingham plant came into the picture at all, so that ICI's scheme would have to rely entirely on the export trade. That would have been bad enough at any time. In 1930 it was catastrophic. By the mid-thirties some ten per cent of ICI's capital had been lost, nearly all of it represented by redundant fertiliser plant at Billingham.

For this collapse Sir Alfred Mond – Lord Melchett from 1928 – bore a heavy share of responsibility, and there is no doubt he felt it. As the weakness of Billingham became more and more inescapably apparent, Lord Melchett become more and more ill, almost as if the sickness at Billingham had transmitted itself to Billingham's most influential backer. On 27 December 1930, Lord Melchett died. The downfall of Billingham must surely have hastened him towards his grave.

Melchett's death left McGowan on his own. The dual monarchy gave way to sole empire. The Directors made haste to elect McGowan Chairman, on 31 December 1930, and they made him sole Managing

Director as well, on terms no less all-embracing than those on which he and Melchett had held the office jointly. There was a Nobel precedent, as there was for so much in ICI's early organisation. McGowan had been sole Managing Director of Nobel Industries before the merger, but to hold the same position in ICI was a much bigger task, especially at the beginning of that grim year 1931. McGowan had strong nerves. He showed no sign of self-distrust or of any wish to share his authority or his responsibilities, either then or later. Instead, he accepted every opportunity to confirm and extend his power. In an age of dictatorship, McGowan was a dictator. The Directors met him half way. The early centralised constitution had over-burdened them, and before Mond died there were moves afoot to release the Directors from managerial responsibilities, ostensibly so that they could become advisers on 'major questions of policy'. In ceasing to be executives and becoming advisers they gave up power, but either the point did not strike them or they thought the exchange a good one : at any rate, they co-operated whole-heartedly in bringing it about. Under the new scheme of organisation (Figure 2) the chain of executive responsibility was made to by-pass the Board altogether, except insofar as Directors remained members of certain committees, but of the two most important, in his capacity of Managing Director, McGowan was Chairman, so that he was not only omnipotent but very nearly omnipresent as well. Below the level of the Board a Central Administrative Committee was set up, reporting – naturally – to the Managing Director. It had a Director as Chairman, but all the other members, fifteen or so, were senior departmental officials.

So much for Head Office. Outside it, even more importantly, the Directors moved away from the management of the Company's operating units. Manufacturing Groups were set up, Divisions in all but name, which were run by Delegate Boards on which ICI Directors did not sit. Their retreat from executive responsibility was complete. McGowan, in a document introducing the new scheme, made its underlying principles succinctly clear. Paying no regard to any kind of collective responsibility shared by himself and the Board, but expressing himself sturdily in the first person, he wrote :

> After consideration of many schemes I have come to the conclusion that any new organisation . . . should delegate all possible authority to the Group Delegate Boards and should liberate the whole-time Directors of ICI from direct executive control of individual Groups, with the corollary that the various Departments at Millbank [Head Office] shall function as Service Departments and not as Executive Departments as hitherto.[22]

This was the system by which ICI was governed from 1931 to 1938.

It was about as near to one-man rule as you could expect in so large a business (Figure 3). It suited McGowan because he could keep close control of large issues of central policy and finance; of relations with ICI associates overseas; and especially of the very elaborate diplomacy which regulated ICI's relations with the other Great Powers of the world's chemical industry, particularly the IG and Du Pont. It suited the Groups also, because in running their own affairs, within the general limits of ICI policy, they had a very free hand indeed. Any Group Chairman who was a moderately skilful politician (and he was not likely to be a Group Chairman otherwise) could count on getting consent to technical proposals, and it was technical proposals, usually,

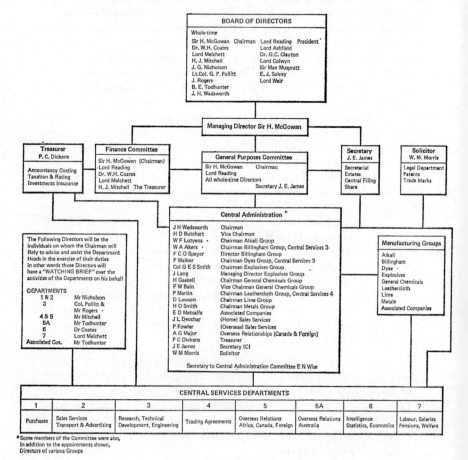

Figure 2　ICI Organisation Chart, 31 March 1931

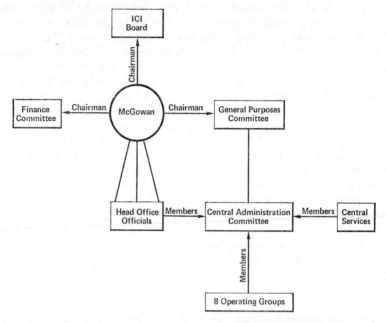

Figure 3 The Mechanics of Dictatorship, 1931–1938

which chiefly interested Group Chairmen, technologists as most of them were.

McGowan's position in ICI invites comparison with Leverhulme's position in Lever Brothers. Each exercised very large powers over very large companies. There was, however, a fundamental difference in the source of their authority. Leverhulme owned his own business : McGowan was a professional manager. Leverhulme could – and did – dismiss Directors who disagreed with him. In McGowan's case the Directors, if sufficiently provoked, might dismiss him.

In the end, that was very nearly what it came to. McGowan treated the Directors almost with open contempt, and they became increasingly resentful. Finally, while he was in the USA in the Autumn of 1937, they gathered courage to revolt, being emboldened by the discovery of some very unwise speculations by McGowan, on his own account, which had turned out badly for him. Like rebellious barons determined to dethrone the King, they had their candidate ready for the succession : Henry Mond, 2nd Lord Melchett. McGowan seemed to be beaten. The leader of the revolt spoke of 'the irrevocable conclusion' that he should go. Then on Christmas Day 1937 Lord Melchett, still under 40, had a heart attack. He survived, but in no condition to step straight into the Chair. The Board at once went into reverse. No more was heard of the 'irrevocable conclusion'. McGowan, on leave of absence while they wondered what to do, remarked to his dentist 'They can't do without me!' and stood his ground. No one on the Board, evidently, was bold enough to demand his resignation. The most they could nerve themselves to do was to get him to sign a new agreement, giving up the post of Managing Director, which was abolished.

McGowan remained Chairman of ICI for another twelve years and lived for another eleven after that, dying in 1961 just after his 87th birthday. The leader of the revolt took to drink, retired from executive duties, made no mention of ICI in his entry in *Who's Who*, and died in 1941, aged 64. McGowan worked his way back to a position of great power, and to the end few, if any, on the Board would stand up to him. When they finally decided that he really must go, they announced their decision to him – he was abroad again – by letter, not by word of mouth. Since McGowan's time as sole Managing Director, ICI has never again had an individual Chief Executive. They tell me it is pure coincidence.

IV

One could pursue this exploration of the effect of personality on the firm much further. Without going beyond the field of my own work, the names of William Weir, 1st Viscount Weir of Eastwood (1877–1959) and of Sir Robert Barlow (b. 1891) come readily to mind. Weir, at the head of a family business – G. & J. Weir Limited – had a ready vehicle for personal enthusiasms. The firm's main business was in pumps and associated auxiliary machinery for steamships, but at one time or another Weir carried it into racing cars (disastrous); steam buses in London (almost equally so); pre-fabricated housing (as a tactical move in a campaign against the craft unions); and into rotating-wing aircraft.[23] Barlow, also operating from a base in a prosperous family firm, was virtually the founder of what is to-day the largest firm, outside the USA, in the world packaging industry: Metal Box Limited. By shrewd and ruthless commercial warfare in 1929–30 he defeated an attempted invasion of the British market by one large American can-maker and then, by skilful diplomacy, he made an agreement with another – Continental Can – which made American can-making technology available to Metal Box so that they could take the lead in creating a canning industry in Great Britain, to say nothing of the canning industries in various British territories overseas and, somewhat later, in Continental Europe. At the same time he transformed a loose association of family firms, each jealous of its independence, into a centrally directed business under a strong Head Office. At that

Head Office, for the better part of thirty years, supreme power lay with Robert Barlow.[24]

V

What can one make of these tales of true grit and high endeavour : these Smilesian success stories in an unfashionable mode – the mode of private capitalism? Have they any general significance or are they simply anecdotes : material for what one reviewer of my history of ICI has called 'a rattling good yarn'?[25] Are 'rattling good yarns' the stuff that serious history is made of? Naturally I think they are, or can be, and for more than one reason. First, the study of human behaviour in any field of activity, and business is by no means a small or unimportant field, has its own intrinsic interest and importance, otherwise novelists, dramatists and biographers, to say nothing of historians, would be out of business. This point, however, is not closely germane to the issues under discussion at this Conference, and having made it I will not labour it.

Moving closer home, let me point out that the businesses which at present represent the businesses on which Leverhulme, Melchett, Mc-Gowan and the others left their mark are none of them small or inconsiderable. Two – Unilever and ICI – are among the largest businesses of any kind in the world and another, Metal Box, is a world leader in its own field : perhaps the same is also true of the Weir Group in some branches of engineering, and in Great Britain it is certainly one of the largest engineering enterprises. Therefore if any of these men can be said to have influenced any of these firms, or their predecessors, strongly, they may be said to have had considerable influence not on the firm alone but on the general field of its activity. They will have affected technology, employment and investment not only on the scale of a single firm, but on the scale of a whole industry or group of industries, nationally and, in some cases, internationally.

If William Lever had never lived, it is conceivable that there would have been a merger between the main European users of oils and fats in order to avoid competion for supplies. The result, however, would not have been much like Unilever, because it is scarcely credible that the leading British soap firm, whichever it might have been, would have come into the merger with the astounding collection of African trading companies and tropical plantations put together by Lord Leverhulme. It would have been even less likely to have acquired on the side, as it were, the gallimaufry of food interests which Leverhulme passed on to Lever Brothers when he had no further use for them himself. In other words, I am not saying that the conditions which brought about the Unilever merger would not have existed if Leverhulme had never lived, nor that some merger of roughly that type would not have come about. What I am saying is that Unilever as we know it would have been impossible and that, as a consequence, the general structure of African trading, tropical agriculture, and various food interests in Great Britain and elsewhere would have been very different. That is a considerable claim, I think, to make for one man's work.

If we pass to ICI, the claims I make for the first Lord Melchett and for McGowan are rather different, and perhaps in a way even more sweeping. The field of their activities was the British chemical industry, which in the early 1920s was in an unstable condition. To survive on any considerable scale – and survival could by no means be taken for granted – some kind of ambitious merger was generally recognised to be necessary. What form it would take was in doubt until the last moment. Mond had plans for an international link-up with German and American interests. In fact, for reasons beyond the control of either of them, it was not Mond's idea but McGowan's which prevailed, producing the purely British ICI.

To the development of ICI, once it was in existence, Mond applied himself as vigorously as McGowan. Between them they undertook one of the most difficult tasks in business: the creation of a durable and successful merger company. Their first major investment decision went disastrously wrong, but in spite of the failure of their strategy, their structure survived, and with it the British chemical industry. If Melchett and McGowan are to be held jointly responsible, as undoubtedly they may be, for the initial gigantic blunder, may they not also be allowed countervailing credit for the ultimate success, in the long run even more gigantic? Success, that is, in laying a foundation strong enough for their successors to build up and retain in British hands a considerable portion of the world's chemical industry, one of the key industries of the world of the present day.

Lord Weir's mark on the Weir Group and on the British economy is less distinct, probably because for a quarter of a century he was chiefly occupied with public affairs, where his main work was done. Of Sir Robert Barlow, however, it may be said that he kept can-making in Britain out of American hands while at the same time gaining access to American can-making technology, and the result of this double success may be seen in Metal Box today. It is impossible to be sure that no one else could have brought off this double, but the fact remains that Barlow was the man who did. His achievement was neither so sublimely idiosyncratic as Leverhulme's nor on so large a scale as Melchett's and McGowan's. Nevertheless it is once again possible to attribute the building up of an important industry of the present day to the force and foresight of an identifiable individual, and both the strategy and the structure of the company through which he worked

were highly personal creations, as I hope the forthcoming history of
Metal Box will demonstrate.

I have perhaps said enough for the present occasion. My theme,
like others in business history, is not one on which much generalisa-
tion has been attempted, though perhaps I have indicated the direction
in which it might go. It seems to me that material is mounting up.
Every company history that is published tells us something about the
kind of people who have made business what it is. Perhaps some one
will be bold enough to cast a net into this rising tide of knowledge
and see what marine monsters (or minnows) he can haul out of it.

NOTES

1   A. D. Chandler and Stephen Salsbury, *Pierre S. du Pont and the Making of the Modern Corporation* (New York: Harper & Row, 1971).
2   Charles Wilson, *The History of Unilever* (London: Macmillan, 1954) I, ch. 3. For the biography of W. H. Lever, see 2nd Viscount Leverhulme, *Viscount Leverhulme* (London, 1927); Harley Williams, *Men of Stress* (London, 1950); *Dictionary of National Biography*, Twentieth Century, 1922–1930 (London, 1937).
3   Wilson I, 22.
4   Private information.
5   Wilson I, 187.
6   Charles Booth, *Life and Labour in London*, 2nd Series, *Industry* v (London, 1903) 329–31.
7   Wilson I, 176.
8   Nigel Nicolson, *Lord of the Isles* (London, 1960).
9   L. F. Haber, *The Chemical Industry 1900–1930* (Oxford, 1971), 284.
10 W. J. Reader, *Imperial Chemical Industries, a History* (London, 1970) I ch. 19.
11 Hector Bolitho, *Alfred Mond, 1st Lord Melchett* (London, 1933).
12 W. J. Reader, *Imperial Chemical Industries, a History* (London, 1975) II, 25.
13 Sir Alfred Mond, *Industry and Politics* (London, 1927) 9, quoted in *DNB* art. 'Mond, Alfred Moritz'.
14 Letter to the shareholders of the four merger companies, quoted in *ICI* I, 464.
15 *ICI*, II, 26.
16 *ICI*, I, chs 5, 7, 9 and generally.
17 Chandler and Salsbury, 569 and generally.
18 *ICI*, I, 384–8.
19 Chandler and Salsbury, 476–80; *ICI*, I, 385–6.
20 *ICI*, II, 28.
21 *ICI*, II, 29–30.
22 *ICI*, II, 141.
23 W. J. Reader, *The Weir Group* (Weidenfeld & Nicolson, 1971), chs 3, 6, 7. See also W. J. Reader, *Architect of Air Power* (Collins, 1968) ch. 6, I and II.
24 W. J. Reader, *Metal Box: a History* (Heinemann, 1976).
25 James Poole in *The Sunday Times*, 17 August 1975.

7 The Early Management Organisation of British Petroleum and Sir John Cadman

R. W. FERRIER

I

Most organisations bear the stigmata of their origins on the conduct of their affairs and BP is no exception to this general rule. The early operations of exploration, production and transportation took place in remote Persia thousands of miles away from the supervising office in London when communications were still rudimentary, so reliance was placed on the initiative and ability of local management in an unfamiliar, if not hostile, environment, to take decisions and establish good local relations without which no progress was possible. The lack of facilities and amenities in the area necessitated the importation of everything required for mechanical effort and human comfort. In an area which was essentially a nomadic society with few settled communities, a large industrial enterprise was introduced requiring regularity of employment and engineering skills. Persia was then in a period of political instability. Such was the nature of some of the early problems encountered in South West Persia where the early concessionary work was undertaken. These problems of communications, co-ordination of effort, local collaboration, importation of supplies, different living standards, employment opportunities and education and government relations recurred frequently.

In London too there were important considerations. William Knox D'Arcy, to whose attention the possibility of acquiring an oil concession in Persia had been drawn, was a solicitor who had emigrated to Australia where he had the opportunity to make a large fortune out of the Mount Morgan gold mine in Queensland when others had despaired of success. More responsible than a speculator, less suited to be an entrepreneur, D'Arcy was granted his concession on 28 May 1901 in

Teheran and set about transforming it into a commercial enterprise, with little comparable experience to guide him. A lesser man would have lacked the determination and persistence without which D'Arcy could hardly have coped with the wide range of difficulties and disappointments he encountered, raised the finance required and sustained the interests of those involved. He was well served by his chief adviser, Sir Boverton Redwood, the only notable figure on the English oil scene who was technically competent and had a wide circle of serviceable acquaintances trained in geology, engineering and refining. He trusted his engineer in Persia, George B. Reynolds, a brusque practical character of great endurance and courage who displayed a real talent for adaptation and improvisation provided he was left to get on with the job, but who was scornful of office 'wallahs'. The brunt of the enterprise in Persia fell upon Reynolds, and the discovery of oil on 28 May 1908 was primarily due to his fortitude and technical competence.

The more routine business matters were initially taken care of by Mr Jenkin, of the Mount Morgan Gold Mining Company London office, his assistant, Mr E. H. Nichols, and Mr G. W. Marriot, secretary and adviser to Mr D'Arcy. The major responsibility was, however, Mr D'Arcy's, and already in August 1901 he felt the burden onerous for he wrote, 'I find the work of such dimensions that it has already surpassed or, in any case, will surpass before long, my isolated powers'.[1] He hoped that a syndicate could be formed to relieve him. Not until his financial affairs had seriously deteriorated and the concession was endangered did the Admiralty, whom D'Arcy approached, become interested in its survival under British auspices and proposed that the Burmah Oil Company should take an interest, and only then did D'Arcy receive any real assistance. Negotiations between D'Arcy and Mr John T. Cargill and Mr C. Wallace of the Burmah Oil Company began on 10 August 1904, and on 5 May 1905, the Concessions Syndicate, which was henceforth to manage and finance the concessionary efforts to discover oil and arrange for a company to be formed to exploit it, was officially incorporated.

In Persia, in addition to drilling difficulties, other problems of a more administrative nature were emerging with some urgency. Reynolds, who had had a very close working relationship with Mr D'Arcy, never felt quite at such ease with the Concessions Syndicate. He warned of the importance of the need for the closest understanding between the home office and the operations in Persia 'and with no reservation, freely exchange any information obtained. It is only by an absolute confidence existing between these two offices . . . . that a united front can be presented to those who wish to exploit the Company'. Reynolds was a realistic, perceptive man but impatient of people who ran round after him instead of letting him get on with the job and when, after the formation of APOC on 14 April 1909, he found that his title of Fields General Manager did not bring immunity from what he considered interference, he reacted understandably but unreasonably in neglecting instructions and following his own councils. His agreement was eventually terminated by 'mutual consent'.

This incident posed at an early stage in the Company's history the dilemma of a technical or administrative approach to management. In contemplating a successor to Mr Reynolds, Mr Charles Greenway (who had virtually assumed the management of the Company, after being principally responsible for the work involved in its formation) commented in 1910 that, 'it has been suggested that the next head of the Field shall not be a *technical* man such as Reynolds but a good office man, who would have under him all the necessary technical men'. He criticised Reynolds for lacking 'the administrative ability necessary for successful management'. The problem is still with us. What constitutes successful management? What are the qualities which need to be exhibited? What training best stimulates managerial ability? How is successful management exercised? How is technical ability to be combined with administrative capacity in a manager? The performance of G. B. Reynolds is an early test case of the interface between managerial authority and the executive function. It also raised the basic question in the first year of the Company's existence of how the Board in London was to exercise and maintain effective control over the activities carried on in Persia.

II

Once oil had been discovered in commercial quantities at Masjid-i-Sulaiman, just in time, because patience and finance were beginning to fail, it became necessary to transform the somewhat *ad hoc* Concessions Syndicate into a properly constituted company. Fathered by William Knox D'Arcy and conceived by the Burmah Oil Company, the Anglo Persian Oil Company was born on 14 April 1909, and inheriting traits from both parents resembled most closely its Scottish parent until its teens. Mr Wallace, a director of Burmah, was the guiding hand, Vice-Chairman as well as Managing Director, in the first instance, ably assisted by Mr Greenway who did most of the routine business. Both had been prominent in Indian commercial circles through their association as senior partners in the important managing agents' firm of Shaw Wallace and Co., which, inter alia, was the Indian distributor of the products of the Burmah Oil Company. They were merchants not technicians. Whilst the general affairs of the company were run from the London office, a branch was opened on the premises of the Burmah Oil Company in Glasgow principally for dealing with engineering matters. Indeed Burmah dealt with all such matters and their staff provided most of the early management and advice over the refinery; and through their contacts with G. and J. Weir and Co. they handled most of the first pipeline construction.

On the crucial question of managing the Company's affairs in Persia, it was decided at first to follow the traditional trading arrangements by appointing managing agents. Strick, Scott and Co. remained as management agents till APOC assumed direct responsibility in 1922.

It is not necessary within the context of this paper to describe the circumstances in which the British Government took a majority shareholding in the Company or the Admiralty made a fuel oil contract with it. It continued to be true for many years that the Company was primarily a producer, dealing with bulk outlets of one kind or another in a relatively narrow range of products. Until the post Second War period it never developed, or at least never gave full play to, an aggressive marketing strategy on the forecourt or elsewhere. Initially it relied on the Admiralty contract, on a ten year agreement with the Asiatic Petroleum Company, a subsidiary of Royal Dutch-Shell, for offtakes of benzine, kerosene and some fuel oil from the refinery which had been constructed at Abadan between 1910 and 1913, and on local outlets. It is also to be remembered that the Burmah Oil Company had its own commercial interests in the area which they were not anxious to see affected by more competition. They recognised and openly admitted that, 'it was primarily the protection of its Indian investments that took the Burmah Oil Co. Ltd into Peria'. The shareholding of the British Government guaranteed at the time the continuing existence of the Company, but not necessarily its success, prevented its merging with or absorption by a larger competitor possessing more extensive marketing outlets and contributed indirectly to the early predominant role of the Company as a producer rather than a marketer.

Admiral Slade and Viscount Inchcape were the first Government directors in 1914. In July 1914, Mr Greenway, who had conducted the negotiations with the Treasury and Admiralty, was chosen as Chairman to succeed Lord Strathcona, the first Chairman, who had died at an advanced age the previous January. The day to day business of the Company was entrusted to Mr Duncan Garrow, who had previously served with the Burmah Oil Company in the Far East and who became a Director of APOC in November 1914 and Mr E. H. Nichols who had been very closely associated with Mr D'Arcy for many years and who became a Director in May 1915.

In Persia during the war the management structure hardly changed. The production and refining of oil continued at an increasing tempo,

80,900 tons were produced in 1913 and in 1918 the figure was 897,402 tons, a tenfold increase. In London, however, in spite of the war, there were considerable developments taking place. Admiral Slade, partly reflecting his responsibilities as a Government director, and partly expressing his own convictions, in October 1914 suggested a refinery in the United Kingdom, out of which evolved the National Oil Refineries Ltd, as a subsidiary of APOC in March 1917, and the eventual construction of the Llandarcy Refinery, which was inaugurated in 1924. The difficulties over meeting the Admiralty specifications for fuel oil led to *ad hoc* testing and investigations with the co-operation of Sir Boverton Redwood, Dr A. E. Dunstan and Dr J. B. Thole. It was finally agreed, probably on Admiral Slade's initiative, that these temporary arrangements be placed on a permanent basis. So in 1916 a research station was opened at Sunbury with Dr Dunstan as Chief Chemist and Dr Thole, his assistant.

On 30 April 1915, APOC registered a new subsidiary, the British Tanker Company, to own and operate its tankers. Mr Greenway justified the acquisition of a fleet instead of using the open market by the dangers of relying 'upon the chances of securing freight at reasonable rates in a market so restricted as that for Oil Tankers'. 'Even before the war', he argued, 'with our then comparatively small requirements of tonnage, the cost of our transport was fully 50 per cent more than it would have been had we been running boats of our own.' There was still one glaring defect in the policy and structure of the Company for its own self-sufficiency, or, in later terminology, for complete vertical integration, namely the possession of its own distributing organisation. It was foreseen that in the post-war world the lack of marketing facilities, techniques and staff would be a severe handicap in competing with the other large oil companies such as Standard Oil of New Jersey or Royal Dutch-Shell. In May 1915, Mr Greenway entered into preliminary discussions with certain Belgian interests concerned in the British Petroleum Company, which had been registered in November 1906 in London as a subsidiary of the Europaische Petroleum Union GmbH, with a majority German shareholding. It had been taken over by the Public Trustee as an enemy concern. Associated with the British Petroleum Company and in the same predicament was the Homelight Oil Company and the Petroleum Steamship Company Ltd. After long negotiations the APOC eventually purchased all three companies from the Public Trustee on 13 June 1917. It was an important addition to the Company's assets for the two distributing companies had over 850 depots and employed nearly 3000 staff between them, whilst the tanker company owned eleven tankers and had interests in others.

As if to reflect the growing diversity of interests it was decided in

December 1916 to transfer to the London office all the business that was being handled by the Glasgow office, thus consolidating all the Company affairs in one office. Another result of the widening range of interests was the appointment to the Board at the beginning of 1917 of Mr Frank C. Tiarks, a Director of the Bank of England and a partner in the firm of J. Henry Schroeder and Company, and Mr F. William Lund who possessed an extensive knowledge of shipping. Partly as a result of the expansion of the Company's business and partly as a result of personality differences, there emerged a challenge to Mr Greenway in November 1916 from Admiral Slade, who proposed that Mr Greenway should resign as Chairman and Managing Director, to be succeeded by himself. Mr Greenway, whatever he thought of the merits of the proposal, took no action. Lord Inchcape, the other Government director, was not impressed and suggested that, 'it would not be to the interest of the Company that Mr Greenway should at the present stage withdraw from active association with the administration of the Company', and that they should wait for two years before taking any further steps in the matter. It was decided just over a year later on 24 January 1918, that 'Mr Greenway shall continue to hold the position of Chairman for an indefinite period, and to fulfil the duties of Managing Director until such time as satisfactory arrangements can be made for relieving him of those duties and that Admiral Sir E. J. W. Slade shall henceforth hold the position of Vice Chairman only, without being responsible for, or taking any active part in the administrative work of the Company'. The Company had survived its first Boardroom clash, but although a Field Marshal and an Air Marshal have been appointed to the Board, there have been no more Admirals!

APOC at the end of 1918 hardly resembled the Company it was at the beginning of 1914. It had paid its first dividend in December 1917 and raised its capital again in the same month by £1,125,000 in 1,000,000 Preference shares at a premium of 2s 6d per share, to £5,000,000. It had become a fully integrated oil company, but it was still very much a one man band, for it was Charles Greenway who called the tune and played most of the instruments. The Company had begun as a simple organisation to develop the large potential oil production it had acquired in its concessionary area. Certainly with a purpose, hardly yet a strategy, it had expanded the size of its operations and the number of its employees and formed some wholly owned subsidiary companies. There was no sign of much recognisable structure, but then the war had speeded material development but impeded adequate measures to administer it. This was a vital issue in the next decade.

III

Mr Greenway recognised the need for certain changes in the administration of the Company's affairs and in January 1919 decided that effective control could best be secured by a co-ordinated division of responsibility, by his resignation as Managing Director in order to concentrate on his position as Chairman and by the formation of a Managing Committee consisting of Managing Directors meeting frequently to co–ordinate policy and administration. He proposed five managing directors, Mr Garrow for the Oil Fields, Refinery and Pipeline, Mr Nichols for commercial and engineering matters and three new ones, including Mr J. D. Stewart, a partner in the Glasgow shipping business of Messrs Gardiner and Co. in charge of shipping, and Mr J. B. Lloyd, then the Senior Partner in India of Shaw Wallace and Co., who had been one of those instrumental in setting up Lloyd Scott and Co., to be responsible for finance, accounts and company work. A fifth director was in the event not appointed, and his responsibilities, mostly political in kind, were re-allocated. These proposals took effect from September 1919 but Sir Charles Greenway – as he had by then become – agreed to take part in the meetings of the Managing Committee at their request 'particularly in regard to new undertakings and general questions of finance and policy'. Colonel Wallace was sent as the first Company Representative to Tehran and Mr Garrow was to visit South Persia to inspect the operations there, to be followed by Mr Nichols the following year, the first visit by a director since 1910.

A beginning had been made, but it was only a tentative one, a picking up of the loose ends after the war had finished, an initial reassessment on which future policy would have to be based. Already in 1919, the Company was embarking on a world-wide network of bunkering installations to anticipate a fall off in Admiralty demands for fuel oil and to take advantage of the increasing use of oil in merchant ships. In the same year it had acquired its first continental distributing interest in the Belgian company L'Alliance. With its own growing secure supplies of crude oil it was approached by other European groups in Sweden, Norway, Denmark and France to supply them in return for shareholdings in the companies which were to be formed. In such cases in general the policy was to obtain representation on the Boards of the companies, put in a Company administrator and leave the day to day routine in the hands of the various local managements. Not always completely satisfactory, it was the only alternative until such time that a proper co-ordinated approach was made towards an overall policy. Occasionally, as in Australia, on the formation of the Commonwealth Oil Refinery with the participation of the Commonwealth Government, an APOC member was appointed Managing

Director to set up the organisation, but local interests were always well represented on the Boards. At this time the object of its policy was the acquisition of marketing outlets to ward off competition and provide increasing outlets for the crude oil production, rather than for their profitability.

Another look at the organisation of APOC was taken at a special meeting held in Glasgow in July 1921 of Sir Charles Greenway, Sir John T. Cargill and Mr R. I. Watson, a director of the Burmah Oil Company who had become a Director of APOC in 1918. It was agreed that provisions for the future should be made and that Mr J. D. Stewart should deputise for Sir Charles and, subject to certain provisions, be 'the final arbiter . . . on all questions, Departmental or otherwise, requiring decision'. Furthermore, Mr Stewart, after full consultations with those concerned should 'immediately set about the reorganisation and defining of the duties and responsibilities and spheres – departmentally – of each of the Managing Directors . . . in such a way as will make the best use of the experience, etc. of each and will secure that each undertaking of the Company is definitely and clearly put under the charge of a Managing Director'. So while it was expected that each Managing Director should efficiently and completely run the Departments entrusted to him 'on his own', in addition an *ad hoc* Committee was to be formed of the Chairman, Messrs Stewart, Lloyd and Nichols, acting on a unanimity principle to take 'decisions involving new, serious commitments by the Company or heavy capital or other expenditure', subject to certain safeguards. The whole object in short was 'to secure better organisation, greater control and the clearer definition of Departmental spheres besides giving effect – or at least assisting in that direction – to the greater relief of Sir Charles from the day to day management and control of the Company'. Meetings of Managing Directors were to continue with other co-opted members in attendance from time to time as it was intended that 'these should form the medium of keeping all *au courant* with every aspect of the Company's operations', and a Managing Director was to visit Persia each year.

This showed a clearer appreciation of the need to place the structure of the Company on a departmental basis, with certain groups of departments or subsidiary companies reporting to a single Managing Director who carried his responsibilities to the executive Management Committee meeting weekly for decision-taking, which could also be exercised in certain circumstances by the *ad hoc* Committee, subject to the approval of the Board. Mr Stewart held his consultations, made his recommendations, which were accepted, and it seemed that he would succeed Sir Charles Greenway on his retirement. His position was confirmed in August 1922 when the Board stated that he was 'empowered to give decisions on all matters, subject only to reference to the Chairman of the Company on matters of importance and without such reference in cases of urgency'. The General Committee, now termed the Managing Committee 'for convenience and co-ordination of working' and composed of nine members under the chairmanship of Mr Stewart, met on Wednesdays at 11.30 am.

The objectives of the Glasgow meetings were admirable, but the results were disappointing, Mr Stewart obviously did not have the respect or the confidence of all his colleagues, among whom was now to be numbered Sir John Cadman, who had joined the Company in October 1921 from the government's Petroleum Executive of which he was the Director. On 23 March 1923, at the same time as Mr William Fraser, he was elected a Director of the Company. On the same day Admiral Slade voiced his concern that the non-executive members of the Board were being kept insufficiently informed about the Company and its affairs. This was discussed a month later and a special Committee was appointed to look into the matter 'regarding the operations and financial position of the Company as they may require and to discuss any other questions of management which the executive members of the Board may wish to bring forward'.

The Company must not only be operating, but must be seen to be operating without secrecy and in confidence and the Committee acted on this principle. It admitted the difficulty of laying down a 'hard and fast basis of a practical character', but made certain recommendations mostly concerned to ensure that members of the Board should be kept informed more adequately and regularly about the affairs of the Company.

These recommendations were approved on 29 May 1923, but the impetus for reform was growing as discontent with the existing state of affairs was becoming more apparent and on the same day the Board appointed yet another special Committee, almost ominously 'to consider and determine questions of management (past and prospective) in view of the near expiry of the Managing Directors' agreements'. These had originally been made early in 1919 for a five year period. The post-war period was closing, improvisation was giving way to planning.

IV

Admiral Slade in a long memorandum on the 'Organisation of the APOC' of June 1923, stated that the terms and conditions of Directors could not 'properly be solved until the preliminary question of the principles which should govern the organisation of the Company be decided', which he believed had not changed since the Government became a shareholder. Questioning the value and scope of the measures taken in the previous few years as the Company grew he asserted that 'no review of the organisation has taken place to ascertain whether the principles on which it has been built up are now the best suited to the conditions of the far reaching business which it has to conduct'. He explained that 'the APOC has not followed any one system in the development of its business, but works a portion through Departments of the Parent Company, and a portion through subsidiary Companies', which produced a lack of co-ordination and control. Therefore 'we should then have one system running through the whole organisation and a more efficient financial and technical control could be constituted'. He advocated a kind of holding company system with APOC as the holding company controlling subsidiaries such as the Producing Company, the Transport Company, the Refining Company, the Distributing Company, etc. The Board would have control of the finance and general policy of the whole Group. Admiral Slade proposed an early form of budgetary control to ascertain revenue and expenditure laid down by a Finance Committee entirely independent of Departmental managers, which could only be overruled by the Board as a whole.

In contrast to such opinions were the conservative views of Mr Stewart. In a short statement on Management to the Special Committee on 7 July 1923, he suggested 'the appointment of a single Managing Director, with power to make decisions, the other heads of departments being given the title of "Managers" and to be responsible to the Managing Director, but stated that he would have no objection to the present Managing Directors retaining their title for the time being, but that he was of the opinion that no Administrative officer of the Company should be on the Board'. After such an uncompromising stance little doubt remained why it was necessary once again to reopen the question of management or why Mr Stewart had some difficulty in retaining the esteem of his colleagues.

Much more significant was the contribution of Sir John Cadman to the same Committee two weeks later, when he gave his comments on the management of the Company. Since much of the drive and inspiration of the Company for the next thirty years came from Sir John Cadman and Mr William Fraser, Sir John's comments carry particular weight. He professed that :

as a new-comer he gathered that some change was necessary in the management of the business with a view to obtaining more harmonious working among those in control of the Management. At the present time there is not sufficient collaboration. Each department seemed to be working separately without consultation with the other departments, and working on its own account without any financial control. He stated that as far as he was in a position to judge the rapidity of the growth of the Company was such that it had been impossible in the time to complete an adequate and well balanced organisation, which would have been easily done had the Company developed along normal lines and, in more normal times; considering that the greatest relative expansion had occurred in the war period, when, owing to shortage of staff it was not practicable to delegate work as it otherwise would have been. The consequence was that the Chairman had necessarily taken a more energetic part in the management of the Company than apparently he had intended to do when he constructed the executive machine with the appropriate heads of departments.

So he was of the opinion :

(a) That the Company should, as far as possible, work to a settled annual programme which should be linked up with a budget of estimated expenditure.

(b) That the general direction should be exercised through several executive heads, each having full administrative powers within the limits of the programme of work and expenditure thereon allotted to his department.

(c) That these executive heads should be charged with the preparation of the annual programme and budget and with periodical reports to the Board of progress of work and state of expenditure against annual estimates. That the Board, in turn, should construct a special finance committee for the consideration of these matters.

(d) That the senior executive head should have powers to see that the programme approved by the Board is adhered to, with distinct responsibility to watch the financial side and to ensure that there is due co-ordination.

(e) That the senior executive head should decide whether any departure from the approved annual programme which may be recommended from time to time by one or more executive heads shall be dealt with off hand, or kept for general Board decision.

(f) That a detailed scheme following the above general principles should be prepared and submitted to the Board.

The result of these deliberations was a further set of recommendations to the Board for the future management of the Company sent on 28 June 1923, which represented a change from the existing procedures including the formation of a Finance Committee which was to meet weekly or more frequently if necessary. Otherwise, it was agreed that 'the management shall be vested in a "Management Committee" working departmentally', with much greater collaboration and the exchange of information.

It was also agreed, probably to satisfy Mr Stewart, that the title 'Managing Director' be dropped in favour of Director, but if that was so Mr Stewart was not appeased. He refused to take the chair or help in the meetings convened by Sir John Cadman, as Secretary of the Committee, to implement the recommendations submitted to the Board and claimed he would table a separate report himself, which he never did. The report of the Committee with the allocation of responsibilities among seven members was presented to the Board and accepted. The main provisions included the following points :

(1) Whilst each Head of Department will be entirely responsible for the working of his Department, within any limitations that may be laid down by the Board, all matters of importance . . . shall be referred to a Management Committee, in whom the management of the Company subject to the Board, shall be solely vested.

(2) The Chairman shall generally direct and co-ordinate the work of the Departments, and he shall see that any matter brought up by any Head of Department for consideration of the Committee is promptly dealt with and a decision arrived at, and that such decision is given effect to. The Chairman shall be available for consultative purposes by any Head of Department without in any way relieving the Head of Department from responsibility.

Procedures and the general character of questions to be handled by the Committee were agreed. Perhaps the most important single item was the establishment of the Finance Committee which came to fulfil an important role in the strategy and structure of the Company. Sir John Cadman already was putting in to practice a simple cost analysis control, but this would have remained either an isolated departmental experiment or ineffectual on a Company basis without the resources and co-operation of the Finance Committee. The first comprehensive budget of the APOC was in respect of the financial year 1 April 1925/31 March 1926, and it followed the system initiated by Sir John Cadman for the previous year for his own Fields, Refineries and Geological Department. It also had the undoubted effect of reinforcing a conservative tendency towards expenditure which had been in evidence already in the Burmah Oil Company and became an aspect of the Company's character. Value for money was the principle and there were few entreprenuerial gambles associated with APOC.

It was not, however, till the end of 1923 that a final list of departmental allocations was approved by the Board. This pattern of management lasted for some eighteen months until the resignation of Mr Stewart on 26 September 1925, on the apparent grounds of ill health. The opportunity was then taken to clarify the position of Sir Charles Greenway and nominate his successor, Sir John Cadman, who was appointed Deputy Chairman, a highly important decision ending much uncertainty. As one looks back at all the discussions over management in the postwar period there is a feeling of drift, of the lack of a steady firm hand on the tiller, with the crew raising and lowering the sails according to their own impressions of the direction in which they were heading.

V

Mr Nichols commented very pertinently in a report on Abadan written after his visit in 1921 that, 'I would again urge that we cry a halt in the direction of further increasing the throughput, and that we give the staff time to consolidate what we have got. Looked at in another way, I think we have enough eggs in one basket. We have always had to aim at the maximum throughput : let us now organise and organise and, whilst still maintaining that throughput, aim at economy of running and so on, as the time will come when the cost of refining per gallon is a far more important matter than it is at present'. What was true at Abadan was equally true elsewhere in Persia : expansion had outrun organisation, the operation had become unbalanced, un-co-ordinated. It was perhaps the greatest single achievement of Sir John Cadman's first years in the Company that he gave to organisation in Persia a clear direction, that he understood the nature of the technical problems that had to be solved and that he imparted to the staff an enthusiasm and interest in their work which eventually resulted in outstanding production techniques, notable geological advances and significant refinery processes. His primary objective was 'to secure a unified technical policy by means of the closest co-operation between the various services concerned'. He also recognised 'the need for much closer general contact between Persia and London than has taken place in the past, since I am very definitely convinced that this is a first condition of sound administration'. He himself visited Persia in 1924 and 1926 and had extensive consultations on all aspects of the operations.

Sir John Cadman engaged in a massive educational and organisational task to interrelate the various stages of the Persian operation into one efficiently functioning unit on a sound profit-earning basis which was administratively cohesive. The management, he was convinced, had suffered from ill-defined responsibilities which militated against practical control of the Company's affairs, policy arose from opportunism and expediency rather than intention. He therefore proposed a single Chief Administrator with proper line management reporting to him with clearly defined responsibilities. He maintained and insisted that such a large undertaking could only be efficiently managed if there was a system of proposed annual expenditure to which estimates the operations had to be geared, for only such a system ensured the full application of business principles to purely technical control. Properly approved and widely accepted standards of prudent business management had to apply to all phases of the Company's operations, whether in Persia or Head Office, so that there was a unifying and reinforcing application of the same principles throughout the Company. It was, therefore, extremely important that the Board itself gave the lead in effective staff collaboration which would permeate throughout the Company.

The spirit and the letter of the recommendations made by Sir John Cadman were accepted by the Board and implemented with the full co-operation of the management in Persia, notably of Mr Jacks on the administrative level, who became the Resident Director there, and of Mr Jameson the General Manager, with three assistant general managers who looked after the technical side. The geological services were reorganised with the active assistance of the eminent Hungarian Professor Hugo de Boeckh as consultant. The foundations so laid were the basis for all subsequent Company developments in Persia. Sir John's visits marked a turning point in the Company's affairs, for technical excellence allied to administrative efficiency and financial control became a matter of primary concern. His enduring legacy to the Company was the high standard of its technical services, exemplified, for instance, in its notable exploratory, and production success.

VI

Sir John Cadman let no time elapse from his appointment as Deputy Chairman to addressing himself to the principles which were to guide the Management Committee following the retirement of Mr Stewart, as was agreed by the Board in November 1925. One of the notable features of this management reorganisation was the small number of directorates that Cadman considered appropriate for running the affairs of the Company and which has remained a conspicuous feature of the Company ever since. The principle was established that the Managing Directors were full-time appointments working very closely together with no outside directorships and owing their appointments to promotion from within the Company. On broad lines it was laid down that the executive control of the Company's operations fell into four main categories :

(*a*) Production and Refining
(*b*) Distribution and Marketing
(*c*) Finance
(*d*) General services, i.e., duties not specifically included in the foregoing although, in most cases, affecting them all.

The duties and principles of each were defined and the Managing Directors allocated as follows : Sir John Cadman (*a*), Mr Heath Eves (*b*), Mr J. B. Lloyd (*c*) and Mr. Nichols (*d*). It was accepted that each Director would appoint a deputy, who would be competent to assume complete charge in his absence. The Management Committee was to comprise the Directors above-mentioned and Mr Fraser, and its con-stitution and *modus operandi* were generally similar to what had already been agreed. The Finance Committee was strengthened by the inclusion of the Chairman, Government Directors and other non-execu-tive Directors and was to review :

(*a*) Annual Budgets
(*b*) Periodical records of expenditure and revenue
(*c*) Statements of financial position and financial proposals
(*d*) Propositions involving expenditure not provided for in the annual budget.

Part of its function was the encouragement of the supply of financial information which was utilised in decision-taking, an early form of management information reporting.

A very clear set of principles was formulated for staff and purchas-ing matters in order to maintain uniformity of treatment. This repre-sented an early attempt to view the personnel function on its own merits for it was 'essential to ensure, throughout the Company's service, a general uniformity of practice in Staff matters and a central re-sponsibility for staff records and the determination of grades and rates of salary. It is equally necessary to ensure that entries, promo-tions, dismissals, etc., and the Staff establishments are in general con-formity with the actual needs of the various directorates, whilst not exceeding what is strictly necessary for the proper conduct of the Company's business.' Today in an age of industrial consultants such a quotation seems a repetition of the obvious, but fifty years ago such an approach to human relations, whatever its shortcomings in practice, was exceptional.

The effect of these November 1925 proposals was to place the direc-torial organisation of the Company upon a more clearly defined departmental basis designed to bring about a recognised and recognisable allocation of duties and to afford full opportunity for control by, and collaboration among, the Heads of Departments. In a Memorandum which accompanied his new organisational responsibilities and principles to cope with the challenge of the increasing complexity of the Company's business, he defined his objectives and methods. 'What is now required', he wrote, 'is to determine, for each successively important stage in the control of the Company's affairs, how that control can in future be most effectively exercised and co-ordinated, where co-ordination is needed, up to the final stage where actual Board Control is involved. The unit for the purpose of this note is the executive Branch (or Department) – the personnel of which may be large or small – each under the direction of a Manager or other experienced and responsible employee of the Company.'

These various units including different but related phases of the Company's operations were grouped together into Directorates under a member of the Board, who had to ensure cohesion among the departments for which he was responsible, and co-ordination with his fellow managing directors. Previously the various activities were scattered in different offices in the City but with the building of the first Britannic House these were now centrally housed, greatly facilitating contact between them. Inter-departmental matters requiring collective consideration were expected to be dealt with on an *ad hoc* basis at which it was not normally necessary for managing directors to be in attendance but who could be furnished with reports on which to give their decisions. By such devolution of responsibility it was hoped that 'subordinate collaboration' was properly directed, economically dispatched and, 'did not degenerate into sterile debate or the convenient shelving of executive responsibility'. The Directors were supposed to direct not manage, a recurring executive dilemma. In short, Sir John Cadman recognised very perceptively 'the necessity, imposed on the Company by the constant expansion of its activities, of periodically overhauling its systems of management in order to keep its perspectives up to date and to maintain a timely adjustment of means to ends. Otherwise – figuratively speaking – the progressive organisation of today may be in danger of becoming stationary tomorrow, and retrograde thereafter'. Here at least can be noticed a recognition of the interdependence of strategy and structure, whether appreciated in these terms or not. There was not then, nor indeed for many years, if ever, an absolute distinction between executive and functional authority, but there was a clear appreciation of the problem and as a result there was a noticeable improvement in the cohesion of the Management Committee and the efficiency of its work. In time there was a withering away of the formalities and a more instinctive informality governed the relations between the Managing Directors, but after the changes

and uncertainties of the early 1920s it took time for confidence to
return, for the procedures to become so operative as not to be noticeable and for the authority of Sir John Cadman to be unmistakably
accepted. He succeeded Lord Greenway (as he had recently been
created) as Chairman on 27 March 1927.

Although Cadman had already stamped his image upon the Company in the previous three years to a greater extent than his predecessors, he determined that his authority should be unchallenged.
He succeeded in creating the impression and the reality of the chairman's dominance which was amply inherited by his immediate successor, Mr Fraser, who worked so closely with him. A year after
becoming Chairman, Cadman submitted another Memorandum on
Management to the Board on 24 November 1928, for their approval,
summarising much that had already been previously agreed but also,
as he indicated, 'incorporating such suggestions as I feel will best
promote a further advance in efficiency and unity of procedure'. The
main alterations amending the previous Memorandum of 24 November
1925 concerned the role of the Chairman, the enhanced status of the
Finance Director, Mr J. B. Lloyd, and the less functional responsibility
of the Committee of Management. The position of the Chairman was
unequivocal for he 'will exercise general supervision over the entire
executive operations of the Company. The Chairman and the Management Directors will, whenever possible, confer daily. The Chairman
will act as the chief instrument of the Board in ensuring to the
Management Directors the maximum day-to-day authority in their
executive operations as pursued in terms of Board policy.' On the
Chairman and his managing directors depended the success of the
Company, for they constituted its management, though they were
members of the Board and ultimately responsible to it.

As for the Committee of Management, this was an instrument of
the Chairman who laid down its procedures, but it was not intended
to have any executive powers. It was not in fact to act in any way
as a separate power base, nothing was to detract from the authority
of the Chairman. It was laid down that 'The functions of the Committee are deliberative, consultative and advisory, and nothing in its
constitution or proceedings shall impair the direct responsibility of
individual Management Directors to the Board.' It was not overlapping
responsibility but the exercise of individual responsibility in concert
that made for collective responsibility. Once that individual responsibility was recognised and practised the *raison d'être* for a formalised
grouping disappeared. Sir John Cadman reported to this effect to the
Board on 29 May 1929 : 'almost daily touch is now maintained between individual Management Directors; and the benefit of full co-
ordination of view and exchange of opinion – without impairing direct

responsibility to the Board of individual Management Directors – is secured under the authority of the Chairman, or in his absence, his Deputy. In practice, recourse to the more formal machinery of Management Committee Meetings is proving unnecessary.' It was, therefore, agreed that it should be dissolved. The Deputy by then was Mr Fraser. Just over eighteen months later the Chairman informed the Board of 'the admirable manner in which the administration was functioning'. To a very large extent it was this same form of administration which was responsible for the growth of the Company and lasted almost unchanged after Cadman's death in office in 1941, when he was succeeded by Sir William Fraser, till the loss of the Company's concessionary position in Persia in 1951, when there was a reappraisal of the Company's affairs. In administrative no less than in technical terms the Cadman Management legacy was real and enduring.

NOTE

1 All quotations in this chapter are from Company Archives and appear by permission of the British Petroleum Co. Ltd.

Part Three

SECTORAL STUDIES

8 Institutional Response to Economic Growth: Capital Markets in Britain to 1914

WILLIAM P. KENNEDY

If it is alleged that manufacturers and commerce find abundant [resources] for their successful pursuit [of expansion] in the hands of individuals in this country, I will answer – England cannot stand still.

Edwin Moss, 1856

The social object of skilled investment should be to defeat the dark forces of time and ignorance which envelop our future. The actual, private object of the most skilled investment today is 'to beat the gun', as the Americans so well express it, to outwit the crowd, and to pass the bad, or depreciating, half crown to the other fellow.

John Maynard Keynes, 1936

I

It is becoming increasingly clear that the organisational structures of economic institutions evolve in response to the market environment in which the institutions operate. Thus, for example, Alfred Chandler has shown that the adoption by firms of the multi-divisional form of organisation in the US, beginning in the first quarter of the twentieth century, was an explicit response to the problems and opportunities of rapid growth and change in the US economy.[1] It is similarly becoming clear that the relationship over time between the organisational structure of such economic institutions as firms and banks and economic development is not simply one in which the impact of growth and change determines institutional structure but rather it is one in which the suitability of the organisational structure adopted by institutions affects the ability of the economy to achieve and maintain a satisfactory rate of economic growth as well.

This paper focuses on an aspect of the relationship between growth and the organisation and operation of economic institutions. It is concerned with the relationship between British economic development and capital markets in the years from the mid-nineteenth century to 1914. Capital markets are defined very broadly for this purpose. They are seen to be not only such familiar institutions as banks, insurance companies, and stock exchanges but also the facilities for resource allocation provided within firms and among men who are close business associates of one another. This concern with capital markets is premised on the belief that they constitute one of the most important components in the economic environment of a society. The efficiency with which they operate determines the extent of the commitment of an economy's resources to those activities which most increase the welfare of the society. It is highly misleading for historians to assume that capital markets as a whole operate efficiently or that they perform different tasks with equal competence. It is difficult to believe that even an approximation to an efficient capital market has ever existed anywhere. It is therefore a central task of historical research to evaluate the consequences of various types of sub-optimal performance in capital markets. This paper argues that the institutional arrangements in British capital markets before 1914, while offering very good facilities for the trading of first-class securities, provided especially inadequate information on the riskiest investment possibilities and failed to encourage or facilitate efficient diversification of wealth-holders' assets.

II

The sub-optimal operations of British capital markets before 1914 occurred because all investors did not share the same information and all could not acquire the same degree of knowledge with equal ease. Consequently, rates of return, allowing for risk, were not equated at the margin in all alternative uses. This is not surprising, for the developing theory of rational decision making under uncertainty, assuming that risk and return are the relevant considerations, has shown that the necessary information requirements for optimality are quite extensive. It is necessary to have an informed estimate of expected mean rates of return on *all* feasible projects, as well as an estimate of the expected variance of the distribution of possible yields and of the relationship of all the covariances of all projects with each other.[2] A central implication of this analysis is that no investment project can be valued in isolation from all others. This is true in general and not only in the obvious case where the one project is directly dependent on another such as might be the case where the successful sale of electricity depends on the successful manufacture of lights and equipment which use electricity. Even if all projects whose yields are perfectly correlated with one another's are treated as being effectively only one project, the value of relatively uncorrelated projects can only be efficiently determined simultaneously. This is the justification for the central role of diversification in rational allocation.

The ramifications of this argument might be made more clear with a simple example suggested by Mossin[3] showing how a financial system initially in equilibrium would adjust to a disturbance. Suppose that firms specialise in production so that all firms are not identical but are exposed to different circumstances. Consider a firm which faces a borrowing rate of 10 per cent on its outstanding debt in a perfect capital market through which all members of the economy may equally accurately assess the firm's prospects in terms of a distribution of outcomes of the firm's risky activities. Since everyone is assumed to have identical knowledge (but not perfect foresight) and to interpret this knowledge in the same way, everyone agrees on what the distribution of possible outcomes is and what it is worth. Let the riskless rate of time discount be 4 per cent. Suppose that the firm then discovers an investment opportunity unanticipated by the firm's management or anyone else which will yield 8 per cent return with certainty.[4] Mossin shows that the addition of this new opportunity to the firm's activities alters both the feasible borrowing rate and the risk of default. Most importantly, because the project is certain in its yield, inclusion in the firm's activities reduces the overall expected variance of the firm's earnings. Since the value of the firm depends on the yield and variance of its activities, the value of the firm is altered and the firm should, for efficiency, convert (and be encouraged to convert) its outstanding debt from a rate of 10 per cent to a rate of, say, 9 per cent. This new borrowing rate is still higher than the yield on the new opportunity at 8 per cent but the reduction applies to *all* of the firm's existing debt, not only to the part incurred to secure the new opportunity. For concreteness, assume that the initial debt of the firm was £1500. At 10 per cent interest, the firm was obliged to promise to pay its debt-holders a total of £1650 at the end of the relevant period. Let the new, riskless opportunity cost £250. If undertaken the principal of the firm's debt would be raised to £1750 but, if correct recognition of the reduced default risk caused by the addition's low variance is taken, the firm's borrowing rate would drop to 9 per cent, making the amount to be paid, both principal and interest, £1907·50 (1750×1·09) which is an increase of £257·50 over the original debt position of £1650. Note that the effective interest rate on the new project, because it allows a reduction in its previous debt by reducing the default risk, is precisely 3 per cent. (£257·50−£250 = £7·50; £7·50/£250 = ·03). Mossin concludes :

Thus, the effective *marginal* borrowing rate is 3 per cent, and it is not surprising that the proposed investment should be considered profitable.[5]

In order for the investment to be undertaken, however, the impact of its addition to the firm's activities must be known. If it is not known the firm will incorrectly reject the project as too expensive and the firm and the economy, under the assumptions of the model, will be worse off than if the refunding of the firm's debt took place.[6]

Thus both the composition and level of capital formation are extremely sensitive to the extent of differential information which exists in an economy.[7] Risk is an intrinsic characteristic of capital formation for capital goods themselves are generally highly use-specific and have limited second-hand value. The services from a machine cannot easily be secured on a short-term basis, as can labour, but must be obtained by purchase of the machine, plant, equipment or facility itself, that is by making a long-term contract to consume the services of the good throughout its life on fixed terms. Thus, capital formation is inherently risky, since the capacity for short-term adjustments to unfulfilled expectations is limited. If investors are risk averse, as introspection and casual observation strongly suggest, the possibility of efficient diversification of risks in order to avert disaster is essential if substantial amounts of risk are to be borne. More risks will be taken collectively than individually and more collective risks will be taken if the probability of all risks failing simultaneously is virtually zero. Segmentation, by creating differences in information and opportunities, restricts the opportunities for effectively bearing risks.

Diversification is not a function which must be performed through formal institutions. Important examples of diversifying behaviour can be found in the histories of both firms and individual entrepreneurs.[8] Diversification at the firm level is an important element of management's duties. However, diversification for wealth holders is most efficiently carried out on a large scale for there are substantial and important economies of scale in this activity. In the first place, the costs of gathering and interpreting the information on relative alternatives are incurred only once for each institution. These basic transactions costs are a smaller proportion of total operating costs for large firms than for smaller ones.

Secondly, as Mossin's example above indicates, risk can only be optimally interpreted within the context of a very wide array of choices. The larger a portfolio of either real or financial assets the more opportunities that exist for laying risks off against each other; that is, the set of optimal feasible choices may be more favourable for large portfolios than for small portfolios, even ignoring transaction costs. Closely related to this point is the probability that important thresholds in the process of physical capital formation exist, such that the ability to complete a project, even when substantial unexpected difficulties arise, is an important element of eventual success. Therefore, the greater the total resources relative to the largest project undertaken by a firm, the better the prospects that every worthwhile project will be undertaken despite the potentially discrete nature of some undertakings.

These considerations offer a persuasive rationalisation for the proliferation of financial intermediaries and for the tendency of firms themselves to behave as diversifying agents. The cost of capital is not uniquely determined but depends on the structure of each firm's portfolio of risks and will vary with every investment decision whether financial or real which changes the characteristics of the distribution of possible outcomes which each firm faces. Projects which are unacceptable to one firm may be highly desirable to another, identical in managerial skill and resources, simply for the reason that the second firm's existing structure of risks is improved by the opportunity while the first's is not. Such possibilities emphasise the value of institutions which gather and transmit the information relevant to such decisions.

From this brief discussion of the requirements of information on returns, variances and co-variances necessary to ensure rational, efficient allocation of resources under uncertainty, it is clear that in reality *no* capital market is or ever has been free from the serious distortions of substantial segmentation, where segmentation is understood to mean the partition of a larger market area into sub-divisions which permit differences in risk-adjusted rates of return to exist. The segmentation of markets is thus a universal problem. Nor is it a new problem. There was, of course, a strong incentive in all developing economies in the nineteenth century, as there is now, to reduce the obstacles to efficiency raised by segmentation. Capital markets in all the advanced countries in the last century have changed constantly in an attempt to offer their users, owners and managers more efficient choices. The institutional history of these markets may be interpreted as a search for improvement, and the growth in the wealth and scope of financial intermediaries and diversifying firms is an important indication of progress. Yet the various national paths toward improvement differed sharply and it is only to be expected that the consequences of the improvements achieved would differ as well. The course which capital market evolution took in Britain bore little resemblance to that taken in either the US or Germany, and changes in those two countries did not closely resemble each other.

These divergent trends resulted in national markets which performed certain tasks with marked differences in proficiency. By 1914, Britain had created a short term money market of unrivalled efficiency and had supplemented this with elaborate institutions, also unmatched, specialising in the trade of first class securities. In these two functions neither the US nor Germany approached the level of performance Britain attained by 1914, although both had progressed far beyond their circumstances in the mid-nineteenth century. Germany and America were compensated for their deficiencies in short term and high-grade security markets, however, by a superior ability to concentrate resources in areas strategic for rapid development at moments crucial to the evolution of new products and techniques.

The reasons for this ability were notably different for the US and Germany. The US, with a rich resource base relative to a rapidly expanding population and a tradition of tinkering, tempered with respect for scientific knowledge, needed only intermittent support from a crisis-prone financial system to achieve rapid, but not optimal, exploitation of new possibilities. Railroads and some New England textile mills depended on funds raised on organised capital markets but the vast majority of industrial firms had little access to them before 1914.[9] When the large banking houses became involved in industrial affairs, it was usually for the purpose of reorganising an industry already in existence. Most firms did depend on bank loans in their initial stages but were generally soon able to sustain further growth from internal resources.[10] Success in the scramble to employ new techniques, offer new products, or penetrate new markets often depended initially on favourable access to external finance. This often led at least temporarily to a monopolistic position for the successful firm. Subsequently it was often only the fear of further entry or the sheer momentum of the logic of a particular form of technical progress which maintained development in some industries, for one of the outstanding features of the emergence of new US industries in the late nineteenth century was the large size and small number of firms which comprised them.[11] Ramshackle as it was, the system was capable of concentrating resources sufficiently to launch, before 1914, a number of new industries in electrical manufacture, chemicals, automobiles, communications, steel and food processing. In a sense, because of the greater level and wider distribution of wealth and the generally buoyant economic environment which this created, formal financial markets were less necessary in promoting a given rate of economic growth in the US than in Europe. The substantial but incomplete progress which was made in the internal organisational ability of firms to cope with the expansion induced by the geographical widening of operations, the increasing complexity and capability of technology, and the burgeoning diversity of products were capable of providing the necessary institutional support for widespread growth before 1914.

Germany, in contrast, was poorer than both Britain and the US before 1914. Without the abundant natural resources of the US it was much less easy for individuals or firms or small, local banks to preside unaided over the creation of entire industries. The German banking system therefore provided much more elaborate formal facilities for concentrating resources than either their US or British counterparts. English financial authorities were well aware of both the hazards and the rewards of this concentration and often wrote favourably of the German system. Thus Lavington wrote :

> An organisation of this kind, [an investment bank] intermediate between the sources of enterprise and the sources of capital must evidently possess machinery for investigating business ventures, financial strength adequate to sustain the heavy risks to which it is exposed and the reputation and business connexions necessary for the efficient sale of securities to the public. An organisation such as the Deutsche Bank possesses these qualities to a high degree. Its practical administration (1914) is in the hands of a body of nine managers, all of them men of wide business knowledge, one or two of them admittedly of exceptional ability. It has a distinct staff of some eight or nine industrial experts, usually drawn from industry itself, and a highly developed department of information, while its system of unsecured advances keeps in the closest touch with the position and progress of business concerns. It is easy to see that, with able management and machinery of this kind, the risks of industrial banking are greatly reduced; business ventures in need of capital can be thoroughly investigated and the development of the more pioneering enterprises may be promoted with a reasonable prospect of success.[12]

Clapham concurred with the tenor of Lavington's argument, approvingly quoting a principal officer of one of the largest German banks :

> 'In Germany,' said Herr Schuster of the Dresdner Bank in 1908, 'our banks are largely responsible for the development of the Empire, having fostered and built up its industries. It is from 1871 that our real development dates and it is since that year that our great banks have been organised.' 'To them, more than any other agency,' he added with pardonable complacency, 'may be credited the splendid results thus far realized.' If his historical summary was not literally accurate, it was accurate in substance.[13]

This is not by any means to be interpreted as a claim that the capacity in the US and Germany to concentrate a large proportion of the economy's resources in the task of utilising new technical and marketing possibilities was without difficulties or costs. To the contrary, throughout the nineteenth century significant regional differences in interest rates on short-term commercial paper and mortgages, let alone on more risky assets, existed in the US.[14] Although a national short-term commercial paper market had begun to appear by 1900, differentials on mortgages narrowed more slowly.[15] The economic development of the southern part of the US, favoured by climate and resources, was probably greatly retarded by capital market imperfections.[16] Similar differentials appeared in Germany. Because the Great Banks 'did not care for that class of business' represented by local deposit banking and the extension of commercial credit to small traders, historians have argued that serious misallocation of resources occurred in Imperial Germany.[17] In contrast, these marked regional and, to some extent, sectoral differences in interest rates on mortgages and short-term commercial credit appear to have been largely eradicated in Britain no later than the 1860s.[18] Furthermore, concentration invited monopolistic abuses in both the US and Germany.[19] The tendency to concentrate control of the nation's rail-roads in the hands of a small syndicate of financiers has not aided in halting the decline of a viable US rail network. Morgan's colossal creation, US Steel, has not been a dynamic, innovative organisation; chaotic management and technological conservatism have relentlessly contributed to the firm's continued loss of market share since its creation. The pre-eminence at US Steel's creation of financial concerns at the expense of production and marketing must bear a major part of the explanation of the firm's subsequent performance. The costs in terms of welfare and foregone growth of these departures from optimality must be of similar magnitiude in Germany. If the Great Banks are to receive much of the credit for stimulating technical change in Germany, they must be held accountable for the failure of industries such as automobile manufacturing to emerge as rapidly as elsewhere. It is obvious, therefore, that economic performance in both the US and Germany was far from equalling that permitted by resources and technology. Yet it also appears to be true that, with all of their documented imperfections, capital markets in the US and Germany, by making resources available to a large group of technologically progressive industries on a scale unequalled in Britain, account for much of the difference in the economic growth performance between those two countries and Britain in the half century after 1865.

III

The evolution of Britain's system of financial intermediaries was very much a product of her early industrialisation. The British system in the formative years of the eighteenth and nineteenth century, had to cope with the fact of growth achieved, not with the desire to expand further. Much argument with little logical basis has held that Britain's 'head start' is responsible for Britain's slow economic progress since the end of the Great Victorian Boom.[20] Little sustained attention has been focused on institutional development,[21] yet it is often within an institutional framework functioning so smoothly that its working is rarely questioned that the most promising areas for innovation occur. Thus institutions successfully created in Britain to ensure the stability necessary to early industrialisation were distinctly less appropriate for the problems of sustaining subsequent development.

As late as the 1790s commerce and industry needed as much funding for stocks and inventories as for fixed capital formation.[22] By 1835, the fixed capital needs of commerce and industry were still only three times that of inventory requirements.[23] It was natural and reasonable then to fear the effects of commodity 'speculation' and to regard fixed capital formation as a largely self-regulating, self-stimulating process best nurtured under a regime of sound money. The Bubble Act was preserved for over a century as a monument to prudence.[24]

The quickening pace of economic development, the increasing demands for long term capital formation, the heightening sensitivity of the entire economy to fluctuations caused by good harvests and bad, buoyant exports and slack, formed the background for fundamental institutional reform of banking in 1844. The purpose of Peel's Bank Act of that year was to eliminate economic disturbances arising out of the 'unwise' actions of the Bank of England.[25]

Three crises in the twenty years after the Bill's passage were required to educate the Bank's Governors in the means of translating the formal mechanism into a device capable of exercising increasingly delicate control over the economy. But as experience in regulating bills of exchange and bank deposits grew, the original objectives of the Bill's authors were increasingly realised and the Bank became a massive force for stability.[26] Stability of the Bank's reserves and the exchanges remained the Bank's objectives until 1914.[27] The state of the Bank's reserves before all else dictated policy. After 1890, the Bank increasingly tried to accommodate business conditions when taking steps to protect its reserves or to anticipate trouble but the Bank's objectives were never widened to encompass actively and continuously the maintenance of full employment or the promotion of growth.[28]

The Bank of England, as it slowly began to fulfil the duties of a central bank, increasingly came to influence profoundly the entire tenor of British banking operations. The Bank's gradual articulation of its role coincided with a fundamental change in bank lending practices in which the strengthening bond between the banking system and industrial long-term finance, which had grown up in the early nineteenth century, was severed. As industrial fixed capital requirements had grown steadily through the early nineteenth century, banks had begun to play a major role in industrial affairs. By the middle decades

of the nineteenth century, the banking system at a local level was playing a role strikingly similar to that played at the end of the nineteenth
century by the German Great Banks on a national level.[29] The un-
remitting increase in the size of plant demanded for efficient use of
evolving technology in most lines of production, however, began to
outstrip the ability of most local banks to respond safely to these new
requests for funds. The rash of mid-Victorian bank failures can be
attributed directly to banks becoming too closely linked with local
firms and over-lending as these firms attempted to expand.[30] These
failures reached a crescendo with the failure of the City of Glasgow
Bank in 1878. This marked a final watershed for British banking before
1914. A point had been reached where the entire system had either to
be re-organised to withstand the greater risks of steadily enlarging
industrial requirements or the system had to withdraw from long term
industrial involvement. The system withdrew. After 1878, no longer
would banks become willingly involved in the long term financing of
industry.[31] Industrial firms, to the extent that a partnership could not
raise the funds, would, in the future, have to resort to the means made
available by limited liability. Jefferys summarises this evolution thus :

> But the shock of these failures [in 1875 and 1878] and the resulting
> turn toward timidity and amalgamation in banking, and the adop-
> tion of limited liability by industry, which lessened the demand for
> long term loans, brought to an end in the 'eighties, this formative
> period of British banking. . . .[32]
>
> The banks were by the 'eighties no longer showing such a readiness
> to act as partners in industrial concerns. They were moving further
> and further away from the concept of long term loans and were
> concentrating on an efficient national short term credit system.[33]

During the same period as the banks were amalgamating and drawing away from long-term industrial finance, the brief tentative foray
of the discount houses into this activity also abruptly ended. In 1863,
the General Credit and Finance Company of London Ltd was launched
with impressive financial support, including that of the most prestigious
London and Paris banks. The aim of this company was to act as a
Crédit Mobilier type of bank, taking long positions in industrial projects. However, despite a very successful start in which an annual
yield on invested capital of 17·5 per cent was recorded,[34] the board's
nerve broke during the panic following Gurney's collapse. Despite
a strong reserve provided by a call on share-holders, the firm went into
voluntary liquidation in November, 1866, reforming into a new company the following January with the well announced intention to hold
only short-dated assets.[35] With the retreat of the General Credit and
Finance Company, an exploratory period in the history of the discount

market ended. The discount houses became unrivalled specialists in short-term accommodation and provided the institutional basis on which the Bank of England was to exert such delicate control over British finances.[36] As long as the discount houses successfully met their objectives and distinguished between bills and mortgages, they did not become a source of long term loans.

The withdrawal of the banks and discount houses from involvement in long-term capital formation left the burden of this task solely to the mechanism of limited liability.[37] There were two main ways in which this mechanism was used. The first, by far the most common and most customary as far as industrial investment for most firms was concerned, used the company law to reduce the risks incurred in the course of investment by friends, relatives and business acquaintances. Reliance on close associates was a tradition well known before the last quarter of the eighteenth century, long before the active industrial intervention of banks and even longer before the advent of general limited liability. Limited liability, by eliminating the most lamentable consequences of investment enhanced the efficacy of the time-honoured practice of entrusting savings to those one knew well. So well did this practice continue to develop that as late as 1904, 3068 of the 3477 new companies registered in London in that year were private rather than public companies.[38] Private companies were those wishing, of the facilities which incorporation allowed, only the advantage of limited liability; in return for exemption from the requirement to publish income statements and balance sheets, private companies were required to make no public issue of their shares, to limit the number of shareholders and to restrict the transfer of ownership. Although many of these firms were small, since the larger ones availed themselves of the flexibility of public ownership, the preponderance of private companies is a telling indication of the preference for finance through private negotiation.

Thus, as had been the case in previous centuries, most industrial capital formation in Britain, probably between 60 per cent and 70 per cent in a typical year of the last quarter of the nineteenth century, was carried out by small groups of men who were well acquainted with each other through personal or business contacts. Private British groups, usually acting without large institutional facilities for diversifying widely and efficiently, achieved the great bulk of the not inconsiderable capital formation and structural change which occurred during the late Victorian and Edwardian eras. In these circumstances, perhaps the most important way in which systematic, organised change occurred in Britain after 1870 was through the diversifying behaviour of established, viable firms with proven technical capabilities and trade connections. These firms accomplished change by using their cash flow from profits and depreciation either to alter the character of the firm's activities by creating new product lines or to enlarge the firm as it was by expanding existing profitable operations. In any event, whether change occurred within firms or through the creation of new firms, it was accomplished by tapping relatively small pools of savings. In the refusal of the banks to play an important, conscious role in long term capital formation, Britain in the late nineteenth and early twentieth centuries differed from the contemporary USA and the Britain of four or five decades earlier. This was a crucial difference, however, for when private or internal resources were insufficient and short term bank accommodation was too limited and risky, British firms and entrepreneurs after the 1880s were forced to turn to the second means of implementing limited liability, that of public quotations on a stock exchange.

Companies, if private resources were insufficient, could use the stock exchanges to raise money more widely. Provincial exchanges, which had been established during the railroad booms of the 1830s and 1840s, were essentially an extension of the close circle of associates since those who traded in local markets were generally well aware of the circumstances of the firms quoted there.[39] Provincial exchanges were an important means of providing liquidity for investors in local business[40] but apparently accounted for raising no more than 5–10 per cent of the annual amount of gross domestic capital formation in the years immediately preceding the war.[41] The London capital market dwarfed those of the provinces and was much more important as a source of new funds, accounting for perhaps 23–28 per cent of the annual amount of gross domestic capital formation in 1911–1913.[42] However, the main functions of the London capital market were concerned with government issues, foreign loans and railroads or other public or semi-public utility securities rather than with domestic industrial finance.[43]

There are good historical reasons why this was so. The London market was an amazing mechanism of great capacity and flexibility. It operated, however, in a legal environment which greatly amplified the information problems which are familiar features even of mid-twentieth century capital markets. This, of course, produced distortions. The extent to which incomplete or misleading accounting conventions and requirements has caused the observed prices of securities quoted by a capital market to be displaced from the complete-information equilibrium cannot be known, but there is some evidence that the distortion is large even for markets well provided with communication links, a vigorous, inquisitive financial press and legal requirements for extensive disclosure of business activities. Marc Nerlove, in a detailed econometric study of the performance of 271 firms quoted on the NYSE for which complete, comparable financial records were available between 1950 and 1964, has found substantial, durable differentials in rates of return *after* allowing for risk and transactions costs.[44] Nerlove attributed this result to the superior perception of investment opportunities within the firm. The management of a firm, he argued, despite disclosure requirements, has a much better perception of the opportunities and dangers within the scope of the firm's activities than do outsiders.[45] This, of course, means that the level and structure of investment will be sub-optimal; managers will know only if internal investment will yield higher returns than some 'market rate', usually the rate on short term commercial loans rather than whether, of all possible investments, the ones within their firm offer the best return for the risks involved. The conclusion of Nerlove's study, that it is not possible on the basis of published corporate accounts to judge investments effectively, has important implications for the historical study of capital markets.

What is true of the recent past is even more relevant to earlier periods, when in the US, Germany and Great Britain, business disclosure requirements were enormously more relaxed than at present. The early days of the corporate form of business organisation were noted for the infinite legal, let alone illegal, elaborations of the art of concealment. By 1900, caustic comments on the great rise in 'ornamental directors', whose function was to reassure the less informed of the worth of a firm and whose services were, not surprisingly, often most prominent when there was much that required reassurance, had become frequent. Judge Emden, in a knowledgeable analysis of the times wrote :

. . . the tempting facilities offered by this modern machinery [of limited liability] now attracts classes that in the past had not tested the flexibility of their consciences in the subject of accounts and balance sheets.[46]

The published data in Britain before 1914 was sufficiently bad that J. B. Jefferys, in his careful study, concluded that the safety of shareholders depended almost entirely on their personal knowledge of the men who ran the businesses in which they invested.[47]

In light of these inherent difficulties it is not surprising that the money ventured in the London markets went very largely to the purchase of 'known' securities. There were a number of ways in which securities became 'known'. They might be the oldest securities traded on the exchange, government stocks. The price of these could certainly vary, but the instrument itself was well understood and obeyed known laws of behaviour. In the first quarter of the nineteenth century the securities of foreign governments began to appear in London in large quantities. Their number grew rapidly and at first they were rather indiscriminately confused with domestic government stocks but this was quickly changed in the 1820s as governments and firms began to be more rigorously classified according to their past record. It became increasingly difficult for a defaulting government or a peccable issuing house to repeat a raid on British finances. The same evolution occurred in the marketing of home railroad securities which had by the 1890s become thoroughly respectable as the memories of the excesses of the 1830s and 1840s faded under the impact of a long succession of dividend and coupon payments successfully met. The unmistakeable sign of grace was extended to selected home railway debentures in 1889 when they were accorded trustee status.[48] The next group of securities gradually to win a favoured place in London were foreign rails, with colonial issues most preferred, followed by the issue of proven North and South American lines. Domestic non-rail companies began to appear in the 1860s; most of these issues represented established coal, iron, steel and heavy engineering firms taking advantage of the new provisions for limited liability to ease the burden of their relatively large fixed costs. These issues, too, were attended by unscrupulous promotions but the prudent Victorians who made up most of the investing public seldom strayed for any time from familiar securities. Finally, there was throughout the nineteenth century an accumulation of other foreign securities primarily those of land, finance, and investment companies, mining and other raw material extracting concerns, and a few industrial and commercial enterprises. What is striking in the great rise of the London exchanges is not that spectacular frauds occurred but that they were of such small magnitude compared with the volume of securities purchased. The Victorians and Edwardians circumvented remarkably well the dangers which tenuous control of managers and unreliable information imposed upon them by buying carefully.[49] In this they were aided by a set of institutions which performed almost a pure intermediary function of a special sort and which undertook, with rare but notable exceptions, almost no managerial responsibility.

The manner in which investment trusts, insurance companies, company promoters, stockbrokers and related enterprises functioned, combined with the withdrawal of the banking system from long-term industrial capital formation, had two far reaching implications for the overall efficiency of financial intermediation in Britain. First, it meant that there was no institutional means of forging tighter links between owners and managers. In Germany, and to some extent in the US, banks acted to evaluate managerial performance by rewarding good results and punishing bad ones, in short acting as a very large shareholders' protection agency, of which the banks were the major beneficiary. In addition the extensive commercial intelligence of such large banks provided the management of client firms with information of relevant production and investment decisions taken elsewhere in the economy and also with suggestions for the firm's own investment and marketing operations as well as providing the banks with a ready measure of their clients' successes and failures. Financial intermediaries closely linked to industrial concerns by ownership and creditor status thus often were in a position to play an informational role of great significance at a time when data publicly available were so often deliberately misleading. Intermediaries did not play such a role in Britain, however.

Intermediaries also failed to play a second role in Britain, which operationally was probably of even greater significance. This role was the systematic provision of the facilities for efficient diversification whereby investors could be sure, for any level of *ex ante* risks which they took, that they would obtain the highest possible return which the system, as a whole, was capable of producing. The absence of institutional facilities for wide-scale diversification combined with the means for exercising appreciable control over individual undertakings therefore increased the inevitable risks which British investors had to bear.

After they had effectively withdrawn from long term capital formation, the banks and discount houses as a group achieved great stability and solvency, the solid, visible proof of the success of the Bank of England in imposing its objectives, but only at the cost of making other institutions' portfolios more risky by effectively monopolising the market for low variance assets. Diversifying institutions in the form of investment and finance trusts did indeed appear but they were too small in proportion to the volume of traded securities to have seriously affected the prices of securities through their activities, accounting for only £90m of the £8000m of securities traded in London in 1913. Furthermore, of more importance for domestic capital formation, their portfolios were almost completely composed of foreign assets.[50] The first important investment trust, called significantly the Foreign and Colonial Government Trust, had appeared in 1868.[51] Similar institutions multiplied and grew rapidly in spite of the well known difficulties in making informed choices. They obviously served a clearly felt need. But even in the middle of the 1890s, a decade of little foreign investment, a typical trust such as the International Investment Trust with assets valued at about £3·5m in 1896 had only 22·4 per cent of its holdings in domestic securities; 44·8 per cent were in North America, 26·6 per cent in South America, and 6·2 per cent elsewhere abroad.[52] Furthermore, only 30 per cent of the portfolio was in ordinary or deferred shares.

The reluctance of investment trusts to have large positions in domestic issues can probably be explained by two factors. First, most trusts appear to have acted as vehicles for conservative clienteles and therefore restricted their own purchases to high grade securities.[53] Secondly, information costs involved in holding domestic industrial issues were probably prohibitively high. The most efficient means of gathering information on industrial firms was undoubtedly that employed by the German banks, unsecured short-term advances.[54] US firms monitoring the progress of branches, divisions or subsidiaries achieved with varying degrees of success the same effect. Because investment trusts were not also banks or firms, they were not able to use the profitable information-gathering devices which the banks had constructed through the laborious process of amalgamation and firms through expansion and merger. The preference of investment trusts for large prestigious foreign issues is therefore readily explained. The most favoured foreign issues, as their early succession to respect on the London exchanges suggests, were close but not perfect substitutes for their well-known domestic counterparts. Hence the preferred foreign assets, in terms of increasing expected risk, were colonial governments, selected foreign governments, colonial rails, American rails, foreign rails, and finally, foreign company issues. Investment trusts selected the best portfolio, then, not from among all assets but rather from a subset of well-known securities. By substituting the foreign equivalent of a well-known domestic asset, expected yields could be raised with only an imperceptible increase in expected risk. The investment trusts were undoubtedly a valuable financial innovation but their impact on domestic capital formation was distinctly limited.

Nor was the institutional gap thus left by banks, discount houses and investment trusts filled by insurance companies. They too faced problems of information through lack of steady flows of commercial intelligence and were guided above all by a sense of prudence and caution.[55] Thus when the yields on the mortgages and government stocks with which they constructed their portfolios fell in the last decades of the nineteenth century, the insurance companies moved into foreign government securities and into proven foreign debentures but not in any substantial way into ordinary corporate shares. The cult of the equity was to be a mid-twentieth century phenomenon[56] and the undeniable emergence of life-insurance companies consistently as major decision makers in corporate investment planning has not occurred yet. The insurance companies as a group had extremely small holdings of ordinary stocks and shares[57] and, while they held appreciable quantities of debentures (about 25 per cent by 1910) the failure of the Royal Exchange Assurance, a large, well run company, to earn an average yield on its portfolio of more than 4 per cent from 1895 to the outbreak of the First World War indicates that the increased debenture holdings were not enterprising to the point of earning yields sufficient to restore the profitability levels of earlier years.[58]

With the established institutions of banks, investment trusts and insurance companies thus removed from an active, direct role in private industrial capital formation by the late nineteenth century, savers were left to bear the risks of such investments through stock exchanges individually. As the first wave of conversion of private partnerships took place in the late 1860s and 1870s, intermediaries appeared which helped otherwise ignorant investors to discriminate among issues and which aided business owners to find funds cheaply for expansion or liquidation. The success with which one of the first of these intermediaries fulfilled these roles helped to convince prudent capitalists of the worth of the innovation of limited liability. This was the famous firm of Chadwick, Adamson and Collier.[59] As early as the 1870s, Chadwick's had established a clientele of perhaps 5000 wealthy subscribers willing to invest in companies promoted by the firm.[60] The operations of Chadwick's, however, differed sharply from the operations of the promoters and stockbrokers who were to take over home industrial issues during the 1880s and after. Chadwick's did not seek out firms to promote but rather offered their services on a selective basis when requested to do so. Their services consisted of a knowledgeable financial and technical check of the prospective company which they presented to their clients together with an assessment of the firm's future. The amount of 'new' money they raised was typically only 25–30 per cent of the value of the issue, the remainder being the value of the vendor's or issuing group's assets.[61] Furthermore, Chadwick's stayed with the company it had formed as auditor, (Chadwick was an accountant) thus providing a vital reassurance to those whom it had encouraged to invest.[62] These services were astutely and cheaply rendered; Chadwick's failure rate by 1877 was but one firm in ten[63] and the commission was only 1 per cent of the issue, and this for companies with a capital as small as £100,000.[64] By the 1890s, the standard rate for less discriminating services was at least 2½ per cent and often more. But promising as this line of development pioneered by Chadwick's was, it was not long pursued. Chadwick's firm disappeared honourably by the 1880s[65] after having promoted and sold more than £40m of joint-stock securities; successor companies were either much less prominent or concentrated on dealing in established securities rather than floating new issues. Firms such as Richardson, Chadbourn and Company; Alfred Whitworth, Clemesha and Company; Joshua Hutchinson and Company; and George White's of Bristol continued in the same tradition as Chadwick's but without ever matching its status, importance or volume of business even as the field of opportunity expanded. Other successor firms such as George Gregory and Sons and the Investment Registry Limited arose to serve clients seeking a higher rate of return than could be had with perfect security but they, as did the investment trusts, concentrated their attention on foreign debentures and bonds, steering clear of common stock.[66] George Gregory, for example, centred its promoting efforts in the 1890s in the West End of London, Brighton and Hastings, as far from the turmoil of industrial activity in England in distance as in investment intent.[67]

While the intermediaries most closely linked to long-term industrial capital formation remained small and select, investors were not without other facilities to aid in disposing of their funds. By the 1890s the age of the company promoter, often working with stockbrokers, had clearly begun. The promotion activity of the 1890s, however, involved a commitment of much shorter duration than did Chadwick's promoting of a decade or two before. The promoter now was often offering a chance for a bonanza, and bonanzas by their nature were more a matter of vision than of a reality which could be certified by an accountant. Thus, Lavington has characterised the British capital markets of the last quarter century before 1914 :

> In the absence of strong intermediary agencies with machinery available for the investigation of industrial propositions and the organization requisite for the efficient marketing of their securities, the work of selecting profitable new ventures, of capitalizing their prospects in terms of securities and of selling those securities to the public, falls mainly to the company promoter; while that of marketing further issues of existing companies is undertaken by the companies themselves.[68]

The trouble with this system, for new companies or old, however, was the promoter; Lavington again notes :

> The promoter is not a very definite kind of person. He may be a parent company engaged in the formation of a subsidiary or allied business enterprise; he may be, and very often is, the vendor of the assets purchased by the new company; or he may be a financier whose contact with the new company ceases when he has completed its flotation and sold any shares which may have been alloted to him. But whoever he may be, his interests *as promoter* are quite distinct from those of the company he forms.[69]

It is no surprise then, that despite the ability of some promoters, underwriters, and stockbrokers consistently to launch new and profitable companies successfully, the stock exchanges as a whole had a disconcerting tendency to launch new issues, especially for firms in new industries, disastrously. The difficulties of using the stock exchanges for capital formation were widespread and affected all industries. Two especially important examples, however, may be cited – electricity and automobile companies. The early financial histories of these two industries are surprisingly similar; in both cases early and calamitous issues appear to have crippled subsequent development and the funds for expansion, when they did appear, almost invariably did so too slowly to exploit the periodic booms in demand. The first to pass through this cycle were the electricity companies. In the very early days, the supply companies also produced the equipment which consumed their power output and these early companies therefore encompassed electrical engineering as well.

Speculative promoters were quick to sense the opportunity offered by interest in the new technology. Some £7m were raised in 1882 alone, most of it going for worthless patent fees and promoters' profits rather than the real development of the industry.[70] The consequences of this ruinous start became clearer as time passed. The industry struggled through the continuous technical change of the mid-1880s with a tarnished financial record. Capacity grew slowly, often as a result of mechanical engineering firms opening a line of electrical manufactures. Profits in the industry did not start to become impressive until the boom from 1888 to 1891. Yet as demand surged ahead and output trebled in three years, firms still found it difficult to expand fast enough. The mechanical engineering firms which had started a line of electrical products either did not have the resources or did not commit those they did have with enough conviction to press expansions home. For other firms, the factor perhaps most responsible for hindering rapid advance then was the borrowing constraint; at a time when conditions justified ploughing all firms' net operating receipts into more capacity, electrical companies could not use the equity market but, because of their past record, were forced into the debenture market if they could borrow at all. Equity financing was preferable at this stage because it relieved firms of the need to meet regular debt payments when conditions for expansion were unusually favourable. Thus, Brush, the largest British manufacturer of the late 1880s and possessed of unusually good City connections through stockbrokers Foster and Braithwaite,[71] was unable, despite considerable effort, to meet the boom after 1888 by selling equities and was forced at this time to raise nearly two-thirds of its funds for expansion in the debenture market.[72] Crompton, one of the most innovative firms, was not even this lucky.[73] Its second bond issue during the boom in the summer of 1890 failed with only £10,800 of a £25,000 issue sold by March 1891. Another bond issue and a preference share issue also were not well received. By March 1895, only £83,000 of a £100,000 bond issue of February 1894 had been sold.

The strain clearly showed in Crompton's management.[74] Elaborate experimentation was to be halted and a general manager, 'not a member of the Board [of directors], but open to every possible criticism and under the most complete control', was to oversee technical development.[75] R. E. B. Crompton, who had been a prolific innovator, was repelled by this atmosphere and as the 1890s wore on took progressively less part in the affairs of the company which bore his name.[76]

Unfortunately for the British electrical industry, the boom starting in 1888 was prematurely damped down in the aftermath of Baring's embarrassment with Argentinian securities in the autumn of 1890. Difficulties, already present before the crisis, became much worse, as the events at Crompton showed. Expansion in the industry slowed to a crawl and the major developments of the period, polyphase a.c. motors and traction motors, were ignored. The liquidity problems of the manufacturers were augmented by the behaviour of their main customers, the new supply companies, who were also pressed for cash and paid for plant in illiquid and depreciated securities which they themselves could not sell on open markets. The industry and the economy were temporarily depressed. The industrial potential of electricity, however, was too great to be long suppressed and by 1896 the great home boom ushered in the beginning of an electrical boom that lasted until 1903, when foreign investment once again became extremely popular and acted to terminate the housing boom, the driving stimulus behind much traction construction,[77] which in turn was the prop of Britain's electrical industry at the time. The liquidity problems of the early 1890s, however, had left an indelible mark. When the boom and the profits anticipated in 1882 and 1888–90 finally arrived the British industry was exhausted from thwarted anticipation. It had neither the capacity nor the technology to meet the boom and the long-sought gains were reaped largely by foreigners who poured in exports and finally followed with high levels of direct investment in the industry. The established British electrical firms were illiquid and by 1896 in the hands of cautious men who used the affluence which the boom brought to restore their companies rather than expand them.[78] Thus, of the increase of £4·1m in the value of fixed assets in the British electrical industry between 1896 and 1904, 67 per cent were supplied by foreign firms.[79] The industry, especially the new foreign arrivals, faced difficult times as domestic investment, and with it the demand for electrical equipment, fell by a third between 1904 and 1908. Yet as Britain once more fell behind foreign technology, the foundation for a catch-up spurt was once more laid; the upturn duly came in the three years just prior to the war. Foreign firms were then still in their dominant position.

One might go farther and argue that many of the peculiar characteristics of the British electrical engineering industry which made it periodically unprofitable were closely associated with a financial system which concentrated resources for risky domestic ventures only with difficulty. One drawback of British arrangements was that electrical manufacturers did not have a dominant holding in supply companies, although in the early 1890s the struggling manufacturers were often paid in the shares of the struggling new supply companies, which usually did not add general electrical engineering to their burdens. Unlike the situation in the US and Germany, where the financial control of manufacturers and supply companies was frequently unified, often through a bank, the practice of inserting an independent consulting engineer became established. These engineers were frequently considered by contemporaries, probably correctly, to impose needlessly rigid and unique specifications on manufacturers,[80] thereby raising costs. This did not always happen. Charles Merz, consulting engineer for the Newcastle Electric Supply Company, followed a very enlightened policy[81] of close co-operation with manufacturers, but Merz was *sui generis* and there is much to be said for an institutional arrangement which can often act as a substitute for talents which are all too rare by any standard. The electrical industry is one where the costs paid by the US and Germany for great concentration were by far outweighed by the benefits.

It is also possible that greater effort on the part of intermediaries could have helped soften the problems created when municipalities with substantial political power insisted on operating their own supply facilities even when the area served was clearly too small to benefit from the economies of scale so brilliantly demonstrated by foreigners abroad and Merz in Britain. One way of circumventing the problem would have been for the power companies to have pushed ahead with their schemes without municipal support, relying on the ability to use the concrete fact of power cheaply generated by their efficient plants to find municipal customers after the plants were built. This would have clearly been a risky proposition, for it hinged on the successful outcome of a rate war and the odds for the thirteen companies which had commenced supply by 1906 were not helped by engineering defects in at least five of their number.[82] The power companies, however, were not enthusiastically received by financial intermediaries[83] although powerful financial and technical resources were necessary to make the schemes feasible at all. British capital markets did not lend themselves to the necessary form of concentration.[84]

Failure to concentrate resources, to expand plant facilities and technological capability, especially during recessions, meant that British firms were always caught short of capacity and backward in products when the booms came. Since it was recognised by the perceptive no later than the early nineties that electricity was the power of the future, the only explanation of the poor state of the industry in the boom beginning in 1896 was the unwillingness or inability to translate the force of technological convictions into physical capital, a risky business but one in which the stakes were correspondingly high. Furthermore, the reluctance to commit resources to investment until a boom had materialised, if widely practised, was ultimately self-justifying and guaranteed the lengthening of recessions. This reluctance on the part of such an important supplier of inputs to the rest of the manufacturing sector had implications far beyond that implied by the size of the electrical engineering industry. The drawbacks, furthermore, were cumulative; when most of the innovations in electrically powered equipment were foreign, British firms, especially the smaller ones for whom electricity was to mean an added flexibility which ultimately offered great hope for the future, became aware of the potential of such equipment more slowly than their foreign counterparts. The slower spread of power equipment reduced the demand for electricity, the supply of which enjoyed substantial economies of scale. High electricity supply prices then further discouraged the spread of electricity usage. The failure to break this vicious circle satisfactorily was in part due to entrepreneurial deficiencies. But it was in large part the failure of financial intermediaries to find the successful men and back them with resources sufficient to weather the recessions and enter the booms with a chance of competing with foreigners on equal terms.

The lamentable financial circumstances of the launching of the electricity industry were repeated less than a decade and a half later for automobiles. S. B. Saul's concise description has a familiar ring:

> The first British motor company was launched in 1896 by a group of financial speculators, headed by Harry J. Lawson, almost as an appendix to their disastrous speculations with the cycle industry, though by that time the automobile industry was already well established in France. The first five years were unrewarding in many ways; little positive progress was made, companies such as Daimler and Humber had to struggle for years to overcome the burden of watered stock imposed upon them by Lawson, and the public soon became shy of investing in the industry as a result.[85]

The subsequent development of the industry also parallels that of electricity. The industry consisted of a host of small producers and it intermittently faced financial difficulties. After a bad beginning, the industry could not easily again obtain capital market support until 1904–1907.[86] Then, beginning in 1904, with many successful foreign examples before them and the extent of the home market sharply outlined by burgeoning imports, new money did flow into the industry. Output began to rise, although this was a product as much of new entry as of established firms expanding sharply. This burst of well-supported expansions and vigorous initiatives, however, was short lived. In 1907, overseas troubles, this time in the US, once again suddenly disrupted the market, forcing several firms into liquidation. This disruption was even worse for the automobile industry than the Barings crisis of 1890 had been for electricity, for a world-wide boom in automobile production was under way. Output in the US itself was barely affected by the crisis, which was resolved with unusual speed. US production more than trebled between 1908 and 1913.[87] Yet during most of this feverish boom, the domestic British industry could not use the stock exchanges.[88] Little was raised in 1908 and nothing at all in 1909–1910. Imports poured in, and by 1911, as the stock market showed signs of recovering its nerve, Henry Ford had settled in to dominate the lower end of the market with the Model-T's gushing from his Trafford Park plant.

The episode from 1907 to 1913 caught the defects of the British capital markets in a harsh glare. The exchanges were then (and are now) extremely fickle with a notoriously high implied discount rate. Thus, flickers of doubt and subtle intimations of difficulties could choke off the flow of funds; while the boom roared on after 1907, the expansion had to come with painful slowness from within the car firms, not from without. On the other hand, when resources were flung into the industry by the market, it was often done without coherence and discipline. With no shortage of potentially successful auto manufacturers, the three firms on which the market lavished funds most readily were the most unprofitable in the industry. Saul is surely too generous in his judgement of the stock exchange's provision of funds to the industry.[89] What was required was a steady, rational, courageous flow of funds to an industry which had technical troubles but also a huge market. What it got was waves of money carelessly supplied, followed by an equally unreflective withdrawal when problems appeared, problems magnified by the previous carelessness. Thus, the electricity industry's experience was repeated in considerable detail. The industry struggled through slack periods and was unprepared for the booms. By the time domestic investment did manage to exert itself, foreign competition was thoroughly entrenched making the investment ultimately less profitable (although still fabulously profitable) and more risky for domestic producers. As with electricity, it was not so much that the slumps were severe but that the booms were so badly exploited. As international markets became more lucrative, the rewards for financial concentrations in the right industry at the right time, grew; the penalties for not concentrating enough grew also.

The stock exchanges did not always perform as badly as they did in some spectacular instances for the electrical and automobile industries and indeed could be valuable devices for raising money for domestic ventures. Some promoters such as H. Osborne O'Hagen, often in conjunction with stockbrokers Panmure, Gordon and Company, launched an impressive number of companies which were fully intended to be (and were) viable. Nevertheless, without stronger, more vigilant intermediaries, the exchanges could never have been expected to play a pre-eminent role before 1914 in domestic capital formation where most of the issues were small. The sheer inadequacy of information guaranteed a massive segmentation.[90] As a consequence of these features an important bias operated in the formal British capital markets, though the bias was not the one most frequently cited, that towards foreign investment. Rather the bias was towards safe, well-known securities in general, many of which were foreign, and away from riskier, smaller, but ultimately from an economy-wide viewpoint, much more profitable ones. Furthermore, the neglect which the organised markets showed towards the riskier ventures was deepened by a lack of good facilities for diversification which would have made the burden of risk and uncertainty lighter. The bias arose because as an alternative to the difficulties, uncertainties and risks involved in real capital formation, the London stock market offered an unusually efficient means of purchasing securities of relatively low risk with attractive yields. Because diversification possibilities for the most dangerous domestic ventures were lacking, the risk was made to appear more stark than it need have been. The London stock exchange offered perhaps the best diversified packages of essentially *safe* securities available anywhere in the world. As a consequence, less knowledgeable risk taking (in the sense of domestic, industrial capital formation, the real risks) took place in Britain than in any of her advanced competitors. A classic problem of the second best appears to have operated in Britain before 1914. A part, but only a part, of her set of capital markets operated better than anyone else's. Had Americans or Germans had the facilities to obtain such high yields with such low risks as did Englishmen, perhaps they too would have taken fewer of the risks which their own capital markets forced upon them. But the Americans and Germans did not have the facilities and they did bear, collectively, the risks associated with later nineteenth century technical change. As a consequence their growth rates were substantially higher than Britain's as their level of per capita wealth surpassed or rapidly approached that of Britain. It is perhaps the case that half a good capital market was substantially less useful than one in which the defects were more evenly distributed.

Michael Edelstein has provided the first estimates of systematic bias within the UK capital markets.[91] Although the pricing model he uses to detect bias is a general one which could, in principle, be applied to any asset, the data base which he has constructed for his test consists only of first-class securities.[92] Since his data base is quite broad in range of industries, the dividends and coupons paid reflect to some extent conditions within the industries in his sample. On the other hand, Edelstein's sample of securities is obviously placed in a special category by the absence of an effective takeover sanction and the requirement that the securities must have exhibited regular pay-out patterns (although equities were permitted to fail to pay dividends for short periods without losing their first-class status). The assumption that all expectations *ex ante* were fulfilled further reveals the special nature of his sample because the selection of first class securities clearly demanded care *ex post*, with large numbers of securities rejected.[93] Therefore Edelstein's conclusions are relevant not for all assets but only for a very restricted subset of assets. Thus, for example, much of the explanation for why Edelstein reports in his thesis a narrowing in rate of return differentials among the comparable securities in his sample must arise simply from increasing market familiarity with assets whose history has been traced for some time. By the time the select group of assets which Edelstein chose, largely on the basis of their similarities to each other, had been observed for twenty or thirty years, price differentials must have moved in such a way that rate of return differentials were largely eliminated.

It is therefore entirely consistent with Edelstein's results that although within the sample group no evidence of bias towards foreign issues appears, the capital markets were in fact deeply biased away from favouring most home industrial projects. Furthermore, some of Edelstein's findings confirm the existence of bias even within his special sample. Edelstein's latest study on the determinants of UK purchases of US railroad securities does not confront the possibility that British capital markets systematically undervalued most domestic industrial securities. Nevertheless, Edelstein does report that he finds a low cross-elasticity of British demand for US railroad bonds with respect to yields on comparable British home securities.[94] While this cross-elasticity remained low throughout the period, it did rise over time but never became elastic. Therefore, even for his restricted sample, Edelstein finds that trading in Australian, Indian and home long term negotiable debt instruments remained partially isolated (segmented) from dealings in their US counterparts.[95] The interpretation of the increase in the cross-elasticity of demand between the US and UK which he does find is not straightforward but it seems clear that only a small proportion may be explained by a heightened British sensitivity to domestic yields induced by the appearance and spread of large scale UK corporate enterprise after the 1880s. UK home industrials, despite the increased demand for resources induced by the major technological advances of the late nineteenth century, would not seem to be the beneficiary of the weakened reception of American securities after 1895. In the nineteen years from 1895 to 1913, UK capital markets were concerned intensively with domestic financing only from 1895 to 1899 and from 1902 to 1905. From 1899 to 1902, the financing of the Boer War dominated the market and by 1905 the greatest surge of foreign investment ever mounted by Britain was well under way, although the US was by then not so well favoured as had been true earlier. Therefore Edelstein's conclusion appears to be only partially valid. The UK capital market surely improved but at best by reducing segmentation *within* the classes of established securities, leaving the segmentation between these securities and the newer, less familiar issues of domestic firms largely unchanged.

Thus, while not proven, there is mounting evidence that a substantially lower growth rate than was feasible resulted from the reluctance of the institutions in the British economy in the fifty years after 1865 to concentrate resources heavily in the industries most favoured by the technological change of the period. Despite some aspects of efficiency in Britain's capital market, efficiency which has impressed many historians, the associated benefits seem in retrospect only partially to compensate for the growth which the capital markets did not sufficiently encourage.

IV

A question that immediately arises from the preceeding consideration of the development of banking and stock exchange operations in Britain before 1914 is that of why the internal organisation of British business firms did not adjust to promote more fully industrial capital formation if this task was not performed by formal organisations. The multi-divisional firm, which has proven itself in the United States as a device for promoting well-diversified patterns of capital formation did not appear in Britain even in its rudimentary form until well into the interwar period. Yet it was in the period before 1914, when foreign portfolio investment claimed such a large proportion of British resources, that perhaps the greatest need for firms to provide internally the resources needed for expansion and diversification existed. The answer to this question is complex and the possibilities suggested here can only be tentative. Nevertheless, Professor Chandler's argument that the organisational structure of firms and the functions which the firm's management undertakes depend upon the economic environment would appear to provide the essential explanation. Most importantly, the massive foreign portfolio investment which flowed from Britain in the years after 1865 greatly affected the level and structure of the demands which faced British industry. By stimulating exports, this foreign investment acted to amplify demand for the traditional staples of British industry, textiles, coal, iron and steel and certain types of machinery and heavy engineering goods.[96] None of these industries either in the US or in the UK readily adopted the multi-divisional framework nor did they pursue a marked policy of product or technological diversification and improvement. Furthermore, the slow pace of structural change which the British economy experienced resulted in a corresponding slow rate of increase of incomes.[97]

Thus, there did not occur in Britain the rapid increases in domestic market demand which could have forced firms into adopting a structure more appropriate to accommodating systematically rapid change. Instead the market growth facing many British firms was determined by the growth of world trade to a much larger extent than was true in the US or Germany. The impact of slow growth may well have been cumulative. Many of the firms which Chandler has examined in the US used funds generated internally from profits and depreciation allowances to finance diversification. Once slow growth became the usual condition of the British economy, the funds for diversification internal to firms were limited at the time when they were most needed. This became even more important as the pace of technological change increased in the latter part of the nineteenth century, enhancing the value of diversifying activities which opened up the new market and product areas which the new technologies made potentially available. In Britain, the short-run incentive to pursue diversification, however, was further reduced since British industry rarely developed export markets for a product *before* establishing a strong domestic market[98]; with British foreign investment stimulating exports produced by well established industries the pressure to diversify was correspondingly reduced even as the potential rewards increased.

In short, it is quite convenient and illuminating to consider the structure of British capital formation, in terms of geographical location, industrial type, and technological characteristics, as the outcome of the operations of a whole array of capital markets, some of which were formal and public, such as stock exchanges and banks, and others of which were informal and essentially private, such as the organisational structure of business corporations.[99] For Britain, the rate of growth and the development of business organisations were fundamentally affected by the operations of those public institutions which directed such a large proportion of Britain's assets abroad. In such conditions the importance of informal capital formation was greatly heightened, but it is surely too much to expect that the institutional response could have been quicker than it was in an American economy favoured by so many circumstances.

NOTES

1   Alfred D. Chandler Jr *Strategy and Structure: Chapters in the History of the Industrial Enterprise* (Cambridge, Mass., 1962).

2   This discussion is based on the emerging theory which relates choice under

uncertainty to financial market operation. One of the most useful surveys is J. Mossin, *Theory of Financial Markets* (Englewood Cliffs, New Jersey, 1973). Mossin clearly describes the importance of investment and production decisions and indicates how these activities may be related to the more extensively analysed problem of demand for risky assets. The literature is still in a state of flux in which few of the major theoretical problems can be considered satisfactorily resolved. However, the theory that does exist now offers the opportunity of approaching the history of capital market development and operation with the prospect of asking questions of fundamental importance. Although the theory is still incomplete, at least the areas of significance are now reasonably well defined and the theory can act as a useful guide to the historian seeking to understand an extremely complex but absolutely fundamental process. Without such a guide, historical studies can only too easily become lost in a mass of uninterpretable data. On the other hand, the historian must exercise care for the theory is, after all, incomplete and is operational, as opposed to inspirational, in only a most limited fashion.

3 Mossin, op. cit., pp. 133–5.

4 This assumption of zero variance is adopted only for convenience of exposition. As long as the risk measure of the new opportunity were either substantially less than the risk measure of the firm's pre-existing aggregate portfolio of investments or if the distribution of unfavourable outcomes of the new opportunity were negatively correlated with the distribution of unfavourable outcomes previously anticipated, the argument would obtain.

5 Mossin, op. cit., p. 134–5.

6 If the firm in the example had issued non-recallable bonds and was unable to reduce the interest rate it was paying it would be unable to take the investment unless the marginal risk of the project alone (in this case zero) were the only relevant criterion for the loan. However, if any of the debt were held in short-term obligations, that proportion would be available for debt reduction. This suggests that firms would attempt to keep a balanced portfolio of debt obligations in order to take advantage of new opportunities without exposing themselves unduly to adverse developments.

7 That the composition of investment is affected by the extent of differential information is perhaps sufficiently obvious to require no additional discussion. This is not the case, however, with the claim that the level of investment is also affected by the extent of information differentials. For example, if a target level of income from investments is sought, the level of investment will be *raised* as a result of misallocations which yield an overall lower average return. (I am grateful to C. J. Bliss for bringing a class of such possibilities to my attention). Behaviour of this type may arise if people at some point experience such a saturation of wealth that any additional wealth does not increase their subjective welfare appreciably. Since this situation, if it ever does occur, is almost certainly only temporary it may be reasonably ignored for our purposes. Furthermore, recent research strongly implies that the level of investment will generally be positively rather than inversely related to the rate of return. Colin Wright has found that increased interest rates in the US will induce a significant increase in savings, holding income constant. (See Colin Wright, 'Saving and the Rate of Interest' in A. C. Harberger and M. J. Bailey (eds), *The Taxation of Income from Capital* (The Brookings Institution, Washington, D.C., 1969), pp. 275–300). Although distinguishing the income and substitution effects of interest rate changes is hazardous, especially since interest rate changes may substantially alter individual's estimates of their wealth, Wright's finding is nevertheless consistent with the observation that over a long period, rapidly growing advanced economies also usually have relatively high levels of savings as a proportion of

national income. (See Tables 7 and 10, Part IV, of U.S. Bureau of Economic Analysis, *Long Term Economic Growth, 1860–1970* (GPO, Washington, D.C., 1973).

8 See Alfred D. Chandler Jr and Herman Daems, 'Introduction – The Rise Managerial Capitalism and Its Impact on Investment Strategy in the Western World and Japan', in Herman Daems and Herman Van Der Wee (eds.), *The Rise of Managerial Capitalism* (The Hague, Netherlands, 1974) 28–32; and Jon Didrichsen 'The Development of Diversified and Conglomerate Firms in the United States, 1920–1970', *Business History Review*, XLVI (1972) 202–19.

9 T. R. Navin and M. V. Sears, 'The Rise of a Market for Industrial Securities, 1887–1902', *Business History Review*, XXIX (1955) 105–38.

10 L. E. Davis, 'The Capital Markets and Industrial Concentration: The U.S. and U.K., a Comparative Study', *Purdue Faculty Papers in Economic History, 1956–1966* (Homewood, 1967) 663–82.

11 See, generally, Chandler, *Strategy and Structure*, chs 1 and 2.

12 F. E. Lavington, *The English Capital Market* (London, 1921) p. 210. The work of the chief administrative officers of the Deutsche Bank, as described by Lavington, is surprisingly similar to the tasks of the general office of a modern multi-divisional firm as described by Chandler, op. cit., p. 9. The practice of interlocking directorates, whereby industrialists sat on the boards of banks and bankers on the boards of firms, greatly facilitated informed decision making. See J. H. Clapham, *The Economic Development of France and Germany, 1815–1914*, 4th ed. (Cambridge, 1963), p. 393.

13 J. H. Clapham, op. cit., 390.

14 L. E. Davis, 'The Investment Market, 1870–1914: The Evolution of a National Market', *Purdue Faculty Papers in Economic History, 1956–1966* (Homewood, 1967) pp. 119–59. It is a reasonable assumption that the financial instruments Davis was concerned with were homogeneous in their risk characteristics even though it is possible that regional fluctuations in economic activity would justify some interest differential.

15 Ibid., pp. 136–7.

16 Ibid., pp. 150–2.

17 Clapham, op. cit., pp. 394–5. H. Neuberger and H. H. Stokes, 'German Banks and German Growth, 1883–1913: An Empirical View', *Journal of Economic History*, XXXIV (1974) 710–31.

18 Davis, 'Industrial Concentration', p. 669.

19 See Davis, 'Industrial Concentration' pp. 680–2 for a discussion of this in the US. Clapham, op. cit., p. 394 for Germany.

20 See Edward Ames and Nathan Rosenberg, 'Changing Technological Leadership and Industrial Growth', *Purdue Faculty Papers in Economic History, 1956–1966* (Homewood, 1967) pp. 363–82 for a discussion of some of the more implausible ways in which a head-start has been alleged to be a handicap.

21 For an exception, see J. R. T. Hughes, 'Wicksell on the Facts: Prices and Interest Rates, 1844 to 1914' in J. N. Wolfe (ed.), *Value, Capital and Growth: Papers in honor of Sir John Hicks* (Chicago, 1968) 215–56.

22 F. Crouzet, 'Editor's Introduction' in F. Crouzet (ed.), *Capital Formation in the Industrial Revolution* (London, 1972) p. 33.

23 Ibid., p. 32.

24 E. V. Morgan and W. A. Thomas, *The Stock Exchange: Its History and Functions* (London, 1962) pp. 38–40. They note, however, that the operation of the act seemed not to hinder company promotion unduly (p. 40).

25 J. R. T. Hughes, *Fluctuations in Trade, Industry and Finance: a study of British economic development, 1850–1860* (Oxford, 1960) pp. 229–31.

26 Hughes, op. cit., pp. 283–4.

27 R. S. Sayers, *Bank of England Operations, 1890–1914* (London, 1936) p. 116–7.

28 Sayers, op. cit., pp. 125–6.
29 J. B. Jefferys, *Trends in Business Organization in Great Britain since 1856* (unpublished Ph.D. thesis, University of London, June, 1938) p. 142.
30 Jefferys, op. cit., p. 17; Davis, op. cit., p. 670.
31 C. A. E. Goodhart, *The Business of Banking, 1891–1914* (London, 1972). Commenting on the portfolio policies of the London clearing banks, which had absorbed most of the local banks through amalgamation, Goodhart notes that: 'The major gap in portfolios was, as is well known, the absence of industrial, especially domestic industrial stocks, from their holdings' (p. 135).
32 Jefferys, op. cit., p. 18.
33 Ibid., p. 119.
34 W. T. C. King, *History of the London Discount Market* (London, 1936) p. 232.
35 King, op. cit., p. 257.
36 Jefferys, op. cit., p. 18.
37 Ibid., p. 119.
38 Lavington, op. cit., p. 201.
39 W. A. Thomas, *The Provincial Stock Exchanges* (London, 1973) pp. 137–9.
40 Lavington, op. cit., p. 208.
41 Thomas, op. cit., p. 139. Compare Thomas' figure of £4–£5 million per year raised on the provincial stock exchanges on average in the years 1900–1913 with the figures for private sector capital formation given by C. H. Feinstein, *National Income, Expenditure and Output of the United Kingdom, 1855–1965* (Cambridge, 1972), pp. T-85, 86. Thomas' figures do not include the £12–£18 million mentioned by Lavington, op. cit., p. 204 raised privately without a prospectus. Such a financial transaction really doesn't require a stock exchange for it is essentially an arrangement among business partners and acquaintances.
42 Lavington, op. cit., pp. 200–206.
43 Morgan and Thomas, op. cit., chs 5–8.
44 Marc Nerlove, 'Factors Affecting Differences Among Rates of Return on Investments in Common Stock', *Review of Economics and Statistics*, L (1968) 312–31. Acceptance of Nerlove's conclusions must be tempered by recognition that he did not use a portfolio model to adjust for differences in risk (*ex post*) among securities and that hence his results are biased by mis-specification. Furthermore the calculation of rates or return of securities based on fairly arbitrary choice of holding patterns causes further distortion. (I would like to thank Marshall Ross for stressing this point.) However doubtful his estimation techniques may be, his conclusions are nevertheless highly plausible and supported by the recent concern on major stock exchanges over insider trading.
45 Nerlove, op. cit., p. 328. Recent proposals to require firms to include in their annual report a forecast of the firm's future prospects may be a useful way to remedy this situation. However, such a forecast may be so conjectural, it is alleged, as to allow management to conceal its true views if it so desired
46 'The Nineteenth Century and After', December, 1900, p. 960, quoted in Jefferys, op. cit., p. 423.
47 Jefferys, op. cit., pp. 409–10.
48 Morgan and Thomas, op. cit., p. 110.
49 An examination of data presented by Michael Edelstein ('The Rate of Return of U.K. Home and Foreign Investment', unpublished Ph.D. thesis, University of Pennsylvania, 1970, pp. 235–7) indicates that no more than 18 per cent of the securities held by UK subjects in 1870 could be classified as risky; this figure had risen to no more than 31 per cent by 1913 and most of this rise was offset by a sharp decrease in securities of moderate risk compared with the proportion of such securities held in 1870. The definition of risk class is based on *ex post* evaluation of the variability of money payments on debt in each class. Hence all

securities bore an interest rate risk, but British government securities were virtually certain not to default from the nominal payment. There were, of course, variations in all classes; for example, not all foreign government securities were of equal safety although by 1913 London was accepting very few doubtful issues. American railways and companies of all regions were a mixed lot; the bulk of their issues were fixed interest rather than variable and most were well established. If anything, the division into classes probably overstates the variability of the expected yields by 1913. The division used here accords with Lavington, op. cit., pp. 193–4; 'It seems reasonable to assume that the investor has fairly adequate bargaining knowledge when he enters the market to buy, let us say, the stocks issued by a Colonial Government, a reputable foreign state or a large municipality or the debentures or preference shares offered by a railway of proved earning capacity . . . Let us make an exceedingly rough division of the whole series of securities offered in the English market, placing on the one side stocks and shares of the kind just described and on the other a large mass of less well-known securities whose main constituents are the stocks and shares of new joint stock companies, formed under the Companies Act.'

50 Jefferys, op. cit., pp. 365–6. H. Burton and D. C. Corner, *Investment and Unit Trusts in Britain and America* (London, 1968) p. 46.
51 Burton and Corner, op. cit., p. 15.
52 Burton and Corner, op. cit., pp. 40–42.
53 Jefferys, op. cit., pp. 365–6. In the absence of transactions costs, this behaviour of course would be non-optimal.
54 Lavington, op. cit., pp. 210–11.
55 Barry Supple, *The Royal Exchange Assurance: A History of British Insurance, 1720–1970* (Cambridge, 1970) pp. 330–48. Also see P. G. M. Dickson, *The Sun Insurance Office, 1710–1960* (Oxford, 1960) pp. 234, 262–3.
56 Supple, op. cit., p. 348.
57 See D. K. Sheppard, *The Growth and Role of U.K. Financial Institutions, 1880–1962* (London, 1971) pp. 154–6. The highest figure given is 3·7 per cent, reached in 1911.
58 Supple, op. cit., pp. 334–5.
59 Jefferys, op. cit., p. 298.
60 Select Committee on the Operations of the Companies Act of 1862 and 1867, *Parliamentary Papers*, England, 1877, VIII, QQ. 1936–2081, cited in Davis, op. cit., p. 671. Davis noted that this clientele rivalled in numbers the list kept by J. P. Morgan twenty-five years later.
61 Jefferys, op. cit., p. 298.
62 Ibid., p. 299.
63 Ibid., p. 320.
64 Ibid., p. 309. The total numbers of failures are cited by Jefferys as 30–50 per cent of all those floated.
65 Jefferys, op. cit., p. 313.
66 Ibid., p. 365.
67 Ibid., p. 365.
68 Lavington, op. cit., p. 213.
69 Ibid., p. 213; emphasis in the original.
70 L. Hannah, 'Electricity in Britain: The Pioneering Years (1882–1913)', (unpublished paper prepared for the History Project of the Electricity Council, 1975) p. 8.
71 Morgan and Thomas, op. cit., p. 111.
72 I. C. R. Byatt, 'The British Electrical Industry, 1875–1914', (D.Phil thesis, Oxford, 1962) pp. 342–3.
73 Byatt, op. cit., p. 343.

G

74 Byatt, op. cit., pp. 347–8.
75 Byatt, op. cit., p. 350. It should be noted that Viscount Emlyn, the Chairman of the company who was quoted on the management reorganisation, was at least partially justified in his desire for control over technological extravagance. Crompton in 1896 had started an electric cooking and heating section which did not have good prospects (Byatt, p. 351). However, complete suspension of experimentation when technological change was as rapid as it was in the 1890s, when British firms were falling far behind foreign developments, was not a satisfactory response to the problem.
76 Byatt, op. cit., p. 350.
77 See Brinley Thomas, *Migration and Economic Growth: A Study of Great Britain and the Atlantic Economy*, 2nd ed. (Cambridge, 1973) for a discussion of the relationships among domestic construction, foreign investment and emigration.
78 Byatt, op. cit., p. 369.
79 Ibid., p. 370.
80 Byatt, op. cit., pp. 471–2.
81 Ibid., pp. 472–3.
82 Byatt, op. cit., pp. 129–30, 133–5.
83 Ibid., pp. 133, 482.
84 Another difficulty was that the power companies, except Newcastle, did not have a solid urban base and hence it was hard to tap the local sources which were the mainstay of British domestic capital formation. The projects were expensive enough to strain all but the very biggest centres. Byatt, op. cit., p. 482.
85 S. B. Saul, 'The Motor Industry in Britain to 1914', *Business History*, v (1962) 22.
86 G. L. Ayers, 'Fluctuations in New Capital Issues on the London Market, 1899–1913' (unpublished M.Sc. Thesis, University of London, 1934) Table 13.
87 Alfred Chandler, *Giant Enterprise* (New York, 1964) pp. 3–4.
88 See G. L. Ayers, *Fluctuations in New Capital Issues on the London Money Market, 1899–1913* (unpublished M.Sc. Thesis, University of London, 1934) Table 13.
89 Saul, 'The Motor Industry . . .', pp. 32, 40.
90 For example, Les Hannah, 'Takeover Bids in Britain before 1950: An Exercise in Business Pre-History', *Business History*, xvi (1974) 65–70, has shown that poor information can account for the virtual absence before 1945 of the takeover bid, a powerful device to insure efficient use of assets, although one which can be abused.
91 See Michael Edelstein, *The Rate of Return on U.K. Home and Foreign Investment, 1870–1913* (unpublished Ph.D. Thesis, University of Pennsylvania, 1970) and 'The Determinants of U.K. Investment Abroad, 1870–1913: The U.S. Case', *Journal of Economic History*, xxxiv (1974) 980–1007. Edelstein's work is an important pioneering effort. Further work along the lines he has suggested will make the analysis of capital market operations much more precise and incisive than has been true heretofore. His thesis has two particularly valuable contributions (1) rate of return data for several hundred issues over a forty-three year period and (2) applications of a rational pricing model to the securities for which he has data.
92 Edelstein, *Rate of Return*, pp. 238–75.
93 A further difficulty is that the pricing model is assumed to apply to an efficiently diversified portfolio and there is much evidence that efficient diversification across all securities did not take place. Hence, first class securities are even more firmly established as deriving their value largely in isolation from the rest of the economy.
94 Edelstein, 'Determinants', pp. 996–8.
95 Edelstein, op. cit., pp. 1006–7.
96 This argument is developed more fully in W. P. Kennedy, 'Foreign Investment,

Trade and Growth in the United Kingdom, 1870–1913', *Explorations in Economic History*, XI (1974) 415–44.

97 In my Ph.D. dissertation 'The Economics of Maturity: Aspects of British Economic Development, 1870–1914' (unpublished, Northwestern University, 1975) I have calculated that had Britain made a commitment of resources to telecommunications, electricity production, engineering (particularly electrical engineering and automobile production), construction and related industries similar to the commitment of resources for these purposes made in the US, the implied increase in growth rates could have been sufficient to raise per capita income in 1913 by as much as 55 per cent over the level it had actually reached in that year.

98 The manufacture of ring spinning textile machinery is an exception, but note that it was the product of an industry in which Britain was a world leader.

99 Chandler and Daems, op. cit., p. 31, recognise this when they call multi-divisional and conglomerate firms mini capital markets.

9 Strategy and Structure in the Manufacturing Sector

LESLIE HANNAH

For the business historian, entrepreneurship is an elusive factor, but it is necessarily at the centre of his subject. Other inputs are also an essential part of the production process – capital and labour being those most commonly evaluated, for example – but these are both more readily defined and more easily quantified[1] than the vital input of entrepreneurial skill which in part determines the extent, and efficiency, of the use of such inputs within the individual firm. There is no general agreement on what in more precise terms constitutes the entrepreneurial function, nor on what determines the supply of, or demand for, entrepreneurs; and there is, as yet, little normative management theory against which to judge the observed performance of businesses in a dynamic industrial environment. In focussing attention on one central aspect of entrepreneurship – the choice of the firm's strategy and the response to strategic innovation through changes in organisational structure – Professor Chandler has therefore done business historians a valuable service.[2]

The purpose of the present chapter is to pursue his method further in the United Kingdom context by examining the record of British entrepreneurs, historically and comparatively. Attention is focussed on one important strategy identified by Chandler as being widely accepted in America : that of the growth of the enterprise by diversification and by expansion in the 'new' industries of the twentieth century such as power machinery, electrical engineering and chemicals. Although there is still a relative paucity of good business history writing in Britain, it was possible to examine the record of a wide range of enterprises using sources such as company reports. For most of the largest companies information was available on whether they did devise such a strategy, and, if so, whether they were as successful as their American counterparts in devising the multidivisional structure which Professor Chandler has shown to be the crucial adaptive response necessary for the efficient management of such a strategy.[3]

I

Dr Channon's findings on the evolution of the strategy and structure of the leading British corporate enterprises in manufacturing industries between 1950 and 1970 are now well-known.[4] In 1950 only a dozen among the largest British firms had adopted the multidivisional structure which has become the dominant form of organisation in twentieth century America. On the other hand research on other European countries suggests that Britain was no slower than France, Germany or Italy in the early introduction of multidivisional organisations and that the transition to the multidivisional form was more complete in Britain by 1970 than in the other three countries.[5] America may have led Britain in the range and impact of its organisational innovators in the industrial system of the 1920s and 1930s, but failure in this respect, if it can be counted a failure, was, it seems, even more marked in continental Europe.

One of the reasons for the adoption of the multidivisional form in Britain in the postwar period was undoubtedly the American cultural and economic penetration of a country with whose manufacturing firms US-based international corporations had increasingly close links. Not only were the American management consultants, McKinsey and Company, involved in introducing the multidivisional organisation in many British-owned companies after 1950, but a number of the largest British corporations which adopted the innovation rapidly were wholly – or dominantly – owned subsidiaries of American parents. The American-owned firms on Channon's list of 1950 classified as having this multidivisional structure were largely so classed because they were organised as geographic divisions of international companies. Thus Vauxhall was the British division of General Motors, and Ford of Britain was also a subsidiary of an American parent. In the oil industry, Esso operated as a subsidiary of Standard Oil of New Jersey, though in this case the British end was also itself organised on a divisional basis.[6] Other American firms on Channon's list were Mars, which was run by the son of the founder of the American confectionery company using a multidivisional structure, and Massey-Ferguson, an Anglo-Canadian company managed on the basis of geographic divisions.[7]

European-based international companies also account for three of the multidivisional organisations in Channon's List. The Swiss Nestlé company was managed on the basis of geographical divisions, whilst the Dutch Phillips company, with its substantial interests in the British electronics industry, had a mixed structure of geographical divisions and product-based divisions. A similar mixed structure was operated in the Anglo-Dutch Unilever enterprise. Unilever, by far the largest food company both in Britain and in Europe, was one of the few in that industry which broke away from the personal dominance of the founder and his family – in this case Lord Leverhulme – and established a professional, largely non-family, management hierarchy. Formed by the amalgamation of the Dutch Margarine Union and the British Lever companies in 1929, its management defies summary. The history of its complicated Anglo-Dutch financial and managerial structure can be traced in the three volumes of Professor Wilson's well-known history.[8] Suffice it to say here that its diversified product range (centred on soap, foods and fats but including fishing and large retail chains) created pressures for a structure based on decentralisation by product, whilst its far-flung markets, by contrast, suggested divisions based on geographical area. (The company sold most of its products throughout Europe, America and the Empire, and was, through the United Africa Company and its Asian subsidiaries, also heavily involved in trade in the rest of the world.) The result was a complex attempt to achieve the advantages of both forms of divisionalisation – regional and product-based – with the disadvantages of neither, in its world wide management. In the UK (Unilever's largest market and production centre), management had by 1950 been divided into four product divisions (known as 'executives') – soap, margarine, oil mills and food – each controlling a range of subsidiary companies.

There were only four wholly British companies in Channon's sample which had adopted a multidivisional structure by 1950. Smiths Instruments was an engineering company specialising in the technically sophisticated and expanding automotive instruments industry, and had diversified into clocks, aircraft instruments, appliance controls and industrial control mechanisms. The company was managed by a system of 4 product divisions established in 1944. Spillers' divisions, on the other hand, were older-established, and regional rather than product-based. The company had been built up by the sequential acquisition of regional, family-owned millers in Britain and abroad. In 1926 the subsidiaries were divided into four regional groups, in each of which an area general manager was given full executive authority, and a fifth regional group, Scotland, was subsequently added.[9]

British-American Tobacco – in which American Tobacco had been forced to relinquish its holdings by a US antitrust action – was by 1950 a wholly British concern, and its international tobacco interests (originally taken over from the (British) Imperial Tobacco and American Tobacco companies) were also managed on the basis of geographical divisions.

Finally, one of the largest companies in the sample which dominated the UK market in chemicals was Imperial Chemical Industries, with a modified form of the multidivisional structure.[10] The ICI is in many ways the most interesting of the examples, for it clearly exemplifies the link between the strategy of diversification and the multidivisional structure. The origins of the ICI strategy can be discerned in one of its founding companies, Nobel Industries Limited, in the years immediately following the First World War. The original Nobels Company was the dominant producer of explosives in Britain, and, although it was split by the declaration of war from the German explosives trust of which it had once formed a part, it naturally benefited from high demand for its products in the war. As peace approached, however, it became obvious, both to Nobels and to its smaller competitors, that they would suffer from serious overcapacity and thus in 1918 thirty of the major British explosives manufacturers joined together in a merger aiming to rationalise capacity to a level appropriate to the reduced peacetime demand for explosives. The programme of contraction proved highly successful – forty factories were closed by 1924 – but also had a positive side. From a base in metal-working, which some of the partners brought to the merger, Nobel Industries embarked on an ambitious programme of diversification. They maintained profitability at a high level and surplus profits were invested in shares in fast growing companies such as US General Motors, Dunlop (the British tyre firm) and Lucas (a major automobile components manufacturer) as well as directly in the manufacture of chemical and metal products such as artificial leather (then being widely adopted in motor cars), zip fasteners, car radiators and paints. Thus, within a short period the main production of the old Nobels company, explosives, accounted for a relatively small part of Nobel Industries Limited's total output. The new strategy was managed by a strongly centralised, functionally differentiated management structure, with decentralisation of production management to subsidiary companies but tight central control over most other policies.

In seeking further expansion it was natural for Nobels to look to the chemical industry in which the company had already decided to intensify its research effort. The main opportunity arose in 1926 when some difficult negotiations led to the formation of Imperial Chemical Industries. This company, by far the largest merger in British manufacturing industry between the wars, created the grouping which has dominated the British chemical industry since that date. In addition to Nobels, the partners in the company were Brunner Mond, United Alkali and British Dyestuffs. United Alkali and Brunner Mond divided the UK heavy chemical industry between them and Brunners, the senior of the two, was developing some interesting research in high-pressure chemical technology at its Billingham plant, as a consequence of war-time research on the fixation of nitrogen from the air to produce fertiliser. British Dyestuffs had also expanded in the war, as the British government had encouraged the few weak British manufacturers to merge and expand production in order to fill the deficit left by the cutting off of the imports of German dyes (which had held the British market before the war). In its product lines, then, the new chemical grouping was highly diversified within the chemical industry both in heavy chemicals and in the developing fine chemicals side. In order to run this diversified grouping, policies of centralisation were at first attempted and they proved useful in imposing a common policy on matters such as accounting and staffing in all the subsidiaries of the group. Nonetheless it soon became clear that the group was too large and diversified to be run efficiently by what was essentially a continuation, in expanded form, of the highly centralised head office of Nobels, with direct functional responsibilities at the centre for the organisation of all subsidiaries. The first steps towards decentralisation took place in 1928 when the 'Birmingham' end of the business – that is, broadly, those subsidiaries engaged in metals and engineering – was decentralised into a separate division, or, as they were known in ICI, 'group'. Other 'groups' followed shortly to decentralise the management of subsidiaries engaged in alkalis, dyes, explosives, fertilisers and synthetics, general chemicals, leathercloth, and lime, cement and plaster. Whilst some policies – notably the commercial initiatives which created a complex tangle of national and international market-sharing and price-fixing agreements – remained under the control of the ICI head office, the divisions developed as the main decentralised unit of management, with financial control from head office exercising an important discipline.

ICI is an interesting case of the evolution of strategy and structure among British enterprises because it was heavily influenced by American precedents. Harry McGowan, in particular, who was the architect of Nobels' strategy of diversification, was strongly influenced by the similar initiatives of the du Ponts in the United States. They too, for example, had invested in the prosperity of the expanding car industry both through investments in General Motors and in chemical products destined for the automobile industry such as leathercloth and paints. Throughout the decades after its formation, ICI remained in close touch with Du Pont, sharing patents and agreeing on the division of world markets between themselves and the German chemical giant IG Farben. The ICI management can hardly, then, have been unaware of the pathbreaking experiments in multidivisional organisation then being made at Du Pont and General Motors[11] and it seems highly likely that they were influenced by American precedents in devising their own multidivisional structure.

II

Are we to conclude, then, that, except where American ownership or American influence were present, there was little managerial innovation in Britain before 1950? This would of course be going too far. There were in fact important initiatives in developing such modern techniques as budgetary control and mechanised accounting in large scale businesses,[12] and it may be that, in defining multidivisional organisation in too strict a sense, Channon's sample of the largest companies of 1950 underestimates the extent to which large companies had overcome the problems of managerial diseconomies of scale, growth and diversification. Two companies within his sample may be cited which had shown a positive response to the need to develop new strategies and structures in the interwar period : Turner and Newall, and Dunlop. Turner and Newall[13] had been formed as a merger of four asbestos companies in 1920 and in the following decade the company acquired a range of its competitors and suppliers, including a substantial interest in Rhodesian asbestos mines. Its strategy was not, however, limited to vertical integration for, within the area of its own competence, the firm also entered the expanding brake linings and asbestos cement industries. Soon after, it began to develop a management structure appropriate to this diversifying strategy within the asbestos industry. Initially a loose holding company structure was adopted. The Turner and Newall board confined its attention to general matters such as finance, whilst the operating units (branch and controlled companies) retained their own boards or executive directors. Cooperation and co-ordination were achieved through monthly meetings of the directors of the operating units, but the company stressed the absence of interference from head office and the freedom and flexibility of their subsidiaries. During 1929, however, the acquired companies were regrouped, with manufacturing and selling units being placed under one roof where possible, and the problem of consolidation and integration led to the consideration of a divisional structure. In 1931 four 'units' (i.e. divisions) – Mining, Textile Manufacture, Asbestos Cement and Magnesia Insulation – were set up, and the financial relationships in the group were reorganised. Consolidation of the formerly independent companies was pressed ahead by rationalisation schemes within each division, it being envisaged that in the longer run the subsidiary companies would disappear, and operations would be conducted entirely as branches of the parent company. This programme of consolidation within main product divisions continued satisfactorily throughout the 1930s. The company also expanded through subsidiary companies in America and Europe : these reported directly to the Turner and Newall parent board. Turner and Newall thus appears to have had the basic elements of the multidivisional structure almost as early as ICI, though the links between the central office and the divisions seem to have been very weakly defined, and remained so throughout the various reorganisations of the 1950s and 1960s.

A weak multidivisional structure can also be discerned in the Dunlop Rubber Company,[14] the only major British-owned rubber producer. Dunlop began as a specialist in tyres, but its production répertoíre was gradually extended vertically with the purchase of rubber plantations, cotton factories, and wheel companies. After financial collapse in the early 1920s, the company was reorganised by Sir Eric Geddes, and expansion then continued with the growth of the market for car tyres and the acquisition of the diversified rubber interests of the Charles Macintosh Group. By the early 1930s the company had developed a decentralised form of organisation which had some characteristics of the multidivisional structure. Fort Dunlop, the main centre of tyre manufacture in the Midlands, was run directly by the parent company, but other assets in England were organised into four divisions : General Rubber Goods Division, Footwear Division, Garment Division and Sports Division. The divisions controlled their own sales and were responsible to a General Manager of Subsidiary Companies at head office. The Rim and Wheel Company and the cotton mills were run as separate units but under the control of a Fort Dunlop head office triumvirate specialised on functional lines : Sir George Beharrel controlling commercial policy, de Paula controlling finance and budgeting and Collyer controlling manufacturing. Foreign subsidiaries in France, Germany, the United States and Japan were organised as separate units and managed by nationals of those countries. Dunlop did not develop a fully articulated multidivisional structure, however, and by the 1950s was becoming increasingly centralised. Writing in *The Manager* in this later period Sir Reay Geddes commented on the limitations of the earlier divisions : 'Until the late 1950s, the day-to-day control of the Dunlop Group was exercised by full-time directors of the company who had functional responsibilities for specific aspects of the company's business. These directors were supported at divisional level (operating divisions or subsidiaries) by managers who held responsibilities for the same functions and who formed an Operating Committee of equals at the division. In a sentence, the group was therefore highly centralised.'[15]

Without a closer examination of the strategy, structure and financial performance of companies like Turner and Newall and Dunlop in the period 1920–1950 – and there is so far no sign of scholarly business histories from those two companies to match those available in the case of other companies – it is difficult to assess whether the limited multidivisional structures which they adopted were particularly appropriate to their problems. Closer study of such cases may reveal that there were perfectly good reasons why these companies did not develop their embryonic multidivisional structures further. There is already, however, a growing body of evidence from other companies that the poor response to organisational challenges from British firms in this period inhibited change for which there was some rationale. Professor Coleman, for example, has shown that in Courtaulds[16] the growth of rayon production at home and abroad was managed on traditional lines with no major organisational innovations. The company remained essentially a single-product firm, with only minor diversifications into cellophane (jointly with a French company, in the 1930s) and into nylon (jointly with ICI in the War). By 1950, production was managed by four vertically-related 'Groups' (rather than product divisions) – Yarn Mills, Textiles, Spinning Machinery and Chemicals – the latter being a producer of the raw materials for rayon production. The management resisted suggestions for further expansion by acquisition and the adoption of a wider strategy of diversification and a more fully-articulated divisional structure was therefore delayed for several decades.

III

There is also evidence from business histories that some British companies which did adopt a strategy of diversification at an early stage failed to establish the appropriate financial and managerial controls on efficiency which were essential to the success of such a strategy. Vickers[17] provides an important example of such a failure. This company, with its experience of large scale organisation in the engineering trades, ought to have been in a favoured position for entering some of the new, high productivity, rapid-growth industries in the interwar period. Its established position was as an integrated armaments firm, with interests in the production of its raw material, steel, and a final product portfolio ranging from machine guns to warships. This made it a natural candidate for expansion in the First World War and it was involved in the development of important new armaments, thus consolidating its already substantial degree of diversification within the general field of engineering and shipbuilding. By 1918 its products included airships, aluminium, aeroplanes, and submarines as well as more conventional weapons of war and general engineering products. The buoyant demand experienced in wartime would, the Board hoped, be matched in peacetime if they made provision for manufacturing products such as railway locomotives and merchant shipping, using their wartime heavy industrial capacity; on the lighter industrial side they were to diversify into sewing machines and motor car parts and, through acquisition, into optical instruments. Already, much earlier, in 1901, Vickers had made a promising diversification into the infant automobile industry with the acquisition of the Wolseley Company, and both in automobiles and in its other diversifying strategies, the firm might have hoped to derive some benefits from its existing engineering skills and reputation. Yet diversification plans did not stop there – the Board's Peace Products Committee even addressed itself to the relative merits of producing consumer toys such as 'boy rabbits (squeaking)' and 'girl rabbits (non-squeaking)'.[18] In their more traditional field, the acquisition of the Metropolitan Amalgamated Railway Carriage and Wagon Company in 1919 was a more sensible exploitation of their likely area of comparative advantage. The Metropolitan Company had already acquired the British Westinghouse Electrical and Manufacturing Company from American Westinghouse in 1917, and when it was itself acquired by Vickers in 1919, it thus brought to the group an established dominant position in the rapidly expanding electrical manufacturing industry and the hope of a substantial slice of the hoped-for market in equipment for the electrification of Britain's railways.

Seen as a clear sighted search for future growth markets, then, Vickers' strategy must gain high marks – possibly, indeed, higher than the strategy adopted by Nobels, which faced similar problems of a substantial, but temporary, wartime demand for munitions and the need to diversify into peace products with prospects of substantial growth. Yet, for a variety of reasons, Vickers' strategy met with rather less success than that of Nobels. On the armaments side, Vickers faced a catastrophic decline in military and naval demand which weakened its finances, and, on the civilian side, schemes for railway electrification were, with the notable exception of those on the Southern Railway, disappointingly slow to materialise in Britain. Vickers' undoubted stock of skills in heavy engineering proved to be somewhat less transferable than had initially been hoped : the engineering tolerances for civilian locomotives, for example, were less demanding than those for ordnance equipment, and, as a result, Vickers' costs proved to be substantially higher than those of specialist locomotive manufacturers. Their automobile subsidiary, Wolseley, failed to secure for itself a position as a leading mass producer in the hectic expansion of the British motor car industry of the early 1920s, and in 1923–5 made losses totalling £841,000 : in October 1926 the company was unable to fund Wolseley's debenture interest and redemption obligations. The receiver appointed by the creditors sold the business to the rival manufacturer William Morris (who had seized the opportunity to establish a British-owned mass production car company) for £730,000.

This policy of selling off subsidiaries – even the more profitable ones – was soon to become a general one for Vickers, and it is difficult to resist the conclusion that its strategy of diversification had been too ambitious and its managerial response to the problems of diversification quite inadequate. Certainly this was the view of the outside committees called in by the Board to investigate the company's overall strategy and structure in the mid-1920s. Until that time the Vickers Board had attempted to run the group as a holding company. The parent Vickers company had a direct operating interest in the major fields of armaments production, and in other fields the various subsidiaries had varying degrees of independence. In 1925 the company called in Dudley Docker, the industrialist, Reginald McKenna, the banker and Sir William Plender, the accountant, to examine its management difficulties and the reasons for accumulating losses. The three-man committee recommended the separation of the company's assets into five divisions, a structure which might, if properly developed, have enabled a central office to make their overall strategy work through largely financial controls which enabled initiative to be retained in the individual profit centres. This proposal for a far reaching reorganisation was seconded by another accountant, Sir Mark Webster Jenkinson, in a further report commissioned in the same year. Changes in the relationship of the parent company and subsidiary boards were put into effect, but the changes appear to have been both too little and too late; certainly by the late 1920s a clear-cut divisional structure had failed to emerge. The only way to save the company at that stage appeared to be to sell off important interests – a decision which meant abandoning the ambitious strategy of diversification. Vickers' prosperous aluminium subsidiary, James Booth, fell victim early to this policy, as did its Canadian subsidiary, and, in 1928 its electrical manufacturing interests – which had built up a promising reputation – were re-sold to American control. (They were then amalgamated with British Thomson-Houston to form Associated Electrical Industries.) The interests in the traditional, slower growing markets were retained, however, and, with Bank of England guidance, Vickers established subsidiary companies jointly with its major competitors to rationalise excess capacity in armaments, shipbuilding and railway equipment. Hence Vickers became a holding company with a dominant interest in the resulting Vickers-Armstrong, Metropolitan-Cammell and English Steel Corporation groupings, and it was not until decades later that a wider strategy of diversification could be successfully re-adopted.[19] The failure of its strategy was duly registered in share prices. The contrast is particularly clear in the comparison with Nobels, whose management, as we have seen, had followed a similar strategy. By the adoption of a more efficient organisation structure, however, Nobels proved to be more adept at achieving their goals. Early in 1919 Vickers and Nobels had been similarly rated by the stock market, their market valuation at £19·5m and £16·3m giving them, respectively, fourth and seventh rank among manufacturing companies. By 1930 Nobels – by now transformed into ICI – had gained in value, was worth £77·3m, and had risen to third rank; whilst Vickers, despite having a comparable record of expenditure on diversifying acquisitions, had fallen to twelfth place and, even if all the values of its subsidiary companies are aggregated with the parent, Vickers was worth little more, at £19·6m, than it had been in 1919.[20]

It seems clear then that, in the case of Vickers, the strategy of corporate diversification was not able to make its potentially important contribution to the change in the structure of the output of the economy. But how representative was this failure? Without a wider range of company histories on which to base judgement, it is difficult to be precise, but it is clear that there were other, similar examples. Armstrong-Whitworth, the eleventh largest manufacturing company in 1919 (and Vickers' main rival as a naval shipbuilder) had shrunk to a shadow of its former self by the 1930s, despite its attempts to diversify into automobiles and aircraft. Cammell Laird and John Brown, also heavily involved in the shipbuilding industry, failed in their attempt to diversify into electrical engineering. Their English Electric subsidiary (which they had created by merging a number of firms in the closing years of the First World War) collapsed financially in the 1920s as the management failed to consolidate the diverse elements in the merger. In 1929 they recognised their failure by selling English Electric to American interests, and it only recovered in the 1930s by dint of orders from its American owners and with the benefit of a technical agreement with American Westinghouse.[21] The Birmingham Small Arms Company (BSA) was more fortunate and retained its position as an important engineering company in the interwar depression, but its automobile subsidiary, Daimler, did not provide a basis for entry into the mass market for cars. There was an abortive merger with the Associated Equipment Company, which it hoped would allow the Daimler company to consolidate its position as a leading supplier of commercial vehicles, but this was dissolved in 1929 and in 1936 BSA finally disposed of its interest in Daimler.[22]

IV

Even in industries where the management stuck to their main line of business and did not attempt substantial diversification – and in many industries with industry-specific skills the benefits they could have expected from diversifications may have been small or nonexistent – the managerial response to new strategic and organisational needs was also often disappointing. Two examples from the new industries – Associated Electrical Industries and Morris Motors – suggest that, within fast growing industries themselves, such managerial failings may have exercised a retarding influence on structural change. The formation of Associated Electrical Industries[23] in 1928, stemmed directly from the disintegration of Vickers' strategy of diversification, and marked a return to American control for its Metropolitan-Vickers (formerly British Westinghouse) subsidiary. The new American owners – GE – put it together with some smaller electrical concerns and with their own British Thomson-Houston subsidiary. After the initial merger, however, the firm was little influenced by American precedents, for the Americans were uneasy about publicising their ownership of the British company, and AEI's management enjoyed a good deal of autonomy on organisational and other policy questions. After lengthy and heated discussions about the organisation of AEI, it was decided to keep the constituent companies as autonomous units. Thus BTH and Metrovick kept their own bank accounts and trading identity, though large capital expenditures had to be authorised by the parent company's Executive Committee. The parent company also sponsored some inter-company coordinating committees but these had little power, and, extraordinarily, the Commercial Coordinating and Policy Committee was one of the last to be established. The main diversification was into domestic appliances, based on an earlier initiative of BTH, which in 1920 copied its American parent and set up the Hotpoint Electric Appliance Ltd subsidiary. In 1944–5 Lord Chandos reorganised the company, establishing greater financial control from head office and closing down many of the smaller plants and subsidiaries, but the company's managerial structure remained a source of trouble until the takeover by GEC in 1967. By contrast, the American Westinghouse Company and the German Siemens and AEG companies appear to have been more innovative in their management structures and succeeded in rationalising their production lines, avoiding both loss of initiative and excessive duplication, yet achieving successful control through general budgets and production plans and through central coordination.[24]

In the automobile industry, the two major British-owned manufacturers, Morris and Austin, were, until the postwar period, firmly under the control of their founders, William Morris (Lord Nuffield), and Sir Herbert Austin[25]. The Morris Motors holding company allowed some decentralisation of authority to subsidiaries (e.g. to the MG sports car subsidiary at Abingdon) but the style of management remained personal. Another firm, Pressed Steel, which, like Morris, was based in Oxford, used American technology to produce pressed car bodies, and also diversified into consumer durables on the General Motors model. There was much to be said for the integration of Pressed Steel into the Morris company, but it remained a separate company, and Morris was even obliged to relinquish his initial shareholding in it, so that it could more freely sell car bodies to competitors. The basis which had existed for diversification in America was thus less clearly apparent in Britain. Had Morris and Austin been willing to sink their differences in a merged company, which might have rationalised production and grown large enough to integrate backwards into bodymaking by the acquisition of Pressed Steel, the pattern might have approximated more closely to that in the American market. However personal differences between the two men wrecked several attempts at bringing them together, and the merger and the acquisition of Pressed Steel did not in fact occur until the postwar years. The adoption of a multidivisional structure was also postponed until the retirement of the founders. Another British automobile manufacture, the Rootes Group (now Chrysler UK) was built up in the 1930s by a series of mergers, but again the style of management remained a largely personal one. There was thus no equivalent to the entrepreneurial, diversifying management strategy of General Motors in America. The UK automobile companies were smaller, less diversified, and under family management for a longer period than their US counterparts. Even when re-armament and the Second World War brought the diversification of some of them into aeroplane manufacture, this proved to be a temporary phase in their development and they reverted to being specialist car manufacturers on the return to peace.

In the more traditional industries also, the organisational response to strategic innovation frequently appears to have been inadequate. The Distillers Company, for example, was one of the larger British companies involved in the processing of agricultural produce,[26] a position confirmed in 1924 by its acquisition of Johnnie Walker and Buchanan-Dewar, the branded whisky blenders (the value of the merger was the second largest in manufacturing industry between the wars). The business was divided between three main operating groups of subsidiaries: the Distillers Company, Scottish Malt Distillers and the blenders and distributors (basically Johnnie Walker and Buchanan-Dewar). Rationalisation in 1930 removed some anomalies: the Scottish Malt Distillers subsidiary for example, took over some of the malt distilleries owned by the blending companies, and the four bottle manufacturing works previously owned by various companies in the group were centralised under one holding company. In 1932 the parent company centralised the financial surpluses of the subsidiaries. By 1936, however, the pressure on the parent company's managing director had become too great and a management committee of five of the chairmen of subsidiaries replaced him. The company had diversified and its various activities are referred to in reports as being managed by 'departments' or 'sections', including Potable Spirits, Industrial Alcohol,

Chemicals, Bottles, Building Supplies and Carbonic Acid Gas; during the War the chemicals section developed plastics. Despite the sale of their bottlemaking section to United Glass in 1937, this diversification, together with a substantial number of acquisitions in distilling and blending, must have placed further strains on the management. Nonetheless the system based on the old Management Committee seems to have continued virtually unchanged – with another member being added in 1949. Not until 1953 were the subsidiary companies reorganised : it was then announced that to avoid overlapping and dispersion of control, the company's activities would be reorganised into divisions rather than carried out through subsidiaries. Even then, the reorganisation had only limited success, and the company later partly abandoned its strategy of diversification by selling off its chemical interests to British Petroleum.

It is, of course, too simplistic to subsume all major organisational failings of the period before 1950 under the general category of omitting to introduce the Harvard Business School-approved diversification strategy and mature multidivisional structure. This structure – Professor Chandler himself was careful to point out[27] – was ideally suited to some industries which had certain characteristics and problems, but quite unsuited to others. In industries selling semi-finished products to a few large industrial consumers, in particular, the multidivisional structure is often inappropriate. Steelmakers in the United States, for example, found it easy to administer and coordinate large functional departments, and their marketing processes were relatively simple : there was thus no necessity for them to develop a decentralised, multidivisional structure. In Britain also a steel group such as the United Steel Companies[28] established centralised control over its subsidiaries in the 1920s, with strong central functional departments handling administration, purchasing and sales. The individual works were rationalised on a geographical basis from the centre, budgetary control was introduced, and local boards of management retained decentralised power only over production and works management. Multidivisional organisation was neither created nor required. Another industry with similar management characteristics was the textile industry and here too centralised, functional management was the norm. There was one exception which proves the rule : the Lancashire Cotton Corporation[29] which merged almost a hundred firms in 1929–30, and experimented with several methods of managerial control. Despite the fact that its product was a fairly homogenous one – basically coarse cotton yarn – its managing director, Captain John Ryan, who was something of an enthusiast for 'modern' management theory, tried to create a divisional structure. However he met serious opposition from traditionally-minded Lancashire mill managers and from the Board. Ryan was removed from his position and the combine reverted to a centralised, functionally-departmentalised management structure, with production management only being decentralised to individual mills, a structure which was almost certainly more appropriate to an undiversified company selling a standardised semi-finished product like cotton yarn to a limited range of industrial consumers.

V

Even in industries where multidivisional organisation has indisputably proved its value, it may also, as Dr Reader has recently reminded us,[30] have created difficulties for strategic innovation. The separate divisions in a large modern corporation like ICI create vested interests in their own product line which may inhibit innovation requiring cooperation between divisions. Thus when the importance of plastics was first recognised in the nineteen thirties, ICI was slow to create a new division to centralise and expand resources devoted to their development. Indeed, for all the supposed expertise of ICI's head office in evaluating investment projects, their major capital investment of the interwar years – that at Billingham – was fundamentally unprofitable and based on a quite misguided commercial assessment of its prospects by the leaders of the company.

In many other situations, however, the creative managerial innovations pioneered by US firms seem to have demonstrated the usefulness of the multidivisional form,[31] and more recent evidence confirms that companies adopting the multidivisional structure perform more efficiently than those not so doing.[32] Why then was it not more widely adopted in Britain? Part of the answer may be that Britain's firms simply did not require complex organisation structures. They were, in general, smaller than US firms, and thus the older, more personal, forms of management could survive the partial encroachment of bureaucratic, formalised structures with less loss of efficiency than would occur in larger US firms.[33] In both countries in the 1930s, however, there are clear signs that severe managerial problems of large scale were being encountered,[34] but it seems to be in America rather than in Britain that the creative innovations by problem-solving entrepreneurs were devised and more widely adopted. The more concentrated pattern of ownership in Britain may be an important influence here. This not only inhibited a strategy of merger and diversification – as in the case of firms such as Morris Motors[35] or Pilkingtons[36] – but, where such a strategy had been adopted, created a vested interest in preserving existing family managements in power, thus inhibiting rationalisation of capacity and organisation structure. Significantly it was not only the multidivisional structure which was relatively rare in

Britain, but also the centralised, functional structure which had been widely adopted in America. In Britain, and even more obviously in continental Europe, the looser holding company device was the more commonly accepted formal structure of large corporations.[37]

A holding company structure was compatible with a number of practical organisational forms and the existence of a holding company is not, by itself, an indication of inefficiency. Even a holding company with a very weak central office could provide facilities for the diversification of investors' risks[38] and some common facilities such as research and exchange of information. The holding company form could even disguise a structure which was in all its essentials similar to the multidivisional structure – ICI, for example, was formally organised as a holding company, and Dr Alford has suggested that Imperial Tobacco achieved many of the advantages of a multidivisional structure within the holding company framework.[39] Lucas – a major supplier of automobile components – is not classified by Channon as introducing a multidivisional organisation until 1951, but the managerial reorganisation of that date was in fact modelled on the existing structure of subsidiary companies which dated from the 1920s. Thus the company had in some respects operated previously as a multidivisional structure under head office control.[40]

It may reasonably be suspected, however, that a looser form of holding company structure, with few managerial advantages, was common in Britain. Companies like AEI, Hawker Siddeley, GKN, Liebigs, Cadbury-Fry, Stewarts and Lloyds, Tube Investments and Reckitt and Colman appear to have been little more than loose confederations of subsidiaries,[41] and it may reasonably be doubted whether such a structure can have achieved many of the potential economies of large scale. Suspicion is inevitably aroused that they were a form of cartel – albeit a strong and permanent cartel – which could achieve many of the private benefits of monopoly power whilst foregoing the social benefits which strategic and organisational innovation were more likely to generate. Nonetheless, in some confederations of firms, the incentive to innovate could overcome these problems. Fisons, the fertiliser group for example, was organised as a holding company of family firms but, as new investment in large scale plant made it possible to achieve economies, the old family shells were discarded and the smaller subsidiaries were consolidated into the larger ones.[42] Clearly a closer study of such individual cases of holding company organisation is required before they are given a blanket condemnation.

What then, may we conclude from this survey? It would, of course be wrong to suggest that the existence of differences in the strategies and structures of entrepreneurs in Britain from those being developed in the United States necessarily implies entrepreneurial failure on the part of the British, for the conditions in the two countries were clearly different. As in all European countries, wages in Britain were lower than in the United States, and hence markets for goods like power machinery, automobiles and electrical consumer durables were simply smaller in the UK than in the US. A strategy of diversification into these products was thus necessarily more halting in Britain than in America, and new organisational imperatives were perhaps correspondingly less demanding. Yet new products and new technologies *were* being widely introduced in Britain, managerial problems *were* perceived by contemporaries, and response in a number of the cases which we have been able to examine *was* clearly inadequate. In some cases, like Vickers or AEI, structure failed to respond to strategic needs; in others, like Morris Motors, an innovative strategy was not adopted and hence existing forms of organisation were not called in question. With increasing tariff protection after the abandonment of Britain's free trade policy in 1932, and with competitive pressures further inhibited by the operation of cartels and the holding company alliances of family firms, and, finally, with the siege economy of the war and postwar reconstruction, the penalties which these failings might have visited upon individual firms could be postponed. Ultimately, however, whatever the reasons for the situation, the penalties of failing to innovate in strategy and structure were to become all too clear – not only in Britain but in the rest of Europe also. In the free-trading, increasingly competitive world of the 1950s and 1960s, it was the American multinationals, with their superior technology and superior management, which set the pace in European innovation and growth.[43] American cultural and economic hegemony in Western Europe in the postwar era thus had its roots not primarily in political imperialism but rather in the innovating strategies and structures which had gained a firmer foothold in American corporations than among their British – or European – counterparts.

NOTES

1   However, the problems raised by the common definitions and measurements of capital and labour still hold the centre of the ring in economic debate: witness the Cambridge controversies on the theory of capital and the burgeoning literature on theories of human capital and skill differentials between workers.

2   A. D. Chandler, *Strategy and Structure: Chapters in the History of the Industrial Enterprise* (MIT Press, Cambridge, Mass., 1962).

3   The research was financed by the Social Science Research Council.

4   D. F. Channon, *The Strategy and Structure of British Enterprise* (London and New York, 1973). I am grateful to Dr Channon for providing me with a list of the firms which he classified as multidivisional in 1950 among his sample of the largest 92 companies. This list has not hitherto been published. The 12 companies are those mentioned in the paragraphs immediately following.

5 Harvard MBA dissertations by G. P. Dyas on France, C. H. Thanheiser on Germany and R. J. Pavan on Italy, as reported in Bruce R. Scott, 'The industrial state: old myths and new realities', *Harvard Business Review* (March–April 1973).

6 Channon, op. cit., p. 117.

7 However, Channon, op. cit., p. 110, suggests that the structure of geographical divisions was not fully articulated at Massey-Ferguson until 1956. Until 1953 the (Canadian) Massey-Harris and (British) Ferguson parts of the group were still independent.

8 C. Wilson, *The History of Unilever*, 2 vols (London, 1954); idem., *Unilever 1945–1965* (London, 1968).

9 Channon, op. cit., p. 166 and *Annual Reports* of the company.

10 The analysis of ICI which follows is based on W. J. Reader, *Imperial Chemical Industries: a History* (2 vols, London, 1970 and 1975); L. Hannah, 'Managerial Innovation and the Rise of the Large Scale Company in Interwar Britain', *Economic History Review*, xxvii (1974), W. J. Reader, 'Personality, Strategy and Structure', pp. 114–26 above.

11 Chandler, *Strategy and Structure*, chs 2 and 3.

12 Hannah, 'Managerial Innovation and the Rise of the Large-Scale Company in Interwar Britain', pp. 256–9.

13 N. A. Morling, 'History of Turner Brothers Asbestos Co. Ltd.', *Rochdale Literary and Scientific Society Transactions*, xxiv (1961); *Annual Reports* of the Company, 1924–50.

14 P. Jennings, *Dunlopera* (London, 1961); Sir Ronald Storrs, *Dunlop in War and Peace* (London, 1946); and the *Annual Reports* of the Company.

15 *The Manager* (July 1965) p. 31.

16 D. C. Coleman, *Courtaulds, an Economic and Social History* (Oxford, 1969) ii, passim.

17 For a fuller account see J. D. Scott, *Vickers: A History* (London, 1962). The following paragraphs are based on this account and on the author's own research in the Vickers' archives.

18 Scott, op. cit., p. 137.

19 Channon, *Strategy and Structure of British Enterprise*, pp. 155–6. Even in the 1950s the firm still encountered problems and not until 1965 was a structure of product divisions introduced, on advice from McKinsey and Company.

20 L. Hannah, *The Rise of the Corporate Economy* (London, 1976) Tables 8.1 and 8.2.

21 R. Jones and O. Marriott, *Anatomy of a Merger, The History of GEC, AEI and English Electric* (London, 1970) ch. 7.

22 St J. C. Nixon, *Daimler 1896–1946* (n.d.) pp. 159–61; Daimler also seems to have diversified into aircraft parts and radio manufacture, see (Balfour) Committee on Industry and Trade, *Survey of Metal Industries* (1928) p. 275.

23 Jones and Marriott, *Anatomy of a Merger*, especially chs 5 and 8. See also p. 193 above.

24 Chandler, *Strategy and Structure*, pp. 363–8; R. Brady, *The Rationalisation Movement in German Industry* (University of California Press, 1933) pp. 175–6, 178–9.

25 On the automobile industry, in this period, see G. Maxcy and A. Silberston, *The Motor Industry* (London, 1959) ch. 1; P. W. S. Andrews and E. Brunner, *The Life of Lord Nuffield* (Oxford, 1955) pp. 87–255.

26 This account is based on the Company's *Annual Reports*, 1922–50.

27 Chandler, *Strategy and Structure*, pp. 326–42.

28 P. W. S. Andrews and E. Brunner, *Capital Development in Steel* (Oxford, 1951).

29 This account is based on unpublished research by the author on the history of the Lancashire Cotton Corporation.

30 Reader, *ICI*, ii, passim.

31 Chandler, *Strategy and Structure*, pp. 342–78.

32 R. P. Rumelt, *Strategy, Structure and Economic Performance* (Harvard University

Press, Cambridge, Mass., 1974). Dr Channon also reports that preliminary results of his study of British service industries (see pp. 213–34 below) reveal a correlation between structure and performance (private communication September 1975).

33   In my *Rise of the Corporate Economy*, ch. 6, I have stressed the role of innovation in overcoming managerial diseconomies of scale, and this is also the focus of much of the current discussion by economists of multidivisional organisation. However, in his *Strategy and Structure*, Chandler explicitly placed more emphasis on the diversification (rather than the scale) of output as a source of managerial problems which the creation of divisions could overcome.

34   Hannah, *The Rise of the Corporate Economy*, ch. 9; Hannah, 'Managerial Innovation and the Rise of the Large Scale Company', pp. 226–9.

35   pp. 195–6 above.

36   Compare Pilkingtons (pp. 85–94 above) with Pittsburgh Plate Glass which was more diversified (see Chandler, *Strategy and Structure*, p. 342).

37   Channon, *Strategy and Structure of British Enterprise*, p. 69. On continental Europe, see Chandler and Daems, op. cit., in Daems and van der Wee (eds), *Rise of Managerial Capitalism*, p. 9.

38   On the importance of this, see W. P. Kennedy, 'Institutional Response to Economic Growth; Capital Markets in Britain to 1914', pp. 151–83 above.

39   B. W. E. Alford, 'Strategy and Structure in the UK Tobacco Industry', pp. 73–84 above.

40   Channon, *Strategy and Structure of British Enterprise*, p. 158; *Annual Reports* of the Company, 1924–50.

41   This is suggested by an unpublished study by Mr D. Fox of the annual reports of the largest 50 companies of 1930.

42   *Annual Reports* of the company, 1924–50.

43   The *locus classicus* of this view is, of course, J. J. Servan-Schreiber, *Le Défi Américain* (Paris, 1967).

10 The Strategy of Sales Expansion in the British Electricity Supply Industry between the Wars

ANDREW WILSON

In his examination of the evolution of new forms of organisational structure, Professor Chandler suggested that they were the result of stresses imposed by the adoption of a new strategy. But why did the new strategy arise in the first place? Chandler's answer to this question is in two parts. The first refers to factors external to the firm : the new strategy came 'in response to the opportunities and needs created by changing population and changing national income and by technological innovation'.[1] The second element suggests that the new strategy depends on the ability of the existing management to perceive the situation and to respond appropriately : '. . . the awareness of the needs and opportunities created by the changing environment seems to have depended on the training and personality of individual executives and on their ability to keep their eyes on the more important entrepreneurial problems even in the midst of pressing operational needs'.[2] This essay focuses attention on the second part of Chandler's answer, in the context of the British electricity supply industry between the wars. It isolates facets of the entrepreneurial character and of the ownership structure of the industry which had a crucial influence on the sales strategy that was chosen.

I

The public supply of electricity had become a commercially viable proposition by about 1880. Most of the technical problems had been solved, and in particular the incandescent lamp was now available. Nevertheless electricity was used exclusively for lighting, and its price put it definitely in the luxury class. Only in areas with a concentration of wealthy people could electricity hope to succeed. Thus the earliest developments were in the south-east, especially in central London. These rather speculative early enterprises were in the hands of companies, but there was at this time a strong measure of support for municipal activity and also considerable resentment against the monopolistic powers of some of the gas and water companies.[3] The desire to avoid similar exploitation led to early legislation for the electricity supply industry, and the 1882 Act gave a substantial amount of support to the interests of local authorities at the expense of those of companies. The 1888 Act eased this burden slightly but the bias in favour of municipal activity remained. It was enacted that company undertakings would eventually pass into the hands of local authorities on terms which were greatly resented by the companies. This provision certainly hindered the early development of company undertakings, and local authority activity was held back by a desire to protect existing gas interests.[4] The legislation also had important long term effects because it imposed on the industry a division into two distinct camps whose mutual antipathy survived at least until nationalisation in 1948. This antipathy is important in explaining the lack of cooperation that existed within the industry. These two forms of organisation, the company and the local authority undertaking, were associated with different types of supply area. The local authorities took advantage of their favoured position to secure for themselves the areas of greatest potential demand. Thus the larger towns and cities were served by municipal enterprises. In smaller towns where the local authority could not be confident of success, company undertakings were typical. London became a mixture of the two types.

Relations between the two forms of organisation varied. At a personal level they might be excellent, but there was little movement of personnel between the two types, and their public positions were a long way apart. Cooperation was desirable on many technical and economic grounds, but combined action was achieved only when the industry as a whole was threatened by external control which would have imposed a unified structure.[5] The companies resented bitterly that undertakings which they had laboured to improve should pass out of their hands, and attitudes to surpluses were understandably very different. The contrasting characteristics of the areas of supply meant that their problems were often dissimilar. Each type had its own trade organisation, the companies had several which catered for different types, and these bodies tended to reinforce the separate identities. The unanimity which is sometimes apparent in companies' attitudes is partly explained by the close links that existed between companies, either through formal connections,[6] or through directoral interlocks.[7] Such contacts did at times influence managerial decisions in the generation and transmission sectors as some electricity supply undertakings were under the control of electrical engineering firms, or had representatives of such firms on their boards.[8] There is evidence that prices paid to these engineering firms were at times excessive, and local authority undertakings were not immune to this problem. A price-fixing ring operated in heavy electrical engineering, and local authorities which tried to obtain lower prices by purchasing their equipment from abroad faced a campaign of vilification from the British Electrical and Allied Manufacturers' Association.[9] This situation does not seem to have applied to anything like the same extent in the distribution field. In general, despite certain common problems, the two types of undertakings resisted efforts to produce combination and this stubbornness in one respect was taken by many as a symptom of a more general lack of enterprise.

At the end of the First World War there were about 560 authorised undertakings, with about 330 run by local authorities and the rest by companies. However, because local government boundaries had been the basis for establishing areas of supply, many undertakings were too small to achieve high levels of efficiency and as a result prices were high compared with other countries and sales per capita were low. Growth had therefore been slow up to 1914, and towards the end of the First World War the industry was subjected to critical scrutiny.[10] Pressures for reform were great, but opposition from within the industry, especially to reorganisation enforcing cooperation between the two types of undertaking, was sufficient to deprive the proposed legislation of any effective power.[11] Nonetheless British backwardness was becoming increasingly evident and criticism was heard from those very close to the industry. In 1925 the President's Inaugural Address at the Institution of Electrical Engineers pointed to Britain's low international standing in terms of sales, and to Britain's high prices. Annual per capita consumption of electricity in Britain was only 190 units, at an average price of 1·9d; in Canada consumption averaged 1,190 units, and price only 0·72d per unit sold.[12] The growing support for change allowed the passing of the 1926 Act which provided for the building of the national grid and for the creation of the Central Electricity Board to control generation and transmission. By the early 1930s the CEB was in operation, regulating the running of power stations, buying and selling power from and to the undertakings, and thus substantially reducing costs on the generating side for many undertakings.

II

The companies and municipalities finally acquiesced in this state intervention, but the success of the policy still depended on the sales strategies of the undertakings which retained control over the distribution of electricity to consumers. Since electricity cannot effectively be stored in large quantities the CEB had to plan for sufficient generating capacity to meet the peak demand on the system at any one time. This meant that a substantial proportion of capacity was idle for long periods. The object of the CEB therefore became the achievement of as even a demand as possible throughout the day or year. The undertakings were encouraged to work towards this ideal by the CEB tariff which incorporated a maximum demand element in its charges for bulk supplies, but it is interesting to note the concern that the CEB felt over the possible 'psychological' impact of its tariff structure on managers of electricity undertakings.[13] Nevertheless the paramount objective of a flatter demand remained; what had originally been the problem of the individual undertaking, and had then apparently passed into the hands of the CEB, was now clearly dependent upon the strategic decisions of the undertakings acting as distributors of electricity. Since it was industrial demand which was creating the peaks, one of the methods of achieving a more even pattern of demand was to fill the valleys by encouraging the domestic consumption of electricity. A great debate raged over the desirability of attempting to stimulate domestic demand, and it is this question which will form the core of this discussion.

There were two main factors operating on the demand side to limit the size of the market. The first was the high cost of electricity : if the price of electric lighting could be brought anywhere near that of gas, then the convenience and cleanliness of electricity would give it a strong advantage. In the case of heating or cooking by electricity the high cost was not the only objection, but it remained an important one throughout the period. The second influence was the fear and confusion that existed about electricity. Many fires were blamed upon electrical faults, and appliances were often regarded as potentially lethal, sometimes quite fairly, for merely spilling liquid on the tops of some cookers could make the whole casing live. Misunderstanding about the practical uses of electricity was rife and mistrust of the complex tariffs in use was usual. Nevertheless a huge potential market did exist and it could be tapped by energetic policies to overcome this consumer resistance. Shortages of factor supplies do not appear to have posed significant problems. Land, in the sense of suitable sites for power stations, did present some difficulty, but solutions were found albeit at a slightly higher cost : cooling towers were the answer to the shortage of water on some sites. Neither did labour present important difficulties : disputes were usually brief and there were no noticeable problems of recruitment. Capital sources varied in that local authorities had access to corporation funds or to other sources on favourable terms. Companies at times found share issues not taken up, but at other times they might be very substantially over-subscribed. Overall, shortages of finance were not seriously complained of. The sometimes excessive prices that have been mentioned with respect to heavy electrical engineering equipment were not paralleled in the appliances sector where a large number of firms were competing. Nevertheless cookers and other such equipment were beyond the means of most consumers and hire or hire-purchase schemes were run by the enterprising undertakings. In general, however, despite occasional increases in cost, the conditions on the supply side did not impose any serious constraint upon the choice of courses of action that might have been dictated by other factors. It should be remembered, however, that the existence of a constraint may depend on the prevailing strategy: an ambitious strategy is more likely to run up against constraints in this area than a conservative one.

Both the generation and transmission side of the industry, which from 1927 came increasingly under the control of the CEB, and the distribution side, which remained under the control of the municipal and company undertakings, were characterised by high fixed costs and by heavy costs of expansion. An extension of the area of supply beyond the densely populated regions of towns and cities would involve a higher cost of distribution per consumer – a cost that had to be met well in advance of revenue. If the industry were to expand it was therefore necessary to sell more units at lower prices. This would help bring down costs, but in the meantime the undertakings faced increases in capital costs before more units could be sold.

What has been presented so far is a generalised view of the conditions that individual enterprises in the industry were facing. Naturally there were substantial variations which were partly a result of the split into local authority and company undertakings. The impact of access to capital has already been mentioned, but differences can be seen in other fields too. The market situation that the companies faced in their small towns was rather more difficult than that for local authority undertakings in their larger towns and cities. The companies were faced with a smaller potential demand and a more rapid transition to low population densities. Differences in the conditions faced by the two types of undertaking might be expected to influence significantly the view that managers and engineers had of their product, but there were other factors at work too. The combination of all these factors produced attitudes within the industry that differed between the two groups. There were wide differences within both groups, and a considerable degree of overlap too, nevertheless the extremes of attitudes are clear and the occupation of those extremes could usually be predicted with confidence. One extreme saw electricity in an almost Messianic fashion; it brought light, heat and power, and freedom from dirt and drudgery; it was the fuel of the future and it was the duty of the undertaking to further its use at all costs. This would have been a local authority position, and although the view might be held in its entirety by individuals, in practice the attitudes of the more progressive local authorities were a slightly diluted version which nonetheless saw the encouragement of the use of electricity as a social duty.[14] At the other extreme the view existed that electricity was a commercial product like any other and that the measure of achievement was profit. The former position found expression in 'all electric' houses, attempts to encourage the widespread use of electricity, and sometimes a total inability to understand that a product so beneficial should need help in being sold. The other extreme, normally held by companies, was epitomised by a policy of high prices and high per unit profits on a small volume of sales, rather than low per unit profits on a high level of sales. Such a view normally carried with it the idea that expansion was intrinsically dangerous. The contrast between these views is illustrated by the Oxford undertaking which changed hands from company to municipal control in 1931. The table below shows the tariffs that operated before and after the transfer. Under company control the undertaking had had none of the sales expansion devices such as two-part tariffs, assisted-wiring, hiring or hire-purchase schemes, which were common by the late 1920s. After the change these were introduced. Sales rose rapidly and by 1935 were more than 200 per cent up on the last period of company activity, with a higher rate of return on capital. The contemporary view of company policy was that it had been profit-maximising;[15] it was certainly risk-shunning.

Thus companies tended to be conservative, and municipal undertakings more aggressive, in selling electricity. Even in the most pro-

TABLE 1   Oxford Tariffs Before and After Reorganisation

BEFORE – Lighting, up to 260 units $7\frac{1}{2}$d/kWh
next 3,500 units   6d/kWh
next 2,000 units   5d/kWh
rest $3\frac{1}{2}$d/kWh
Heating $2\frac{3}{4}$d/kWh
Power, up to 2,000 units $3\frac{1}{2}$d/kWh
next 1,000 units $2\frac{1}{4}$d/kWh
rest $1\frac{1}{2}$d/kWh

AFTER – Fixed quarterly quota of 10–250 units at $4\frac{3}{4}$d, the rest at $\frac{1}{2}$d.
In summer, with certain approved appliances such as cookers, any above quota at $\frac{1}{2}$d.

Source: Prof. M. Walker, 'The Prices for Electricity Supply', *Journal of the Institution of Electrical Engineers*, LXXIX (1936) 510–11.

gressive undertaking, however, there was a strong representation of a force that was present in the most backward. This force was very important, not so much because it deliberately obstructed attempts to sell electricity, but because it epitomised a view of electricity which saw attempts to sell the product as almost irrelevant. This outlook essentially saw the supply of electricity as the prerogative of engineers. Any interference with these rights was bitterly resented and commercially-minded people within the organisation were seen as of insignificant importance, or sometimes more specifically as 'scum'.[16] The importance of this for the enterprise was considerable because the strength of the engineering position was sufficient to obstruct the development of new outlooks. A hierarchy came into being – generation engineers were at the peak, transmission and distribution engineers slightly lower, and commercial engineers, if they existed at all, a long way below that. This status that went with the generation of electricity is exemplified in the wage cuts that were typical if an undertaking ceased to generate its own electricity but bought it in from elsewhere instead.[17] The preoccupation with engineering at the expense of sales can be seen in the refusal of some undertakings to send a sales representative to firms that had made enquiries about taking a supply of electricity. The firms were expected to come to the undertaking, not the other way round.[18] There were, then, conflicting pressures for the encouragement of sales, and for the restriction of sales to avoid risk and maintain profits. This struggle took place against a general background in which engineering achievements were valued more highly than sales achievements.

III

The agency through which these at times conflicting pressures passed, and which had the task of determining what response the enterprise should make, was the administrative structure and in particular the controlling body whose form depended on whether the undertaking was run by a company or by a local authority. In the former case the controlling body was the board of directors which would often know little about electricity supply, in the case of the local authority it would be the electricity committee of the council, and again ignorance of technical matters was typical. Beneath these bodies the organisation of the enterprise would be similar whatever its type. There would be an engineering and administrative staff almost invariably headed by an engineer, and it would be the Chief Engineer who would report to and advise the controlling body, and manage the day to day running of the enterprise. The board of directors was responsible to the shareholders who were not normally consumers of their own company's electricity, whereas the electricity committee was responsible to the town council and ultimately to the electors who were at the same time consumers. The local authority undertaking was, therefore, at times sensitive to public pressure in a way that was unlikely with a company. On the other hand the company's possible financial difficulties might lead either to the representation on the board of possibly helpful contacts, or increasingly to the effective control of one company by another. There are examples of electrical engineering companies integrating forwards to ensure outlets for their products,[19] and control by holding companies could be strict.[20] Nevertheless despite the limits to individual action that both types of undertaking faced, in each case the Chief Engineer was in a position of great power.

In practice the Chief Engineer's power extended to commercial matters too. He was responsible for the overall performance of the undertaking, and was therefore closely involved with all aspects of the enterprise. Moreover it was a characteristic of the industry that any discussion of commercial issues necessarily involved the consideration of technical matters as well. The consideration of tariffs, for instance, bristled with engineering technicalities. The cost of supplying electricity to a consumer varied throughout the day, not just because of the additional generating capacity that might be needed for a new consumer at the demand peak, but also because the efficiency of equipment, and hence the cost of generation or distribution, varied with the load upon it. Thus even the question of tariffs, which might have been thought to have been the preserve of the commercial man, required a good grounding in the theory and practice of electrical engineering. The position of the non-engineer was weakened further because it was quite impossible to work out the costs of supplying an individual consumer.[21] Attempts to do so provoked derision at professional meetings,[22] and for the most part the territory was left under the control of the engineer. Thus the Chief Engineer was a person of great importance and power, and the personality and prejudices of such a man could have a great impact on the performance of the undertaking. Within the enterprise the rest of the formal structure reflected this engineering dominance. Accountants, secretaries and even commercial managers were employed, but they were typically on a level with the deputy chief engineer rather than with the chief engineer himself. Progressive undertakings, such as the Hull Corporation Electricity Department, often had some quirk in the administrative structure. In the case of Hull it was the presence near the top of the hierarchy of a particularly able man, Mr D. Bellamy, an accountant interested in selling electricity. More typically such interests were represented at a much lower level.

IV

Do the structure of ownership and management organisation provide adequate explanations for the differing strategies adopted by undertakings in the electricity supply industry? The answer appears to be that they do. Most units within the industry were slow to adopt techniques to stimulate domestic sales despite the well-known benefits demonstrated by a few active undertakings. The condition of the market, especially in the early 1920s was certainly a factor in some cases, and there were valid doubts as to whether demand was sufficiently elastic for price reductions to bring increased revenues. These conditions, however, applied generally and it is difficult to explain the differences between undertakings in terms of the more or less favourable nature of market conditions. In the case of Hull the high proportion of working-class housing was more likely to have been a handicap than a help. It seems, then, that the undertakings that were successful in stimulating domestic sales were those that tried hard to do so, and that the perception of the product within the undertaking and the administrative structure were crucial in determining the strategy adopted. In some companies the passive extreme held sway and prices were deliberately kept high to achieve high profits on low sales at minimum risk. In some local authority undertakings missionary zeal ruled and electricity was enthusiastically sold in the poorest homes. For the most part, however, the engineering view prevailed, and selling electricity was not seen as important. A study of strategies, in the electricity supply industry at least, suggests that a large part of those strategies can be explained, if not by the administrative structure itself, then certainly by the operation of that administrative structure upon the ideas and information that necessarily flow through it.

NOTES

1   A. D. Chandler, *Strategy and Structure* (MIT Press, 1962) p. 15.
2   Ibid.
3   H. H. Ballin, *The Organisation of Electricity Supply in Great Britain* (1946) ch. 1.
4   A. G. Whyte, *The Electrical Industry* (London, 1904) p. 28.
5   Ballin, op. cit., passim.
6   Political and Economic Planning, *Report on the Supply of Electricity in Great Britain* (1936) pp. 140–1.
7   E. Garcke, *Manual of Electricity Undertakings*, Lists of Personnel in the Industry.
8   Ibid.
9   A. H. Swain, *The Economic Effects of Monopoly on British Power Stations* (Leicester, 1929) passim.
10 Ministry of Reconstruction, Coal Conservation Sub-Committee, *Interim Report* (Cmd 8880, 1917); Board of Trade, *Report of the Committee Appointed to Consider the*

Question of Electric Power Supply (Cmd 9062, 1918); Board of Trade, *Report of the Departmental Committee on the Position of the Electrical Trades After the War* (Cmd 9072, 1918); Ministry of Reconstruction, Advisory Council, *Report of the Committee of Chairmen on Electric Power Supply* (Cmd 93, 1919).

11   Ballin, op. cit., p. 115 et al.

12   W. H. Eccles, 'Inaugural Address', *Journal of the Institution of Electrical Engineers*, LXV (1927) 1.

13   Central Electricity Board, Tariff Committee, *Minutes*, 11 October 1934.

14   A representative of this view was Mr D. Bellamy of the Hull undertaking. Bellamy Papers and *interview* with Mr H. W. Young, who was in charge of the Hull Assisted Wiring Scheme, 20 August 1975.

15   Prof. M. Walker, 'The Prices for Electricity Supply', *JIEE*, LXXIX (1936) 510–11.

16   *Interview* with Mr J. C. Williams, former Assistant Chief Engineer of the South Western Electricity Board, 5 February 1974.

17   Ministry of Transport, *Report of the Committee Appointed to Review the National Problem of the Supply of Electrical Energy* (HMSO, 1927) paragraph 107.

18   *Interview* with Mr W. E. Swale, former Consumers' Engineer of the Manchester Area of the North Western Electricity Board, 27 March 1974.

19   PEP, loc. cit.

20   *Interview* with Mr K. Meiklejohn, son of the former Manager of the Penarth undertaking, 27 February 1974.

21   D. J. Bolton, *Electrical Engineering Economics* (London, 1950) p. 52; H. M. Sayers, *The Economic Principles of Electrical Distribution* (London, 1938) p. 148.

22   See comments after papers presented at the IEE such as Major E. H. E. Woodward and W. A. Carne, 'An Analysis of the Costs of Electricity Supply and Its Application in Relation to Various Types of Consumers', *JIEE*, LXXI (1932) 893.

11 Corporate Evolution in the Service Industries

DEREK F. CHANNON

Today the economies of developed countries are no longer primarily concerned with manufacturing industry. While the production of manufactured goods remains an essential feature, the largest sector of the modern economy is the service industries. Yet surprisingly the vast majority of the attention devoted to economic policy by politicians, economists. and management theorists is concerned with the relatively declining manufacturing sector. Indeed, while specific service sectors have merited investigation, no major study of the strategic management problems of these industries has been attempted. Further, many politicians, economists, and the like seem not only unable to recognise the importance of the service sector, but to consider that it is only investment in the manufacturing sector which essentially contributes to economic and thereby social development.

This study is, therefore, a first attempt to begin to redress the balance. It examines the evolution over a period of some 25 years of some 100 major British service industry corporations in the postwar period since 1950.[1] A number of specific variables were examined, but attention was principally focused upon three. These were the strategies adopted, as measured by the patterns of major moves over time; the top management organisation structures chosen by the companies to manage these strategies, supplemented by investigation of the internal controls, planning, information and reward systems; and the resulting financial performances achieved.

I

Perhaps one reason why studies of service sector corporations are few is that the area presents a number of serious methodological problems which are not apparent in manufacturing industry. Firstly, there is a difficulty in defining precisely what is meant by a service. Some industries such as banking, insurance, and retailing clearly fall within the service sector. Public utilities such as gas and electricity are more

H

ambivalent, as is the construction industry. These industries were, however, included in the companies examined. The definition of a service industry chosen was thus deliberately left wide, starting from the classification adopted by *Fortune Magazine* that a service industry was essentially one that was neither manufacturing nor mining. As a result the study examined companies engaged in transportation, distribution, banking, insurance, construction, property, hotels and leisure, communications, and the public utilities.

A second and more serious problem arose in defining size. In manufacturing industry it is possible to measure firms using a single comparative variable such as level of sales, assets or number of employees. None of these measures used individually provides a suitable measure for all service industries. As a result a mixture of size variables was adopted according to the relevant industry characteristics and judgement used in the final analysis to decide on cut-off points. In the event, all the companies examined had sales of over £120m and/or net assets of more than £100m in 1973–4.

The ultimate sample of companies chosen for examination was as shown in Table 1. The breakdown by industry is, however, crude, since by 1974 many of the companies had already substantially diversified their activities, and for a significant number this evolution had proceeded so far that they were perforce defined as conglomerates. These concerns make up the majority of the 'miscellaneous' category. Utilising the variation of Scott's Stages of Corporate Growth Model[2] developed from the work of Wrigley, Channon et al.[3] the strategic and structural histories of the companies were built up over the period 1950 to 1974, based on annual reports, various other published data, company histories, and, in almost 50 per cent of cases, interviews conducted at Board level with the companies themselves.

II

In the postwar period the role played by service industries has considerably increased in importance as a contributor to GNP, as an employer, and in terms of contribution to the balance of payments. In 1955 the numbers employed in manufacturing industry in the United Kingdom were 9·4m or 40·1 per cent of the total population in civil employment. By contrast the service industries in combination employed 10·7m (45·7 per cent) of the working population. In 1973 the numbers employed in manufacturing industry had exhibited a substantial decline to 7·8m (31·4 per cent) while employment in the service industries had risen to 12·5m or 50 per cent of the working population.

Similar trends can also be observed in terms of contribution to GNP

TABLE 1   Service Companies by Industry 1974

	No.	No. with MD Structure
Clearing Banks	8	3
Merchant Banks	7	5
Other Financial Institutions	7	3
Property	4	–
Hotels and Leisure	3	3
Non Food Retailers	11	7
Food Retailers	5	1
Construction	5	3
Merchanting and Commodities	7	3
Public Sector	9	3
Insurance	23	–
Miscellaneous	10	6
	99	37

as shown in Table 2 where the percentage share of GNP produced by manufacturing industry has steadily declined while that from the service industries in aggregate has similarly increased. Not all the service industries have recorded significant growth however, but rather have undergone reorganisation as for example in the distributive trades where the postwar period has seen rapid growth in self service and multiple retailing with a corresponding decline among small shopkeepers. Financial services, the gas industry, the tourist and leisure industries and many professional services on the other hand have all recorded well above average growth. Elsewhere experience has been mixed; in transportation a significant decline took place in rail transport with a corresponding increase in road and air transportation.

The contribution of the service industries to Britain's trade balance has also increased substantially, especially from the financial service industries. Although the City has traditionally been a net contributor from insurance and the like, the earnings from banking, brokerage, and merchanting have increased dramatically from £67m to £253m over the decade from 1964. Overall the net contribution from the service industries from 1964 to 1973 increased from £186m to £974m, excluding portfolio and direct investments from the private sector. Unfortunately, over the same period the public sector invisible deficit also grew from some £550m to £985m. Nevertheless, Britain's overall invisible balance has expanded almost 10-fold in the past decade to reach £1,165m by 1973.

Against this brief background, then, what patterns of strategy and structure can be observed amongst the service industry companies in

TABLE 2 GNP by Industry 1950-1970 (£ million)

	1950	1955	1960	1965	1970
Agriculture forestry and fishing	679	778	915	1056	1348
Mining and Quarrying	412	575	675	726	718
Manufacturing Industry	4377	6535	8168	10805	14551
Service Industries					
Building and Contracting	629	956	1388	2224	2640
Gas, Electricity and Water	252	397	615	1041	1322
Transport and Communication	982	1394	1957	2615	3548
Distributive Trades	1600	2115	2772	3688	4524
Insurance Banking Finance	331	493	684	997	1552
Other Services	1244	1876	2567	3496	5879
Public Administration and Defence	1100	1577	2330	3205	5033
Total	11637	16821	22767	30904	42819

Source: Central Statistical Office.

the postwar period? Further, how similar are these problems to those exhibited by manufacturing companies? Finally, does the strategy-structure model developed from the study of manufacturing companies apply generally to corporate evolution or does the study of service industry companies suggest any necessary modifications to the original model?

III

The pattern of corporate evolution observed by Chandler[4] and later researchers amongst manufacturing firms indicated that companies whose original markets began to mature continued to grow by diversification into new products or geographic markets or by some combination of these strategies. This trend was observed amongst many of the service companies, but for the financial corporations the adoption of a strategy of diversification seemed to be leading to the creation of a new type of company where previously there had been a series of specialist activities. Moreover, companies were approaching the multi-market financial service enterprise from a number of directions, leading to new competition and confrontation.

In 1950 the financial institutions each enjoyed a relatively well defined role and position in the market place. Such a specialist task was in turn usually protected either formally or informally by a cartel mechanism which restricted competition, inhibited the emergence of new competitors, and permitted the perpetuation of almost feudal organisation structures and inefficient administrative systems. Thus, the clearing banks operated their widespread branch networks, concerned with short term deposits and loans, and operating an official interest rate cartel. The merchant banks were small, highly personalised, usually family-dominated institutions, dealing with acceptance credits and lending arrangements for medium and long term finance for both public and private sectors. Like the banks other financial corporations also tended to be specialised in a particular market segment : C. T. Bowring in insurance broking, Lewis and Peat in commodity trading, United Dominions Trust and Mercantile Credit in the fledgling consumer finance industry.

The 1950s brought only limited change to these arrangements. The clearing banks were especially slow to adapt. Although some began to recognise the growth of and need for new financial services, their response tended to be one of taking an investment shareholding in other specialist concerns such as the finance companies, rather than direct entry into new activities.[5]

At the end of the 1950s a combination of circumstances began to cause change amongst the merchant banks. Firstly, in 1958 fully convertible sterling was introduced which became formalised in 1961. Secondly, the introduction of Regulation Q by the American Federal Reserve, which limited interest rates on time deposits with US banks from 1958, coupled with the growing US payments deficit on trade with Europe, led to the formation of the Eurodollar market. Thirdly, the rapid growth of US direct investment in Europe and especially in the UK led to the need for new corporate banking services. Finally strategic changes among British corporations led to a rapid increase in the numbers of mergers and takeovers. These factors gave the merchant banks a new *raison d'être*. But in order to take advantage of these new opportunities change was initially necessary. Thus a series of complementary mergers took place in the early 1960s which tended to bring together those banks strong in the new corporate finance skills and those with a large deposit base.[6] Such moves led to the creation of Mercury Securities embracing S. G. Warburg and Seligman Bros.; Schroders, from J. Henry Schroder and Herbert Wagg; Kleinwort Benson, an amalgamation of Kleinwort and Co. and Lonsdale Investment Trust; and Hill Samuel, which was the end result of a series of moves culminating with the merger between Phillip Hill Higginson and M. Samuel and Co. Groups like Morgan Grenfell and Lazards (a subsidiary of S. Pearson), which already enjoyed strong relationships with associated banks outside the UK, found such moves less necessary, while for a few banks such as Hambros, the potential loss of family sovereignty proved too high a price to pay for this route to expansion and new strategies had to be forged.

Amongst the other financial institutions the 1950s offered an opportunity for rapid expansion by the finance houses as consumer spending increased. However, for those more concerned with foreign trade, such as the British overseas banks and commodity traders, the gradual dissolution of the Empire and changing trade patterns began to pose a threat to existing strategies.

As the 1960s unfolded, the clearing banks slowly began to awake themselves in the face of growing indirect competition for deposits from the revitalised merchant banks, building societies and others as a result of the interest rate cartel. Further competition came from the rapid build up of American banks in the UK, who quickly followed the USA multinationals in establishing a direct presence as London became the centre of the Eurodollar market. Finally there was a growing customer dissatisfaction with the banks' services fuelled by criticism from official bodies such as the Monopolies Commission who called them 'soporific'.[7]

Faced with new competitive threats, although the interest rate cartel remained between the clearers, the big branch banking systems began to rationalise their operations. A final wave of mergers reduced the London clearing banks to five, the end coming with the creation of the

National Westminster in 1968, since the later move to link Barclays and Lloyds was blocked by the Monopolies Commission. The banks began to offer a wider range of services directly to their customers. Led by the Midland, personal loan schemes were initiated; some banks took direct ownership of finance companies with which they had previously been associated; some moved into the rapidly growing unit trust and investment management areas initiated by the merchant banks as an alternative to insurance; leasing and factoring operations were imported from the USA; and a growing tendency to develop international connections became apparent.[8]

These strategic changes in turn led to pressure on administrative systems. Previously the typical clearing bank structure consisted of a large board overwhelmingly made up of industrialists, former military officers and civil servants and members of the peerage, few of whom had any knowledge whatsoever of banking, although occasionally representatives of old banking families might appear whose banks had long since disappeared. By contrast the executive members of the bank, traditionally called general managers, were usually completely excluded from the board. These men, virtually all career bankers, had developed through the branch system, and exercised essentially tight centralised functional control over operations. Decentralised decision making was severely bounded by tight rules laid down by the top management in central office, and managerial initiative was stifled below the level of the small cadre of senior banking officers.

In the late 1960s McKinsey and company were employed to review the structure of the Westminster bank, and were subsequently retained to advise on a suitable structure when the merger with National Provincial was announced. Thus, the first multi-divisional organisation was introduced in a clearing bank in 1968. National Westminster continued to diversify rapidly both by product and geography into the 1970s, buying its own finance house, extending into leasing, factoring, insurance and building up the County Bank as a full merchant bank. Barclays and the Midland rapidly followed with reorganisations as they too expanded their range of banking services, especially after the new policy encouraging increased bank competition, introduced by the Bank of England in 1971.[9] The Midland acquired Thomas Cook Travel Agents, and moved heavily into merchant banking via the acquisition of the Montagu Trust, as well as developing leasing, factoring and insurance operations. Meanwhile, Barclays acquired full control of Barclays DCO, its former Dominion and Commonwealth based overseas bank, renamed it Barclays International and proceded to move heavily into banking operations in Europe and the USA, while attempting to build an international merchant bank based on London. By 1974 the four major London clearers had all diversified dramatically over the previous decade, and three had adopted a multidivisional organisational format.

The remaining clearers were basically Scottish. The Bank of Scotland was still predominantly a clearing bank, with a large shareholding held by Barclays, and had undertaken limited diversification, while National and Commercial, only formed in 1968, still operated as a holding company, and was partly owned by Lloyds.

The diversification exhibited by the major clearing banks was largely repeated by the leading merchant banks. These concerns, too, moved to increase the services they could offer, expanding especially into investment management, leasing, factoring, insurance services, and, in some cases, property, as well as extending their overseas interests.[10]

These changes led to some organisational reform as the former family-dominated, partnership relationships began to break down under the need for increased specialist knowledge and spread of services. A number of banks thus began to adopt divisional systems, often with the aid of consultants.

By the mid 1970s the diversification of both the clearers and the merchants was bringing the two increasingly into competition with one another especially as the clearers became market oriented, and extended their skills in merchant banking, investment and longer term corporate finance. This threat was posing difficulties for the merchant bankers since their own expansion was restricted due to their size and deposit base. As a result several of the merchant banks had sought mergers with non-banking institutions. Thus Hill Samuel acquired Noble Lowndes before trying unsuccessfully to merge in 1968 with Metropolitan Estates, a property company; Guinness Mahon merged in 1972 with the diversifying commodity merchants Lewis and Peat; Singer and Friedlander were acquired by insurance brokers C. T. Bowring in 1971; and William Brandts were finally completely acquired by overseas bankers National and Grindlays in 1972.

Apart from their moves to acquire merchant banks, the other financial institutions had also diversified from their specialist positions. Leading finance houses United Dominions Trust and Mercantile Credit had both extended into leasing and factoring, and even, in a limited way, into automobile distribution. C. T. Bowring, which had originated as a colonial merchanting and shipping company, had developed insurance broking as its major operation prior to going public in 1964. Having adopted a strategy of diversification in financial services the company had entered credit finance and leasing via the purchase of Bowmaker prior to its acquisition of merchant bankers Singer and Friedlander. The new entrants into banking, Slater Walker and First National Finance, were also diversified across a range of financial services.

By the mid 1970s, therefore, the diversification policies adopted by a variety of specialist financial corporations were leading to the emergence of a series of what have been loosely called 'financial conglomerates' offering 'department store' banking and financial services. The precise nature of the winners and losers in the pursuit of this strategy has still to be determined. Nevertheless, the changing strategy has already begun to result in significant modification of administrative structures. Although holding companies seem to have been the easier administrative form to adopt following the initial diversification by acquisition moves, the fact that the synergistic elements of the new strategy need cooperation between financial specialisms to achieve the advantages anticipated has already led to the appearance of a number of multidivisional structures, and more can be confidently predicted.

IV

Contrary to the widespread strategic changes observed amongst banks and other financial service institutions the rate of change amongst the insurance companies has been notably slower, although by the mid 1960s some movement had occurred, leading to changes in product offerings, marketing methods and managerial practices which appeared to be the forerunners of more widespread change in the 1970s.

In 1974 there were still approximately 500 insurance companies operating in the UK. Some 400 of these were incorporated in the UK with the rest being registered overseas. During the postwar period there has been a significant reduction in the number of traditional insurance companies due to mergers and acquisitions by other insurance companies, or, more recently, by new entrants into the industry from banking and the like. In addition to the companies, there were the 7,000-odd underwriting members of the Corporation of Lloyds, organised in some 270 syndicates, each member of which took a prearranged share of any risk accepted by the syndicate underwriter. The research concentrated on the development of the insurance companies, although a limited study of Lloyds over the period was also made as an essential background to understanding the industry as a whole.

The main services within the insurance industry can be conveniently divided between life and non-life or general. This latter area, in which Lloyds specialises, is traditionally subdivided into three branches, fire, accident, and marine, including aviation. Life assurance in turn can be subdivided into ordinary life, which tends to be essentially a form of investment, and industrial life, which grew out of the old Victorian burial societies.

Despite the importance of Lloyds, the companies dominated the insurance market. They could be generally distinguished according to function. First there were the composite companies which transacted all forms of insurance, although here too there was a tendency to specialise. Thus General Accident was the largest British motor insurer, while Sun Alliance had extensive connections with building societies, and was heavily involved in household insurance. Secondly, there were the general companies which did not write any life assurance. Thirdly, there were the companies which did business in only one area – the most obvious example here being the specialist life companies such as Standard Life and Scottish Widows. Finally, there were a declining number of companies which specialised in industrial life assurance with the majority of these being composites.

A further significant distinction was that between the mutual and proprietary corporate forms. The proprietary company had a share capital, shareholders and operated as a normal joint stock company. By contrast a mutual company had no share capital, its policy holders being its members, and they shared all profits or losses of the company. In theory, therefore, mutual life companies had a built-in advantage over the proprietary concerns which, apart from offering a satisfactory return to policy holders, had also to pay dividends to shareholders. Further, mutual companies could not be owned by any other company. In practice the advantage of the mutual companies was generally not evident, since these companies, not open to external attack, tended to be the slowest of all to change, and actually found expansion quite difficult, since during the extensive launch of a new life fund, finance had to be found from operating profits, which in theory belonged to the policy holders.

Over the period the insurance companies had slowly evolved, but usually innovations had come from outside the industry. Moreover, competition was significantly restricted by the legal framework surrounding insurance, although this was usually designed to protect policy holders. In non-life for much of the period many of the specific markets were the subject of legal cartels – the tariff system, which only began to break down at the end of the 1960s.

In the mid 1960s, following increasing criticism, coupled with new competition for investment funds from the merchant banks and serious underwriting difficulties in non-life, a number of the major companies began to examine their administrative systems. Traditionally, the organisation of insurance companies tended to be on a functional basis. In its most simplistic form, the organisation was subdivided into sales (marketing was virtually unknown in most insurance companies until the 1960s), actuarial and administrative functions. Most such firms later added their own investment management departments. Such a system still persisted in the 1970s in many of the mutual life companies.

Composite companies tended to be somewhat more complex with the sales/marketing function usually subdivided by product or, in the case of those companies with substantial overseas interests, by geography. Nevertheless the actuarial and investment functions were almost always centralised until the 1960s. Further, the boards of the insurance companies, like those of the clearing banks, were usually non-executive and composed mainly of members of the 'establishment'. Where mergers or acquisitions had taken place, holding company structures were the rule with no attempt being made to integrate the portfolios of two or more insurers. Here the industry was partially inhibited by legal constraints on merging like funds, but also was a victim of its own inertia, believing that insurance clients might be lost if any change in policies were put to them.

These organisational forms were dominated by the actuarial profession which established the terms of the basic product lines of the insurance companies. The development of the mutual fund unit-linked life assurance markets in the 1960s by the merchant banks, however, began to place increasing emphasis on investment return. Despite the vast funds available to the insurance companies for investment, the depth and skills of their investment management in many cases were pathetic, and their investment return records poor. Faced with new competition, only by the late 1960s did long term investment portfolios begin to shift from their traditional heavy emphasis on fixed interest and government securities (70 per cent in 1947 *v.* 37 per cent in 1970), and into ordinary stocks and shares and real property.

In addition to improving investment performance some companies went further and adopted full scale organisational reform, often with help from consultants, but the need to maintain central control over investment ensured that no multidivisional structures emerged. Instead a hybrid structure, defined as a 'critical function' organisation, developed, where marketing and actuarial activities were grouped by product or geography and administration was significantly simplified to offer standardised product packages, while the investment function remained strictly centralised. Thus Guardian Royal Exchange – one of the more progressive composites – adopted such a structure with help from McKinsey in 1968. Other more recent moves have seen the beginning of significant diversification. The most common move here has been for the companies to expand their investment management units, and several have added property specialists or even acquired development companies to enable themselves to undertake direct property development rather than working through established developers. The most advanced companies have indicated further that, recognising the trend amongst the banking community toward the 'department store' financial service concept, they too will be emerging in this direction by seeking entry into banking and other such services. This is likely to occur in the latter half of the 1970s, and at this point it would seem logical that true multidivisional structures will also emerge.

V

The increased interest of the insurance companies, and many of the banks, in property is no accident. This sector has shown remarkable growth in the postwar period. Excluding insurance and the public sector corporations, no fewer than 19 of the remaining 67 service companies were still led by their original founding entrepreneurs. Perhaps more remarkably, many of these companies had not only reached the top 100 service companies, but had only been founded in the late 1950s to mid 1960s. Many of these new entrepreneurial firms grew either directly or indirectly on their basic skill and knowledge of the property market.

Most early property companies were investment concerns buying completed properties to obtain a yield for rental income. After the war the established property companies continued this policy, but the newly formed concerns, exploiting loopholes in the new Town and Country Planning legislation, took the higher-risk and much more potentially lucrative strategy of becoming a development company. That is to say they acquired low yielding properties at relatively low cost, demolished the existing buildings and rebuilt larger, high yielding property with a much greater capital value. The risks in this could be quite high when developing provincial shopping precincts, but proved to be virtually nil for office developments in central London. Three of the four property companies in the sample had emerged using this basic strategy, and regular revaluations, coupled with mergers and acquisitions, had resulted in dramatic increases in their asset values.[11]

The pure property companies employed few people and were organised usually along simple functional lines. Ultimate decision making commonly rested in the hands of the founding entrepreneur or his family, who were still usually large, although not controlling, shareholders. Other entrepreneurs built up their activities somewhat less directly. These men recognised the underlying value of property assets in companies which perceived themselves as being actively engaged in some other business such as brewing, hotels or retailing. The market capitalisation of such firms was based upon their earnings and in particular on their dividend flow, rather than on the true underlying asset values, which tended to be much higher. Such firms were, therefore, vulnerable to corporate raiders who recognised the real as opposed to balance sheet values of property which had been acquired over the years and often not revalued since the 1930s. Such men as Clore, Joseph, Collier, Wolfson and the like thus came from virtually nowhere to buy up retail and hotel chains in the late 1950s. Joseph continued to expand rapidly by acquisition in the 1960s building Grand Metropolitan into a giant leisure, hotel and brewing operation by the mid 1970s. In the 1960s Clore at Sears Holdings and Wolfson at Great Universal tended to stabilise somewhat, settling to the management of the large, diversified, retailing-oriented ventures they had built, with later moves tending to concentrate on overseas operations.

The pace was sustained, however, by new arrivals such as Slater who initially built up an industrial conglomerate from asset situations, before reversing into financial services; by Whyte at First National Finance who finessed the property game by establishing himself as intermediary between the developers and sources of finance; by Broakes at Trafalgar House, a new generation property man who first saw the tax advantages of linking property and shipping; and by Goldsmith at Cavenham Foods, who in ten years built a major international food, retailing, property, and finance conglomerate.

In managing their fast won empires these men, surprisingly perhaps, were widespread advocates of the multidivisional organisation structure. Family companies in general have tended to be reluctant to cede power, but the new entrepreneurs were predominantly men who were masters at seeking the potential of a deal rather than becoming concerned with day to day operations. Hence a multidivisional system utilising strict financial controls and a small central team of troubleshooters was for them an ideal managerial system.

VI

Traditionally Britain has enjoyed a substantial merchant shipping industry. By 1974, due only partially to a relative decline in importance by comparison with other industry segments, there were no pure shipping companies left amongst the top 100 service companies. Such companies as Cunard, P & O, and Ocean Steamship had remained undisturbed from the turn of the century until the mid 1960s. Then came the traumatic bid by Trafalgar House, a growing property company, for Cunard. Like other asset situations, the shipping companies had experienced poor financial performance, their management was unimaginative and again largely the same non-executive group who composed the boards of the banks and insurers. In shipping, however, there were no restrictions to prevent outside attack and Trafalgar recognised the substantially undervalued property and other assets of Cunard, which, coupled with the accumulated depreciation charges for ships (charges which were unused since profits were inadequate), gave a combined property/shipping company dramatic tax advantages. After a struggle, Cunard, the doyen of the shipping lines, fell to Trafalgar which, apart from reaping its expected financial advantages, substantially improved the performance of Cunard by the application of sound managerial techniques.

The Trafalgar-Cunard merger proved a threat to all the traditional shipping companies where management had no real experience outside the industry, where administrative methods were usually antiquated and where assets were undervalued and financial skills inadequate. In 1973, P & O came under attack from Bovis, a property and construction company much smaller (in terms of assets) than the shipping line. After a boardroom dispute this bid was fought off, a McKinsey reorganisation introduced, assets revalued dramatically and the following year with a new board, now dominated by line executives, P & O bid for and won Bovis, its former aggressor.

Ocean Steamship of the large shipping concerns had diversified least, but in 1972 had also undergone a reorganisation to shake up its management and move to a multidivisional system. This had been followed by the acquisition of William Cory which moved the company heavily into coal and oil distribution.

VII

One group of companies often closely related to shipping and other City institutions were the colonial merchanting companies. These enterprises are perhaps unique to Britain, and represent a strategy born of an imperial past which could seem somewhat of an anachronism in the post-colonial world.

The old merchant companies were usually created by entrepreneurs developing trade with a particular colony or series of colonies. Usually such trade was centred around the agricultural produce of the colony, shipped back to London and ultimately sold in what became the London commodity markets. The colonial merchant company could in the ultimate be a complete, integrated operation. Thus it could own local commodity producing estates, a shipping line for transport, a commodity trading operation in London, colonial infrastructure management such as retailing and merchanting operations to supply estate and consumer needs, and insurance and ship-broking interests covering transportation to and from the colony. Booker McConnell, for example, which emerged after an amalgamation of two such colonial enterprises, dominated the sugar trade with British Guiana; Inchcape was strong in tea, and, later, textiles, in the Indian subcontinent; Bowring was founded on trade with Newfoundland; and Dalgety concentrated on Australian and New Zealand pastoral activities and the wool trade.

The postwar period brought decolonisation and local nationalism to the former Empire, posing a major threat to the merchanting companies who were usually seen as prime targets for nationalisation. The companies, recognising the new threat, thus began to change their strategies with the objective of reducing their vulnerability to this new political risk. For most this meant the selective build up of various activities in the integrated chain of their traditonal business in less vulnerable political areas and especially in Britain. As the links in the chain of integration became more tenuous and as new activities were in turn added to those built up, many of the merchants thus seemed to be evolving conglomerate strategies covering widely disparate interests. Thus Bowring developed its insurance broking business so extensively that by the mid 1960s this activity dominated the shipping and merchanting interests, and formed the basis for Bowring's subsequent growth as a financial conglomerate. Booker McConnell on the other hand began the progressive expansion of its shipping interests, developing coastal trade in the West Indies and Europe. The company also developed by acquisition wholesale automobile components distribution in Canada, (later sold as a failure), department store retailing in the West Indies, sugar-based liquor manufacture and distribution, engineering (initially of sugar machinery, but later more general), and food retailing and wholesaling especially in the UK.

Companies less concerned with local colonial operations and historically traders in agricultural commodities (such as Gill and Duffus in cocoa, S. and W. Berisford in sugar, and Lewis and Peat in rubber and natural oils) tended to integrate forwards into the manufacture of derivative products. Thus, Lewis and Peat began to manufacture polyurethane foams – a substitute for foam rubber, Berisford packed and distributed specialist sugars and later other foodstuffs, and Gill and Duffus began to manufacture cocoa butter. A few of the merchants, however, still endeavoured to maintain their traditional strategies. Thus, Inchcape, although reducing its dependence on India and Pakistan by merging with the Borneo company in the mid 1960s, still operated as a merchant throughout the Middle and Far East, and was still dominated by the Inchcape family. Dalgety too, although slowly transforming itself, was still heavily dependent on wool and pastoral activities.

The long history of the colonial merchants, their usually extensive family tradition, and the fact that their boards tended to be dominated, in the postwar period, by third and fourth generation, establishment, city families, meant that managerial reorganisation tended to be slow. Most of the merchants still operated as holding companies. Such structures were not without any central management however. Rather there was no central administrative effort to coordinate and integrate activities in an overall strategic sense. The central office consisted of a series of area desks essentially responding to the needs of the local overseas managements, with control being exercised on a personal basis by members of the board who represented the parent on overseas subsidiary company boards. Such central executives had usually grown with the business, and had normally spent many years themselves in far-flung overseas trading posts before returning to take up their positions on the central board.

VIII

The entry of some of the former colonial merchants into distribution in recent years is indicative of a number of new entrants from bases outside the industry. To date, however, such newcomers have not significantly penetrated the ranks of the major operators in retailing and distribution. The large retailers could, therefore, be loosely subdivided into two groups. The first of these had developed on the basis of the organic growth of a successful retail formula, and included companies such as British Home Stores, Marks and Spencer, Tesco, and Sainsbury. The second group were those which had expanded primarily by acquisition, and included the UDS Group, Great Universal, House of Fraser, and Sears Holdings.

Those groups which had developed organically tended to establish a successful retail formula, which, although modernised over time, retained a number of fundamental elements which had given the basic strategy a long and successful life. Such firms were nearly all family based, and indeed still retained family management in most cases, and jealously sought to guard this. Starting from small beginnings, sometimes as single shops, occasionally as market stalls, the early pioneers gradually evolved their recipe for consumer acceptance. Thus British Home Stores, like Marks and Spencer, concentrated on cheap textiles and food, Woolworth translated the US 'five and dime' formula to the UK, John Cohen, founding Tesco, offered good quality food at low prices (quickly coupled with self-service in the postwar period), and the Sainsbury family concentrated on high quality fresh produce offered in hygienic surroundings. From their early beginnings the family retailers grew basically by a pattern of geographic expansion. The older established concerns had thus largely penetrated substantial geographic areas by the late 1930s. In the postwar period, the retailers began both to rebuild and expand their existing operations. In addition, the product range began to increase as store sizes grew bigger, and self-service became the norm in most types of retailing.

The organisational characteristics of this group of retailers, whether in food or non-food, were essentially similar. They all tended to have a highly centralised buying operation which controlled sources of supply, product range, pricing and volume terms. In the case of Sainsburys, Marks and Spencer and one or two others, the retailers had further developed significant research units which laid down quality standards and product specifications for suppliers, so giving retail domination of the distribution chain. While buying was a critical function, other important central responsibilities included site and property development, merchandising, personnel, finance and accounting. Despite the presence of these critical functions, the management of retail store operations was clearly not centralised with regard to day to day operations. Most companies supervised individual store managers by means of a regional organisation, which coordinated the activities of groups of stores.

Companies which expanded by acquisition tended to be more diversified. Such firms had gained much of their growth by purchasing retail chains operating in disparate markets. For example, Great Universal, having started in textiles, had added furniture, menswear, mail order, shoes and fashion wear, while UDS, having started with drapery, had acquired interests in men's outerwear, ladies' wear, suede and leather, furs, department stores and shops. The Burton Group offered an example of a company which had started with an organic growth strategy and later switched to an acquisition mode. Having built itself up as a men's outerwear manufacturer and retailer, finding its original retail formula no longer suitable, Burton had adopted a policy of acquisitive diversification buying its way into department stores, women's fashion, office furnishings, and photographic equipment.

This additional diversification had resulted in multidivisional organisation structures emerging amongst the acquisitive retailers, the earliest example of this being found in Great Universal Stores, where Sir Isaac Wolfson had closely studied the early development of Sears Roebuck in the USA.[12] In contrast, those companies which had grown by acquisition, but without diversification, such as the department store groups Debenhams and House of Fraser, had tended initially to be organised along holding company lines. Even though the form of retailing was similar, individual department store groups were initially left to manage their own affairs, to do their own buying, and to retain their local name. The weaknesses of this administrative system tended to be highlighted, however, as a result of increased competition from the leading variety chains and new competition from supermarket operators moving into non-foods. Thus by the early 1970s the department store groups were increasingly turning to centralised buying, and the establishment of a common corporate identity and brand image.

IX

Ten of the enterprises covered were in the public sector, following the nationalisation programme of the first postwar Labour Government. The nationalised enterprises covered utility production and distribution, the railways, long distance road transport, air transport, and the post office and telecommunications.

Strategically the nationalised concerns operate under a constraint not evident amongst private enterprise, in that their capacity to change their product market scope is severely limited. Such change that had occurred, therefore, had been largely brought about by technological change. In some cases this had led to dramatic results. Thus the gas industry was, until the end of the 1950s, essentially a two-fuel industry, taking in coal and converting it into gas and coke. Production took place at localised plants mainly situated in urban areas, and the organisation of the industry was vested in a series of regional companies each responsible for production, distribution, and, subject to certain constraints, able to determine its own pricing policy. These local authorities were autonomous of one another, although an overall Council for the Industry advised government on aspects which affected the industry as a whole.

In the early 1960s, following the discovery of processes for the gasification of oil, the economics of the gas industry were transformed. In the space of a few years coal gasification was virtually eliminated, and a vast capital investment programme introduced to switch to oil gasification. The new plants were, however, sited away from the urban areas and it also became economic to build a grid system to distribute gas from one geographic area to another. This began to break down the previous area autonomy, leading to increased centralisation and a growth in the power of the Council.

No sooner had the switch to oil gasification occurred, however, than major gas fields were discovered in the offshore North Sea which resulted in a second transformation for the gas industry inside a decade. North Sea gas required a major investment programme in a pipe distribution system, and virtually eliminated the need for local production altogether. By the early 1970s, therefore, after it had been obvious that reorganisation had been necessary for some time, the British Gas Corporation was created out of the former Gas Council, which completed the centralisation of the industry. With centralisation the structure thus became one of centralised finance, planning, some marketing and production, coupled with localised distribution through the old area organisations.

While production in the utility companies tended to be centralised, resulting in further examples of the 'critical function' organisational form, the transport companies had tended to adopt regional division systems by the mid 1970s. However, the land-based transport companies had been subjected to almost perpetual reorganisation since they had first been nationalised. Indeed a feature of the entire public sector was the increasing degree of intervention by ruling political parties for apparently short run political purposes. At the same time there was an increasing tendency to apply economic objectives for performance to the public sector. Thus the ironic situation arose of the managements of these concerns being subjected to economic measurement criteria which were almost immediately being negated by governmental decisions taken for political purposes.

X

In the above sections a brief sketch has highlighted a number of the emergent strategic and structural trends amongst some of the service industry corporations in the postwar period. How do these trends compare with those observed in manufacturing industry?

In the postwar period in Britain the largest firms in manufacturing industry underwent a substantial degree of change. There was a large increase from 21 per cent in 1950 to 60 per cent in 1970[13] in the number of diversified firms and a corresponding decline in the number of concerns operating with a narrow product market strategy. Many of the companies also diversified by geography, the number of firms being defined as multinational rising from 29 per cent in 1950 to 58 per cent by 1970.[14] In order to manage their new diversity the organisation structure initially chosen tended to be that of the holding company or some variant of this. This structure, however, proved unsuitable to the managerial complexities of the new strategies, and from the late 1950s and throughout the 1960s British manufacturing companies turned increasingly to the adoption of a variant of the multidivisional form. By 1970 over 70 per cent of the largest manufacturing concerns had, often with the help of consultants, found and adopted this structure. In contrast to the early US multidivisional systems many of those implementing divisional organisation opted for the variant based on a small central office. In this, finance and planning were the dominant functions, and tight financial controls and information systems became the key tools for top management to keep abreast of progress toward overall group objectives.

The strategic development of many of the service industry corporations reflected similar tendencies to diversity both by product and geography. Amongst a number of the insurance companies, especially the mutual concerns, the property companies, some public sector concerns, and some retailers, however, there had been no great tendency to diversify, thus in 1974 there were still 16 single-business firms operating. In addition, there were 17 firms which were only partly diversified where one business, representing over 70 per cent of turnover or assets, still dominated. These firms which remained undiversified were different to those experienced in manufacturing industry. Except for those in the public sector they were not locked into their situation by necessity, but rather by choice, and there was little need for change since such firms enjoyed either a real or quasi monopoly which avoided the threat of direct competitive attack. The characteristics of the stable dominant-product firm identified as the large integrated manufacturing firm were thus not really found in the service industries, except amongst the public sector corporations which did exhibit similarities to integrated manufacturing concerns. Even firms such as the clearing banks, undiversified retailers, and insurance and shipping concerns had the capacity to shift strategy fairly readily if and when they wished to.

Further, whereas the majority of manufacturing firms had diversified into areas related in some way to an existing business, the service companies showed a much greater tendency to evolve into conglomerates. Indeed by 1974 it was impossible to define 15 concerns as anything other than conglomerate. Moreover, as traditional specialisms in financial services broke down, a whole new group of financial and investment conglomerates seemed destined to emerge. A further difference between the manufacturing and service companies was the large number of firms in the service sector led by their original entrepreneurs. Some explanation has been given of this above in discussing the property-oriented enterprises, but the service sector has certainly proved an extremely fruitful area for entrepreneurial activity in the postwar period.

Perhaps not surprisingly in view of the lower degree of diversification, multidivisional organisation structures were less common amongst service companies. However, the difference was dramatic, with only 37 per cent of the companies having such a structure by 1974 compared with over 70 per cent of manufacturing firms by 1970. In fact most of the 37 firms adopting the divisional system had done so since 1968, and consultants had been largely responsible for this organisational reform. For most of the other firms which, given their strategy, one might expect to have adopted a divisional organisation, a holding company structure still prevailed. Thus it seems probable that structural reform amongst the service companies will persist for some time.

One further structural difference which appeared to be specific to service companies concerned the widespread use of the 'critical function' form of organisation, which represented a hybrid between the functional and divisional forms. In many service industries it was possible to identify one or more critical functions, the management of which was strongly centralised, such as investment management in insurance and central buying amongst retailers. Apart from these functions and the other more normal centralised functions such as finance, planning and the like, the widespread branch or store distribution system was subdivided into regional divisions or groups. Such regional groups in the clearing banks had been granted some degree of autonomy, and, although somewhat more restricted, regional differences could and did occur in retailing and utilities. In insurance, subdivision of the distribution system was usually along product rather than geographical lines. Nevertheless, the nature of this structure, which recurs in several industries, cannot be said to be purely functional or truly divisional. It is clearly functional in part in that critical operational activities are centralised, but it is also partly divisionalised in that the widespread geographic branch distribution systems of many service industries require an intermediate executive function between the local branch and the central office. The structure was to be found in many of the relatively undiversified retailers, clearing banks, diversified insurance, and property concerns and in the public sector. It appeared to be quite stable and only disappeared when further major diversification led to the introduction of a full divisional system.

These preliminary results, reported for the first time above, are still the subject of detailed ongoing analysis. Nevertheless, it seems clear that many similarities exist between manufacturing and service industry enterprises. However, there also appear to be some significant differences, and it is hoped that further explanation of these will help in the further refinement of a prescriptive model detailing the stages of corporate evolution.

NOTES

1 This research has been sponsored by the Social Science Research Council.
2 Bruce R. Scott, 'Stages of Corporate Development', unpublished paper (Harvard Business School, Boston, 1971).
3 See for example L. Wrigley, 'Divisional Autonomy and Diversification', unpublished Doctoral Dissertation, Harvard Business School, 1970. D. F. Channon, *The Strategy and Structure of British Enterprise* (Boston and London, 1973).
4 Alfred D. Chandler, *Strategy and Structure* (MIT Press, 1962).
5 This process is described in detail in: H. Chryssaphes, 'The Evolution of the U.K. Clearing Banks 1950–72', unpublished MBA dissertation (Manchester, 1974).
6 For a description of why particular mergers occurred in this period see: D. Robinson, 'Strategy and Structure in Merchant Banking', unpublished working paper (Manchester, 1975) ch. 2.
7 Monopolies Commission, *Report on Proposed Merger Between Barclays and Lloyds* (HMSO, 1968).

8   See Chryssaphes op. cit. for an excellent summary of the clearing banks' diversification moves into new services and overseas.

9   'Competition and Credit Control', *Bank of England Quarterly*, June 1971. This policy although leading to substantially greater competition was also largely responsible for the secondary banking collapse of the mid 1970s which for a time threatened the entire UK banking system.

10   For a full description of both product and geographic diversification see Robinson, op. cit., chs 2, 3.

11   For a more detailed description of this process see O. Marriott, *The Property Boom*, London, 1967 and D. Booker, *The Development of Leading Companies in the Property and Construction Industries* (unpublished). Note that in a sense the property market became transformed from an original safe income yield base from rentals to a pursuit of capital profits in the form of the increased capital value of the property. Hence the property developers have been subject to severe political attack since it was often better to leave completed property empty rather than let it. This was because capital values tended to increase with time, and, once let, the capital value came to be based on the rental income obtainable.

12   Sears was probably the pioneer in retailing to develop a divisional form of organisation. This was done in conjunction with management consultants, some of which later established McKinsey and Company, the US consultants who have played a dramatic part in spreading the multidivisional form. For further discussion of the development of Sears see Chandler, op. cit., ch. 5.

13   Channon, op. cit., 9, 67.

14   Ibid., p. 78.

Part Four

CONCLUSION

12 Directions for Future Research

WILLIAM P. KENNEDY and PETER L. PAYNE

The papers presented at the Management History Conference in June 1975, and their discussion, provoke a number of thoughts concerning the possible direction of future research in this general field. Some of them have already been adequately considered either in the editorial introduction or in the observations by Dr Alford and therefore require no repetition here; others deserve further emphasis, and several additional issues – the nature of which doubtless reflect our own particular interests – are most appropriately dealt with in these concluding remarks. For clarity, they have been roughly divided into three groups. The first is concerned with the organisation and performance of the individual firm; the second with the relationships between firms and how such relationships affect innovation, competitiveness, and other aspects of the behaviour of the firm; and the third with the way in which firms' activities are influenced by general economic factors, in particular, capital markets, macroeconomic policies and conditions, legal practices, and the social environment.

I

Historians generally study the individual firm by a combination of two basic approaches.[1] The first approach emphasises objective measures such as sales, value added, total assets, the distribution of net earnings actual or imputed, the number of employees and their remuneration, and the firm's share of the markets in which it competes. Although these indicators must be the objective basis of any business history, they gain perspective only when seen in relationship to more subjective criteria. The most important of these is what the historian feels was possible given the firm's resources, the available technology, and the market conditions. In most cases, the comparison of indicators of actual performance with subjective yardsticks proves to be extremely difficult. The performance of competitors, both domestic and foreign, is perhaps the most useful component in the construction of a yardstick, but the firm's own past performance may also be valuable in this task. For example, one might ask how profitability during one period of competitive stress compares with that of a similar episode several years or decades earlier. Despite the inherent difficulties, historians should be strongly encouraged to make explicit the standards by which their judgements are formed. Only thus can their insights be fruitfully shared.

The second approach used by business historians explicitly recognises that the construction of subjective yardsticks is an impossible task without an examination of *the way* in which the particular results were achieved. Alfred Chandler's pioneering investigation into the relationship between corporate structure and corporate performance have pointed the way for subsequent research. Careful examination of the structure of a firm's internal organisation can yield significant results for, if we are correct in believing that choice in the allocation of resources so best to meet diverse demands is the heart of the managerial function, then the means by which a firm's leaders choose to appraise themselves of the firm's operations and to execute their decisions are perhaps the most fundamental acts of management. This is especially so in large firms where there is no possibility that top management can be acquainted on an informal basis with all aspects of the firm's operations.

The information that management requires may be grouped into the two categories of costs and revenues. Each of these may be broken down into its components. Simplest to provide are data on current operating costs and current sources of revenue. Differences between firms in the comprehensiveness of the coverage of these magnitudes can often partly explain differences in the observed performances of these firms. For example, two innovations in cost control in the 1920s gave General Motors a substantial advantage over Ford in their struggle for dominance in the US automobile industry.[2] One was the careful systematic comparison of unit costs in different GM plants. This helped keep average costs in GM plants very close to lowest costs and may have permitted 'super-fast' diffusion of new manufacturing techniques.[3] This cost-comparison method was made possible only by the reorganisation of the firm on the basis of autonomous divisions all using a uniform set of accounting conventions. The other innovation was in inventory control. This was of signal importance in an industry in which the value of each unit of final output was relatively high. Although well-managed American firms had widely adopted monthly forecasts of sales as a control technique early in the twentieth century, GM's management, by putting dealer inventory reports on a ten-day rather than monthly basis, and by giving such reports the highest priority, elevated this tool into a much more powerful control mechanism. This practice also had the advantage, given GM's spread of products over the entire auto-motive range, of heightening the sensitivity of management to market trends and allowing the best use to be made of raw materials stocks and accessory production. Such examples of the impact of organisation innovations can be multiplied. Business history would be richer if such illustrations were to be given a prominent place in future studies.

While the scope for the profitable use of current information is thus great, the long-term performance of the firm depends finally upon choices made with the much more fragmentary evidence of technical reports on production and process innovations and upon market assess-ments for new or current products. The comprehensiveness and quality of those reports for the general office is therefore an important indicator of the emphasis the firm gives to forward planning, and such memo-randa comprise an extremely important complement to data on current operating costs and revenue. Such innovations in marketing and pro-duction are, from a social viewpoint, among the most important of the firm's activities and hence should be accorded very careful attention by the historian. Furthermore such successful innovations should lie at the heart of any explanation of the firm's overall success.

The examination of the organisation of information flows provides a number of areas of research in which historians may make important contributions both to theoretical work and to policy formulation. There is substantial agreement that resources in developed countries are now allocated on non-market criteria to an extent much greater than was common in those same economies before 1914. This phenomena is of great theoretical interest for, on the one hand, there is substantial agree-ment among economists that the outcome of unfettered market trans-actions tends to be more efficient than alternative allocation mechanisms and, on the other, that certain problems are not optimally resolved by market mechanisms, especially in those cases in which the future be-haviour of transactors and prices is unknown and where the goods and services traded possess a wide range of possible qualities. Examination of the way in which successful large firms are organised may provide useful clues in determining how, at any given level of technology, the balance between market and non-market transactions is struck.

A major issue in this area concerns the range of products offered by the firm for final sale to the rest of the economy. Both Du Pont and GM grew rapidly through a sustained strategy of product diversification, yet the management in both firms was acutely aware of the limits to their firm's operations. For example, Du Pont made only a very limited commitment to pharmaceuticals, and refrained entirely from entering the burgeoning branch of chemistry based on petroleum derivatives.[4] Similarly, GM liquidated its tractor division in 1921 and steadfastly refused to enter the market for luxury custom-built cars even though the latter policy precluded GM's participation in a market which other manufacturers found highly rewarding.[5] In part, these key strategic decision turned on principles easy to state but difficult to execute : resources must be committed to sectors only if the anticipated net returns, allowing for risk, are sufficiently high. Too small a commitment of resources to feasible projects threatens to stunt the firm's development through loss of opportunities for profitable growth while too large a commitment courts disaster. Clearly, the solution to this problem on the basis of the fragmentary evidence typically available when decisions had to be made is difficult and the value of many business histories would be greatly enhanced were conscious attempts made to present cases illustrating the skill, or, alternatively, the indifference, with which such decisions were made.

However, this is only part of the explanation for the existence of limits to the firm's operations in diverse final product markets. In the sectors in which Du Pont and GM choose not to participate, other firms operated profitably. Economies of scale or other barriers to entry are not fully satisfying explanations of their decisions.[6] The solutions must lie within the assessment each firm made of its own managerial resources and of the strains which further diversification might have placed upon those resources. This question is necessarily complex, for most firms (and certainly those as large and powerful as GM or Du Pont) were always able, through investment, research, recruitment and promotion, to improve their managerial abilities and expand their options, and were always doing so, thereby altering the extent to which any given change overburdened the firm. In short, the determination by a firm's management of the boundaries within which non-market allocations may work effectively in producing goods and services for final sale outside the firm is a crucial strategic decision, as is the drawing of divisional boundaries. Both of these problems, the number of divisions and their boundaries, deserve the closest attention.

A related issue concerns the extent of vertical integration undertaken by a firm. Chandler has emphasised that one of the most important decisions at GM in the 1920s was to curtail the extent of vertical integration, although such integration had been a predominant characteristic of GM's growth under Durant,[7] and was enthusiastically taken up by Ford. The wisdom of this decision was fully revealed by the difficulties which Ford encountered when full integration was attempted at River Rouge. Only recently have theorists begun to analyse exactly what factors determine the optimal limits to integration[8] and there is little question that business histories could contribute to this analysis by the provision of illuminating case studies.

Since the examination of the organisational characteristics of the development of a prominent company is a highly fruitful approach to the analysis of the company's performance, the researcher must be careful to ascertain exactly how the organisation operated in reality, not simply as it appeared on paper or in logic. One of the authors, on requesting a copy of the formal organisational arrangements prominently displayed in the company secretary's office, was once told 'certainly you can have one, but it is quite misleading. The Chairman simply short circuits these lines of communication and obtains the information he requires and delivers his instructions by telephone. This is a one man show'. (It is said that the first function of this Chairman's successor was to teach the board how to arrive at a decision!) This incident and the papers contributed to the Conference by W. J. Reader and Stanley Chapman made one wonder about the *real*, as opposed to the formal structures of British companies in the past, certainly in the interwar period.

This concern for the substance rather than the shadow of the firm's operations necessitates much more work on the raw materials of informed decision making : the accounting data of the firm. Business historians, anxious to employ quantitative data for illustrative or model building purposes, and rightly urged to give 'greater emphasis to analytical techniques developed for empirical studies of the firm or industry',[9] must, in the absence of (or even to supplement) the original accounts books, depend upon company financial statements for some dimensions of development and change. Such statements are notoriously treacherous and often provide wilfully misleading data, particularly if they are used for the compilation of time series, so often were they manipulated in order to justify encouraging dividend payments and to create totally erroneous ideas of solvency. Not until the famous Royal Mail case did the practice of 'secret reserve' accounting begin to diminish (secret reserves were not expressly prohibited until the Companies Act of 1948);[10] depreciation of fixed assets was extremely arbitrary until, one would guess, the eve of the Second World War; and since we are very concerned in this context with mergers, it would appear that published accounts often undervalued the assets of acquisitions. As Dr Hannah has observed, 'the imperfect state of the law relating to company accounts, and in particular to secret reserves and holding company accounts, allowed common resort to such malpractice'.[11] There must have been many chairmen who followed the practice described – in an unusual outburst of frankness – by one of their number as bringing into the accounts 'just as much . . . as will enable us to pay dividends we recommend and placing to general reserve or adding to carry forward just as much as will make a pretty balance sheet'.[12] Since 1948 the accounting position has improved markedly – business historians now have much more accurate information to go on – but even so much is still obscure and unknown; particularly concerning the critical issues of acquisition and merger activity.[13] Clearly, business historians must support the appeal of the accountants for more research in this area. Ultimately, it must be the historian's task, taking full advantages of historical perspective, to recreate as far as possible the actual financial condition of the firm under examination and in the light of this knowledge to assess the effectiveness and fitness of the firm's crucial managerial decisions.

Research into systems of internal organisation may also suggest the direction in which corporate structure is most likely to evolve in the future. Chandler has emphasised that the successful decision to adopt the multidivisional structure in a number of important firms emerged directly from crises caused by strategies of limited diversification miscarrying and producing losses when there was reason to believe that substantial profits were feasible.[14] The diversification moves which generated these crises in the past, however, often involved the firm in entry into markets rather closely related to its original lines of business. Recently, the 'pure conglomerate' has emerged as a distinct corporate type and although there are some plausible theoretical grounds for believing this to be a useful development, conglomerates have not yet successfully demonstrated the qualities which should attach to them.

It may be that the many empirical studies[15] of the disappointing consequences – in terms of profitability and efficiency – of the British merger boom of the period 1960–8, for example, might be explained not so much in terms of, for example, the overvaluations of a captive firm's assets by an acquisitive diversifier, as by the complex problems of structural adaptation to a new marketing situation. Clearly, fundamental organisational change, usually involving the successful establishment of the multi-divisional form, takes considerable time. The difficulties in integrating new acquisitions into a core structure is a major reason why multi-firm mergers, common at the beginning of the twentieth century in both Britain and America, have virtually disappeared, to be replaced by a much more methodical, drawn-out, sequential pattern of acquisitions by firms with the managerial and organisational capacity to cope with the attendant complexity. Obviously there is, for any core firm of given resources, a sequence of mergers which is optimal in terms of the timing and the nature of each successive acquisition. Furthermore, it would appear that the optimal timing and sequence of successive acquisitions would be quite sensitive to the degree to which new acquisitions were remote from the experience and knowledge of the core firm's managers, although much more research is needed before the precise characteristics of an optimal acquisition programme can be known.

More case studies of both successful and failed attempts at extensive diversification are needed; not least because they might guide theoretical

work into more fruitful areas. From such research it might be possible
to discern how new, more flexible management structures and techniques might evolve to fulfil the promise of the corporate conglomerate.
At the very least, it should be possible to learn whether or not inherent
barriers to the extent of diversification really exist. On the answer may
hinge the welfare implications of a situation increasingly revealed by
current research[16] : that small to medium sized firms are more efficient
at transforming research and development inputs into useful innovations while larger firms, which generate fewer good ideas relative to
their effort, are more efficient at transforming an innovation, once they
find one, into an effectively marketed product or service. Valuable
returns, both to individuals and to society, would result from an organisational structure which could combine the creativity and *esprit de
corps* of the small research establishment with the resources of the
large firm.

Finally, there is a widespread belief that major organisational change
usually takes place only after the onset of major crisis. This is not to
deny the possibility – suggested by Alford – of a relatively slow process
of development through adjustment and adaptation, but at present, the
evidence does appear to favour the dramatic change as the predominant
mode of evolution. The reasons for this invite scrutiny. Is it really the
case that defects in existing systems are not perceived until disaster
compels change? Something along these lines was suggested by S. G.
Checkland when, in reviewing Coleman's *Courtaulds*, he asked, 'Is it
inherent in the growth of a firm and indeed of all great organisations,
that they cannot adjust to change continuously, but must reach some
critical level of vulnerability before a response is forthcoming?'[17]

II

A different but related set of research problems arise when the historian
considers the relationships among firms. These relationships may be
most conveniently viewed as falling in two categories, competitive and
cooperative, where a cooperative relationship is defined as one in which
one firm is either a customer or supplier of another.[18] In both cases
the relationship is mediated through markets. On grounds of welfare
and growth, the most important question to be asked of market relationships is : what are the competitive conditions most conducive to an
optimal combination of rapid innovation and socially desirable levels
of output?

Recent research has cast doubt on the Schumpeterian claim that
monopoly affords the best environment in which to encourage the innovations that are the basis for improved standards of living.[19] Yet
Schumpeter was not entirely wrong, for while it appears that monopoly

is not a good environment for breeding innovation, neither is perfect competition. A balance must be struck between some security in which to exploit a new process or product and so much security that no new products or processes are forthcoming to disturb the profitable peace. The issue is further complicated by the likelihood that differences in demand characteristics (i.e. the price and income elasticity of goods and services) and in the technological bases (i.e. how easy it is to make important discoveries) of industries mean that each industry has a different optimal interaction of competition and security. Furthermore, the relationship may not be stable over time. For example, Scherer has suggested that the Second World War had provided such a powerful demonstration of the practical benefits of applied research that the attitude of entire industries towards formal, systematic research and development was stimulated and transformed. In a passage rich with historical implications but tantalisingly bare of amplification, Scherer observed that :

> It is conceivable that before World War II had its demonstration effect, the organizational slack associated with market power was a more important basis of technological leadership. This could explain why the performance of such firms as du Pont, ICI, I.G. Farben, R.C.A. and A.T. and T. was more impressive relative to that of smaller concerns before the war but not after.[20]

The pronounced trend towards corporate diversification has also had an impact on competitive and innovative performance which is only now being perceived and measured. This trend towards diversification has undoubtedly contributed to the observed increase in industrial concentration, usually measured by value of assets controlled, stock market valuation, or level of total value added relative to an industry or economy. The impact of this increase in concentration is hard to assess. On the one hand, it means that very few industries are sheltered from potential competition by means of large start-up costs alone. If the profit potential exists, it is difficult to imagine large, well funded, diversified firms being effectively kept out.[21] The threat of potential entry by wealthy, technically sophisticated rivals must have kept prices lower and innovation higher in many industries than would otherwise have been the case. On the other hand, a few large firms competing with each other across a wide range of industries may find numerous ways of colluding.[22] While the variety of contacts between large, widely diversified firms produces the heterogeneity of output which complicates collusion, it also produces numerous situations where collusion would be rewarding and possible. How the balance is struck can only be assessed by examining particular cases.

This whole area of the impact of industrial organisation on industrial performance, particularly in terms of innovation, is one unusually well suited for case studies by historians. Innovation does not lend itself to easy cataloguing. What is an important innovation and what is not? Due to such ambiguities, econometric studies of innovation have not been convincing, especially since most of those which have appeared so far have treated admittedly complex situations by single-equation methods which are known to be liable to serious error.[23] What is necessary is a study of the unusual and extraordinary; in studies of innovation the 'representative' firm is not especially interesting. This is because only a few industries have a strategic potential for an entire economy. Freeman[24] has suggested chemicals, electronics (including computers) and electrical engineering. To these might be added machine tools and some specialised branches of mechanical engineering, but the list is surprisingly short. Within this small group of industries it is possible, even on fairly casual inspection, to spot the firms which have either been technological leaders or responsible for a large portion of the observed success. Such concentration of interesting cases invites the skills of the historian who is prepared to sift a wide variety of facts and who is always conscious of the uniqueness of the material.

Co-operative relationships among industries also pose interesting issues for research. Dr Channon[25] has emphasised the importance of the service industries in the British economy. However, it is important to note the important links between the service and manufacturing industries. The service industries tend to be highly capital intensive (utilities, communications, health, transportation, education and defence, for example) and are therefore among the most important consumers of manufactured products, particularly computers. It is noteworthy that while IBM is generally considered a manufacturing firm, it owes its predominant market position and rapid growth not to its hardware so much as to its software capability – that is, to its ability to offer users programming material suitable to their needs.[26] IBM is then, in reality, a huge service organisation and not predominantly a manufacturing firm. As this example also suggests, manufacturing firms are important consumers of services as well as being major suppliers to the service sector. Similarly, advances in communications have been instrumental in encouraging and permitting ambitious strategies of diversification and expansion for both manufacturing and service industries. It is important that historians are sensitive to the way in which new technologies have altered forms of organisation and methods of management and to the manner in which these changes have come about, whether through new tools removing existing bottlenecks and allowing smoother operation of existing management systems, or by opening up possibilities for entirely new systems of greater capability than had previously existed.

I

The close relationship between services and manufacturing suggests that substantial gains in productivity have come about through one industry, often in the service sector, utilising a new good or service produced by a different industry. Further research might provide valuable quantitative data on this subject. The relationships between communications firms and their suppliers and between airlines and aircraft makers suggest that this form of technological diffusion is of substantial importance. Finally, the government's role, both as manufacturer and consumer, in eliciting technological advance is one of obvious importance, although it is a role not yet thoroughly analysed. The importance of externalities in basic scientific research and the government's unequalled ability to spread risks indicate the dimensions of the task of this analysis and the rewards that will accompany its successful completion.

III

The third area of research concerns the behaviour of the firm in the context of the entire economy. There are three subjects under this heading which would appear to promise substantial returns to research. The first concerns the behaviour of firms operating within an environment characterised by particular institutional arrangements, especially those related to financial intermediation. The second concerns the long run implications of various legal attitudes toward industrial and commercial collusion and the impact of various types of macro and micro policies enacted by governments. The final subject is concerned with the social processes involved in determining what sort of men, with what kinds of background, attain positions of importance in the allocation of resources in both firms and in government ministries.

In considering the first of these topics it might be fruitful to think of firms as mini-capital markets, simply because those who control the firm allocate finance, men and material to various projects on the basis of their private calculations of the risk-adjusted rates of return associated with various actions. As Chandler has emphasised,[27] the multi-divisional structure might have been purpose-designed to aid such allocation. The divisions are generally supposed to have sufficient autonomy to permit the operating results of each one to serve as a valid indication of performance. If the company were organised into nothing more than a weak holding company, there would be little or no difference between external and internal capital markets. As we have seen, the essence of the multi-divisional organisation as a successful structure lies in the information flows which the general office establishes to supplement observed market performance. These flows, involving personal links carefully cultivated by the selective staffing of inter-divisional committees and the introduction of conscientiously devised policy and operations review procedures, provide the general office with a better idea of what is happening within the organisation than is ever reported to any outsider, even stockholders. Because of the wealth of non-market data available to the general office, the firm's executives should be, and invariably are, better prepared to make rational allocation decisions within the firm than are any outsiders.

On the other hand, the firm's management is less well informed about affairs within other organisations. They are not, of course, completely ignorant. The accounts required by law and accompanied by informed comment within the financial press provides some important information. Knowledge gained in commercial transactions may provide a great deal more. What is important is that information differentials are known to exist and that because of this there is a strong incentive for individual firms to become as self-sufficient as possible. Thus firms seek opportunities for diversification within their own organisation rather than outside it. Diversification is attempted for two reasons : one is the obvious desire to reduce risk, the other is both to be able to tap (at low cost) new markets which are capable of faster growth than the firm's established markets and to provide new and more varied ways of utilising the results of research undertaken by the firm.

The consequence of firms allocating resources in this manner is that, except by chance, the resulting allocation will be inferior to one achieved in conditions where all allocators had the same information. Nevertheless, interactions between capital markets internal and external to firms are very important. External capital market behaviour provides some important information to a firm's executives. The rate of interest at which they can borrow or lend money compared with the change in revenues caused by an alteration in the scale of operations provide important, although highly aggregated and hence crude, checks of the firm's prospects compared with all others.[28] A firm confronted with very promising prospects compared with other firms will find the cost of borrowing in the open market relatively low. Losses to the economy as a whole, however, arise when the firm with good prospects will not borrow enough. This occurs partly because too many firms with poorer prospects are themselves conducting, through ignorance of alternatives, high levels of internal investment and are thereby keeping all firms' investment costs unnecessarily high. The more easily all firms considered as a group can compete for funds on open markets the less likely is it that social costs will be exorbitantly high.[29]

External capital market operations are obviously strongly improved if good facilities for take-overs exist.[30] Such facilities (and especially the information their operations require) provide some assurance that assets are put to their best uses. This can be of great importance, for numerous examples[31] exist in which managements, protected from competition and demanding shareholders, have directed their firms in an inept, complacent and occasionally incompetent manner. Of course, competitive pressures are never completely absent, and even where take-over bids are non-existent, such managements will eventually be replaced. However, if they control substantial assets and enjoy a secure cash flow, the damage they can cause to the economy is sometimes severe and sustained. A take-over mechanism can shorten their ruinous tenure and, by example, create an environment in which incompetence and inadequacy do not flourish. Another important aspect of 'efficient' use of resources in the presence of some degree of differential information is that firms wishing to diversify can often more easily and effectively do so by taking over a firm already established within the sector in which they want to expand. Another situation where mergers (defined here as an uncontested take-over) are desirable may occur when innovative small firms lack adequate resources to exploit workable ideas. For such firms to be taken over by a larger, but less creative firm represents a reasonably efficient means of capturing some of the potential of the prototype innovation without requiring that the small firm take the idea through all its stages of development, stages which become progressively more expensive as the innovation nears the last stage of marketing. What the 'core' firm provides in these cases is a more stable operating environment due to greater diversification, an established marketing network, a greater supply of available resources for further expansion, and perhaps more experience in large scale but routine manufacture of a good or provision of a service. However, despite these potential advantages of the take-over and merger mechanisms, its use does not guarantee the efficient use of resources, for take-overs only reduce, but do not eliminate, inefficiency.

These considerations make it clear that imperfect capital market operations have powerfully biased the performance of market economies. As a paper in this volume argues,[32] biases unique to British capital markets before 1914 contributed heavily during that time to the much smaller commitment of British resources to technologically progressive and rapidly expanding sectors than occurred in either the US or Germany, countries whose capital markets, while exhibiting distinct imperfections of their own, nevertheless encouraged growth in crucial respects. Since 1914, important changes in British capital market operations have occurred. It would appear that these changes have constituted a substantial improvement. However, without much further research it is possible only to know that the direction and perhaps the extent of biases and imperfections have changed. The quantitative importance of the changes remains unknown.

Three kinds of changes may be identified. Each of them has resulted in an expansion of the information available on investment opportunities. First, the amount and quality of information that firms have been required by law to divulge has steadily increased. The development of the take-over bid in the 1950s and 1960s undoubtedly owes a great deal to enlarged disclosure requirements, beginning with the major reform in 1948. As already emphasised, one consequence of frequent take-over bids is a fuller utilisation of resources, often to a degree commensurate with their market value. Second, a more broadly based shareholding in many firms has occurred and with it a reduction in the power of closely knit families or family trusts to sustain indifferent managerial performance. A situation such as that which occurred during the interwar period at Kenricks, the hardware firm, when outside consultants Peat, Marwick and Mitchell – called in to revive the fortunes of the firm – were unable to conduct an integral part of their investigations because a number of the family refused to allow an independent technical expert to examine part of the plant,[33] now has a decidedly antique air about it. Similarly, the situation that existed in some firms in the heavy industries in the interwar period is no longer possible on such a grand scale. In these cases, founders of businesses that had grown large and had frequently coalesced into holding companies after 1918 sometimes arranged for the creation of trusts in favour of members of their families on their deaths. The trustees – often possessing little or no direct knowledge of the firms in which they sometimes held a controlling or substantial interest – were apt to regard the investment of retained profits with suspicion and structural change with horror, particularly if the second, or even third, generation of senior executives were drawn from outside the family circle. The presence of trustees on the board had a stultifying effect on innovation, particularly in periods of depression, when much needed – even vital – capital investment was apt to be regarded as an unacceptable diminution of the income of the trusts and hence the living standards of the founders' kinfolk dependent upon it. Failing to appreciate the necessity for the replacement of outworn plant or the seizure of new opportunities, the family trustees blocked new investment and inhibited structural reorganisation for fear that any change would be to their detriment.[34] This is a theme that deserves fuller investigation. It may go some way to explaining the loss of vitality of some hitherto progressive firms. It is not implausible that it has greater significance than those arguments concerning waning entrepreneurship that depend upon the mere passage of generations.

Finally, information flows through capital markets and operating procedures within firms have been improved by direct personal intervention by representatives of the Bank of England, many commercial banks and, increasingly, institutional investors. These representatives, acting to protect the investments of their sponsors, demand a performance of the firm to which the firm's board of directors might not other-

I*

wise aspire. The outside representatives also generally have the power to enforce the standards of operational performance which they impose. Such intervention in many firms' internal affairs by creditors and minority owners often had its origin in the 'reconstructions' which the Bank of England and many commercial banks undertook as the price of continued help in the interwar period.[35] At the same time, institutional investors, unit trusts, pension funds and insurance companies, timidly began to protect their assets more persistently. More research is needed to understand exactly what these institutions' role has been and how it has changed. This is an important problem, for these institutions, even more than the banks, depend upon the real, long term value of their assets being maintained and increased.

Until very recently, *it would appear* that despite their increased holdings of equities – something like 70 per cent of all shareholdings in this country are now [1975] held by insurance companies, unit trusts and pensions funds – these institutions have been reluctant to exercise their potential power over the management of the enterprises which they own. They appear to have been prepared simply to sell their holdings when dissatisfied with the affairs of the companies represented in their portfolios. Rarely have they done more than hesitantly 'intervene'. The case of Vickers in 1970 – when the institutional investors led by the Prudential were instrumental in replacing the top management – is almost unique.[36] As the investment director of Legal and General put it :

'The old theory was that if you felt that the management of a company was bad you just sold your shares, but that's a doubtful practice. Either you have to sell at a poor price or you cannot sell at all. Anyway, that's a policy of total defeatism. There are other ways of dealing with one's indifferent investments. I'm in favour of the gentle nudge. It has to be done discreetly because as soon as you turn on the searchlight of publicity, then it's self-destructive'.[37]

What business historians might try to discover is just what constituted a 'gentle nudge' or an 'intervention', and, in due time, it might be possible to date and evaluate the adoption of a more positive policy.

A penetrating study of these three phases of capital market operations promises a considerable yield. For example, it would be interesting to know whether the greatly improved record of innovation in British industry between 1919 and 1945 was due to changes in the operations of external capital markets which caused them to be much more receptive to the needs of domestic financing. Possibly this inward orientation altered the structure of rates of return facing British firms so as to favour technological innovation to a degree unknown before the war. In short, since the process of intermediation was different in the interwar period from what it had been before, it is an important historical task to define the extent of the change and the degree to which the change was beneficial. Such research will illuminate the remaining deficiencies in efficient resource allocation as they existed in 1939. This is necessary both for business histories covering the post 1945 period and for evaluations of overall economic performance.

Another factor which has acted on firms as powerfully as external capital markets, particularly in the twentieth century, is the government. The legal guidelines within which firms operate, the taxes they pay, the subsidies they receive, all have a direct influence on firms. The macro-economic consequences of overall monetary and fiscal policies, which act pervasively rather than directly, are also of great importance. The issues arising from a consideration of the relations between the state and business firms are extremely numerous and wide ranging. A number of conference participants drew attention to the effect of American anti-trust laws on business organisation and some suggested that the absence of such laws in Britain encouraged a less innovative and competitive stance because there existed few if any barriers to overt attempts at collusion.[38] This is an attractive hypothesis but it requires further, more rigorous examination. Perhaps anti-trust laws have simply compelled firms to devise and use more elaborate and expensive means of collusion. If this is true, anti-trust laws may actually be counterproductive. Exactly how, if at all, do anti-trust laws work? Are prices really lower and output higher because of them? Or is their effect mainly to create uncertainty about competitors' plans sufficient to encourage product innovation, innovations that might anyway have been forthcoming? If anti-trust laws are proven to possess the beneficial capabilities attributed to them, do studies of case histories suggest ways in which performance might be improved? Such studies may be a useful means of determining the circumstances and the manner in which direct government intervention in private industry will be beneficial. Furthermore, they might shed light on the appropriate criteria by which firms owned partly by the government may be judged. Similar questions arise in connection with subsidies and the operations of industries which sell most of their output to the government. What examples of fruitful relationships exist and how do they differ from the cases where intervention (shipbuilding? Concorde? the nuclear reactor programme?) has badly miscarried?

An evaluation of the impact of monetary and fiscal policy on firms is a difficult task. There is little question that booms promote growth, yet in a number of case studies it is apparent that a crisis provoked by a sharp national recession, like that experienced in 1920–21 in the US, led to very far reaching, beneficial changes in business strategy.[39] Nevertheless, the obvious waste induced by the world depression of

1929–1933 clearly shows that the degree of creative response does not invariably reflect the seriousness of the challenge. What comprises the right combination of ease and tension? Exactly how does monetary policy operate : only indirectly through changed intermediary behaviour or directly *via* binding constraints on firm activity? So little is known of the impact of monetary and fiscal policies that historians should, when examining the historical record, be particularly alive to the possibility of illuminating this problem.

The last area of research considered here is perhaps both the most difficult and potentially the most rewarding. In the final analysis, whatever the organisation of information flows, whatever the macroeconomic environment, however financial intermediaries operate, individual men must make the final decisions.[40] The competitive-meritocratic paradigm assures us that the best men to fulfil each task will inevitably be found. Casual observation suggests either that this paradigm is incorrect or that the disequilibrium condition is so prevalent that the study of steady state conditions is simply academic. Therefore, even if we accept the belief that eventually there will be a tendency for the best man to be found for every job, it is important to observe the actual process of selection and to judge how close to the theoretical optimum the system is operating. There are a number of ways in which this problem has already been approached. Our purpose is to encourage others to continue to work in this field.

What are the backgrounds of the group of men who make the most crucial allocative decisions in Britain?[41] How were and are such men trained? Since technology is a key variable in economic growth, and hence in the welfare of firms, it is important to examine their attitudes towards, and competence in technology. Do business leaders possess sufficient technical knowledge to appraise the various investment and marketing proposals that come before them? If not, how do they compensate for this deficiency? In the previous discussion of the organisation of the firm, it was argued that the construction of a systematic method of obtaining data on operations and market opportunities was one of the most important functions performed by management. But how do men with widely different experience and outlook go about inaugurating such data flows? Do executives originally trained in classics or law generally have a different system of priorities from those trained as engineers? Indeed, does it matter what the original training was? Chandler suggests tantalising possibilities. He observed that many of the men who made important organisational innovations had scientific or engineering backgrounds and that the relationship between the rationalising and systematising of industrial administration in the US has been close.[42] But the precise relationship is not clear. Some engineers were not good organisers or salesmen and some men with non-engineering or scientific backgrounds became good organisers and marketers. What seems important is the need for a rational, systematic approach to business problems. But how is that engendered?

In view of the interest shown in this conference by participants from business schools, it would be useful to investigate the role of the business schools in promoting more effective organisational structures and operational strategies. Professor Chandler has persuasively argued that the problems involved in the adoption of the multi-divisional structure by the large, usually integrated, American managerial enterprises as they moved into new geographic and product markets were less than those confronting British concerns in the post-1945 period. This was not simply because when the former transformed their structures they were 'already administered entirely by professional, career managers, trained in the methods and procedures developed in the early years of the century to administer American big business'[43] but because a significant number of these professionals had come from the same business schools (typically Harvard, MIT, the Wharton School, Purdue and Cornell) and, as it were, spoke the same language and had learned from the same examples. Thus business schools appear to have accelerated the diffusion of management techniques and practices.

Other issues inviting investigation arise from this. What has been the role of business schools in initiating improvements in business organisation and practice? Might the course structure of business schools perpetuate existing functional structures, thus making innovation actually harder? Or is there a creative interplay between successful firms and the best business schools? Do business schools, by making managers acutely aware of the informational, monitoring, controlling and guiding needs of business structures, engender the revision of existing practices which Chandler has shown to be so important in the history of the firms pioneering the multi-divisional structures? Have the business schools, themselves a growth industry in the service sector, improved their own performance over time? It would be an interesting and useful exercise to try to quantify the contribution business schools have made to economic performance in the twentieth century.

As important to managerial excellence as technological competence and functional business skills is the ability to manage men. Since the labour force in a modern firm generally includes executives, technical personnel, functional specialists, skilled and semi-skilled manual workers (all perhaps organised into different bargaining and intra-firm pressure groups), the breadth of the task is clear. How the skills necessary for this task relate to the skills needed for other managerial functions is obscure. Are the abilities to master new technologies, to devise efficient organisation structures and to manage men sufficiently different to cause a clash of objectives? Although much more work needs to be done in this area, the intriguing case of the successful Swedish ship-building firm, Kockums, suggests that the different skills can be highly complementary. Kockums' shipbuilding labour force of 5000 workers is highly skilled. It has a large proportion of university graduates. Con-struction workers operate in teams of from 4 to 25 members and each team has considerable latitude in organising its assigned tasks and in negotiating production schedules with other teams. Furthermore, nearly 10 per cent of the total labour force sit on committees dealing with manifold aspects of the firm's operations. Through these committees much co-ordination between individual teams takes place and decisions are taken on matters concerning maintenance methods, production, machine operations, outfitting, working environment and health. Co-operating with these teams and committees are workers performing specialist functions, such as design and job-specific material selection. This highly complex arrangement is remarkably flexible, extremely effi-cient, and highly satisfactory to the workers. Perhaps only recent advances in materials handling and mechanised tools permit such de-centralised manufacturing operations to be employed, while industries using established mass production techniques must perforce employ other forms of labour organisation less satisfying to the workers. If so, can changes in technology explain the historical evolution of labour rela-tions in a given firm? If this proves to be so, then the same organisa-tional factors that determine the firm's technology also determine its labour relations; and researchers might expect to find good labour relations highly correlated with progressive technological standards of operations.

It is not only within firms that the attitudes and outlook of decision-makers is important. What are the implications of the training of those who perform the task of financial intermediation upon the operations of those intermediaries? William Reader has emphasised the fact that members of the London Stock Exchange and others concerned with company promotion have not in the past been good judges of advanced technology. What does this mean in operational terms? Does it mean that technologically advanced projects were considered by those with-out scientific knowledge to be more risky than the same projects might have appeared to specialists, or were such projects considered no less risky because the scientifically ignorant managers are unable to estimate potential problems? Indeed, are non-specialists able to tell winners from losers or must they depend upon the advice of the technologically competent? It may be that non-specialists tended to ignore or refuse to tackle certain types of project and that, as a consequence, they were more disposed to lend abroad than were technically trained men.

Examination of the attitudes of those responsible for allocating re-sources and monitoring routine operations invites consideration of the firm as a social mechanism. Firms not only allocate physical capital to different uses but also allocate men. They are mini-labour markets as well as mini-capital markets.[44] The same types of relationships that exist between internal and external capital markets also exist for labour markets. Of particular interest is the process by which firms decide recruitment and promotion policies. Are certain posts to be filled with new recruits or with men promoted from within the firm? This question is of especial interest for the most senior executive positions. At a different level, to what extent are man-power policies of firms determined by unions and how do union attitudes respond to management decisions? How do successful firms weight personality, training and background in recruitment? Are such criteria different in less successful firms? Do changes in the more powerful personnel occur only during crises? If so, are the qualities of the new leaders dictated by the nature of the crisis?

It has been suggested that certain types of problems are best resolved by distinct personality types. The ability necessary to establish a firm is not necessarily the same as that needed to maintain the established company successfully. As Dr Channon has observed :

> The successful entrepreneurs . . . tended to come from socially out-cast sectors of society, tended to run their organizations autocratically, tended to find it difficult to delegate responsibility (even for operations), and tended to hold on to the organisation even when age or product-market complexity would seem to indicate structural change was necessary. By contrast, organisations which successfully underwent the transition from entrepreneurial leadership to managerial control tended to adopt leadership by what might be called administrative personalities who consolidated, restructured, and institutionalised into the organisation the original purpose determined by the entrepreneur. The contrasting styles of these two extreme cases suggest they might be ends of a spectrum perhaps embracing small-sized to medium-sized entrepreneurs and less dedicated managerial personalities on the middle ground. Differences would seem to be apparently some function of personality, and studies of such personalities might reveal meaningful generalisations on the type of leadership required by enterprises at various stages of their evolution.[45]

An assessment of the proficiency with which a firm promotes men capable of successfully directing the firm, as the scale of operation changes and the technical and marketing environment alters, must be given more attention than it has hitherto received in the overwhelming majority of business histories.

IV

Let us end this programme of suggestion for future research by a reiteration of the challenge and rewards of considering firms as the agents of economic growth. It is firms that make most of the basic allocative decisions of any economy. If the output of goods and services rises over time it is because firms produce more of them. Yet change through time raises fundamentally complex issues involving an almost limitless range of problems concerning choice in conditions of uncertainty. As it is not yet possible to simulate these problems they will have to be examined through the medium of actual case studies of what happened in the past. Such historical studies will, we believe, remain indispensable guides to the process of economic development and aids in charting the future.

NOTES

1   That is, of course, when *any* scholarly attempt is made to indicate scale and growth and to assess performance. Numerous studies do little more than provide a straightforward chronological description: these range from 'short (and usually glossy) brochures to bulky bundles of volumes' (Asa Briggs, 'Business History', *Economic History Review*, 2nd Series, ix (1956–7) 486).

2   The following discussion is heavily based on Alfred D. Chandler, *Strategy and Structure: Chapters in the Industrial Enterprise* (MIT Press, Cambridge, Mass., 1962) pp. 130–62.

3   For another illustration of a situation in which a non-market mechanism, in this case a trade association, made possible 'super-fast' technological diffusion, see G. R. Saxonhouse, 'A Tale of Japanese Technological Diffusion in the Meiji Period', *Journal of Economic History*, xxxiv (1974) 149–65. Note that in the case of GM, with an active, talented General Technical Committee, a potential drawback of the Japanese organisation, lack of sufficient independent experimentation due to rapid low-cost imitation, was avoided.

4   Chandler, op. cit., pp. 52–113.

5   Ibid., pp. 141, 143.

6   F. M. Scherer, *Industrial Market Structure and Economic Performance* (Rand McNally, Chicago, 1970) pp. 79–88, argues that in most industries in the US the minimum optimal scale of operations is well below the extent of the relevant markets. Furthermore most economies of scale which do exist are exhausted within plants and are not contingent on multi-plant operations. Of course, lack of financial or other resources could not of themselves keep GM or du Pont out of markets in which they were otherwise capable of competing.

7   Chandler, op. cit., pp. 114–28.

8   See O. E. Williamson, 'The Vertical Integration of Production: Market Failure Considerations', *American Economic Review: Papers and Proceedings*, lxi (1971) 112–23 and K. J. Arrow, 'Vertical Integration and Communication', *The Bell Journal of Economics*, vi (1975) 173–83.

9   K. A. Tucker, 'Business History: Some Proposals for Aims and Methodology', *Business History*, xiv (1972) 1.

10 P. N. Davies and A. M. Bourn, 'Lord Kylsant and The Royal Mail', *Business History*, XIV (1972) 121.

11 Leslie Hannah, 'Takeover Bids in Britain before 1950: An Exercise in Business "Pre-History" ', *Business History*, XVI (1974) 69.

12 Ibid., p. 70.

13 T. A. Lee, 'Accounting for and Disclosure of Business Combinations', *Journal of Business Finance and Accounting*, I (1974) 1–33.

14 Chandler, op. cit., p. 95.

15 See, for example, the studies by G. D. Newbold, 'Implications of Financial Analyses of Takeovers', in J. M. Samuels (ed.), *Readings on Mergers and Takeovers* (London: Elek, 1972) pp. 12–24; John Kitching, 'Why Do Mergers Miscarry?', in Samuels, op. cit., pp. 40–63; John Kitching, 'Why Acquisitions are Abortive', *Management Today* (November 1974) pp. 82–7, 148; M. A. Utton, 'On Measuring the Effects of Industrial Mergers', *Scottish Journal of Political Economy*, XXI (1974) 13–26.

16 M. I. Kamien and N. L. Schwartz, 'Market Structure and Innovation: A Survey', *Journal of Economic Literature*, XIII (1975) 15–24.

17 S. G. Checkland, review of Donald Coleman's *Courtaulds* in *Economic History Review*, 2nd Series, XXIII (1970) 559–60.

18 Competition of a sort may still arise in conditions of monopsony, oligopsony, or bilaterial monopoly.

19 See Kamien and Schwartz, op. cit., pp. 15–24, Scherer, op. cit., ch. 15.

20 Scherer, op. cit., p. 372, footnote 89.

21 C. H. Berry, 'Corporate Diversification and Market Structure', *Bell Journal of Economics*, V (1974) 196–204.

22 For an example of such collusion between ICI and Courtaulds, see W. J. Reader.

23 See G. N. Von Tunzelmann, 'The New Economic History: an econometric appraisal', *Explorations in Economic History*, 2nd Series, V (1968).

24 C. Freeman, *The Economics of Industrial Innovation* (Harmondsworth: Penguin, 1974) pp. 33–7.

25 Channon, pp. 213–34 above.

26 G. W. Brock, *The U.S. Computer Industry* (Ballinger, 1975).

27 Chandler, op. cit., passim.

28 This abstracts from certain types of local market imperfections.

29 This is the logic behind the frequently heard proposal that firms be required to distribute all net earnings rather than being allowed any retained earnings. It is hoped that the competition this would cause in external capital markets for new funds would provide much better information globally for making new investment decisions.

30 Preferably in the presence of an arbiter who can usefully distinguish whether merger benefits simply reflect increased monopoly power.

31 Channon, above, p. 226, cites several prominent examples of firms over-ripe for take-over bids. The most conspicuous of these was Cunard.

32 Kennedy, above, pp. 151–83.

33 R. A. Church, *Kenricks in Hardware. A Family Business, 1791–1966* (Newton Abbot, 1969) pp. 206–7.

34 P. L. Payne, *Colvilles and the Scottish Iron and Steel Industry* (forthcoming).

35 Ibid. See also John Vaizey, *The History of British Steel* (London: Weidenfeld and Nicolson, 1974) passim; Sir Henry Clay, *Lord Norman* (London: Macmillan, 1957) pp. 318–59.

36 See K. Midgley, 'How Much Control do Shareholders Exercise?', *Lloyds Bank Review*, No. 114 (October 1974) 28, 26; *The Guardian*, 6 October 1975; Richard Spiegelberg, *The City. Power Without Responsibility* (London: Quartet, 1973) pp. 47–60.

37 *Investors Chronicle*, 18 December 1970, quoted by H. McRae and Frances Cairncross, *Capital City. London as a Financial Centre* (London: Eyre Methuen, revised edition, 1974) pp. 165–6.
38 See the papers by Chandler, Hannah and Alford.
39 Both GM and du Pont responded to the sharp postwar slump of 1920–1 by thorough-going reorganisation. See Chandler, op. cit., pp. 104–13, 128–58.
40 W. J. Reader has emphasised this point. Historians generally are extremely conscious of this.
41 Substantial work on this has already been done. See Charlotte Erickson, *British Industrialists: Steel and Hosiery, 1850–1950* (Cambridge, 1959); Political and Economic Planning, *Attitudes in British Management* (1955).
42 Chandler, op. cit., p. 317.
43 A. D. Chandler, above, p. 46.
44 See the articles by Spence and Boorman in the 'Symposium on the Economics of Internal Organisation', *Bell Journal of Economics*, VI (1975) 163–280.
45 Derek F. Channon, *The Strategy and Structure of British Enterprise* (London: Macmillan, 1973) p. 248.

Index

(This index lists only the names of persons and firms mentioned in the text; it is not a subject index.)